# INFOCOMP 2017

The Seventh International Conference on Advanced Communications and Computation

**MODOPT 2017**

The International Symposium on Modeling and Optimization

June 25 - 29, 2017

Venice, Italy

**INFOCOMP 2017 Editors**

Claus-Peter Rückemann, Leibniz Universität Hannover / Westfälische Wilhelms-Universität Münster / North-German Supercomputing Alliance, Germany
Ian Flood, Rinker School, College of Design, Construction and Planning | University of Florida, USA
Isabel Schwerdtfeger, IBM Deutschland GmbH – Hamburg, Germany
Christian Simmendinger, T-Systems SfR, Germany
George Beckett, EPCC, University of Edinburgh, UK

**Printed from e-media with permission by:**

Curran Associates, Inc.
57 Morehouse Lane
Red Hook, NY 12571

**Some format issues inherent in the e-media version may also appear in this print version.**



Printed by Curran Associates, Inc. (2017)

International Academy, Research, and Industry Association (IARIA)
412 Derby Way
Wilmington, DE 19810

Phone: (408) 893-6407
Fax: (408) 527-6351

petre@iaria.org

**Additional copies of this publication are available from:**

Curran Associates, Inc.
57 Morehouse Lane
Red Hook, NY 12571 USA
Phone: 845-758-0400
Fax: 845-758-2633
Email: curran@proceedings.com
Web: www.proceedings.com

# TABLE OF CONTENTS

# INFOCOMP 2017

# Forward

The Seventh International Conference on Advanced Communications and Computation (INFOCOMP 2017), held between June 25-29, 2017 in Venice, Italy, continued a series of events dedicated to advanced communications and computing aspects, covering academic and industrial achievements and visions.

The diversity of semantics of data, context gathering and processing led to complex mechanisms for applications requiring special communication and computation support in terms of volume of data, processing speed, context variety, etc. The new computation paradigms and communications technologies are now driven by the needs for fast processing and requirements from data-intensive applications and domain-oriented applications (medicine, geoinformatics, climatology, remote learning, education, large scale digital libraries, social networks, etc.). Mobility, ubiquity, multicast, multi-access networks, data centers, cloud computing are now forming the spectrum of de factor approaches in response to the diversity of user demands and applications. In parallel, measurements control and management (self-management) of such environments evolved to deal with new complex situations.

The conference had the following tracks:

- Biometry, security, access technologies, algorithms, and applications
- Large Scale Energy Efficient Data Center Concepts
- Advanced applications
- Networks/systems measurement, control and management
- Modeling and optimization in complex systems
- Empirical modeling
- Common Grounds for Parallel Interfaces in HPC and Data Science

The conference included the following symposium:

- **MODOPT 2017,** The International Symposium on Modeling and Optimization

We take here the opportunity to warmly thank all the members of the INFOCOMP 2017 technical program committee, as well as all the reviewers. The creation of such a high quality conference program would not have been possible without their involvement. We also kindly thank all the authors that dedicated much of their time and effort to contribute to INFOCOMP 2017. We truly believe that, thanks to all these efforts, the final conference program consisted of top quality contributions.

We also gratefully thank the members of the INFOCOMP 2017 organizing committee for their help in handling the logistics and for their work that made this professional meeting a success.

We hope that INFOCOMP 2017 was a successful international forum for the exchange of ideas and results between academia and industry and to promote further progress in the areas of advanced communication and computation. We also hope that Venice, Italy provided a pleasant environment during the conference and everyone found some time to enjoy the unique charm of the city.

**INFOCOMP 2017 Chairs**

**INFOCOMP Steering Committee**
Claus-Peter Rückemann, Leibniz Universität Hannover / Westfälische Wilhelms-Universität Münster / North-German Supercomputing Alliance (HLRN), Germany [Chair]
Kei Davis, Los Alamos National Laboratory, USA
Malgorzata Pankowska, University of Economics, Katowice, Poland
Subhash Saini, NASA, USA
Hans-Joachim Bungartz, Technische Universität München (TUM) - Garching, Germany
Almadena Chtchelkanova, National Science Foundation - Arlington, USA

**INFOCOMP Industry/Research Advisory Committee**
Bernhard Bandow, Max Planck Institute for Solar System Research (MPS), Göttingen, Germany
Alfred Geiger, T-Systems Solutions for Research GmbH, Germany
Philipp Kremer, German Aerospace Center (DLR), Institute of Robotics and Mechatronics, Oberpfaffenhofen, Germany
Edgar A. Leon, Lawrence Livermore National Laboratory, USA
Lutz Schubert, Institute of Information Resource Management, University of Ulm, Germany
Walter Lioen, SURFsara, Netherlands
Huong Ha, UON Singapore and University of Newcastle, Australia
Manfred Krafczyk, Institute for Computational Modeling in Civil Engineering (iRMB) - Braunschweig, Germany
Hans-Günther Müller, Cray, Germany

**MODOPT 2017 Chairs**

**MODOPT Advisory Committee**
Ian Flood, Rinker School, College of Design, Construction and Planning | University of Florida, USA
Mauro Iacono, Seconda Università degli Studi di Napoli, Caserta, Italy
Jay Lofstead, Sandia National Laboratories, USA
Robert Wille, Johannes Kepler University Linz, Austria
Laura Carrington, PMaC Lab/SDSC/UCSD, USA
Frank Herrmann, Ostbayerische Technische Hochschule - Regensburg, Germany

**INFOCOMP 2017**
**Committee**

**INFOCOMP Steering Committee**

Claus-Peter Rückemann, Leibniz Universität Hannover / Westfälische Wilhelms-Universität Münster / North-German Supercomputing Alliance (HLRN), Germany [Chair]
Kei Davis, Los Alamos National Laboratory, USA
Malgorzata Pankowska, University of Economics, Katowice, Poland
Subhash Saini, NASA, USA
Hans-Joachim Bungartz, Technische Universität München (TUM) - Garching, Germany
Almadena Chtchelkanova, National Science Foundation - Arlington, USA

**INFOCOMP Industry/Research Advisory Committee**

Bernhard Bandow, Max Planck Institute for Solar System Research (MPS), Göttingen, Germany
Alfred Geiger, T-Systems Solutions for Research GmbH, Germany
Philipp Kremer, German Aerospace Center (DLR), Institute of Robotics and Mechatronics, Oberpfaffenhofen, Germany
Edgar A. Leon, Lawrence Livermore National Laboratory, USA
Lutz Schubert, Institute of Information Resource Management, University of Ulm, Germany
Walter Lioen, SURFsara, Netherlands
Huong Ha, UON Singapore and University of Newcastle, Australia
Manfred Krafczyk, Institute for Computational Modeling in Civil Engineering (iRMB) - Braunschweig, Germany
Hans-Günther Müller, Cray, Germany

**INFOCOMP 2017 Technical Program Committee**

Mehmet Aksit, University of Twente, Netherlands
Daniel Andresen, Kansas State University, USA
Raymond Bair, Argonne National Laboratory / University of Chicago, USA
Bernhard Bandow, Max Planck Institute for Solar System Research (MPS), Göttingen, Germany
Hans-Joachim Bungartz, Technische Universität München (TUM) - Garching, Germany
Xiao-Chuan Cai, University of Colorado Boulder, USA
Ralph H. Castain, Intel Inc., USA
Hsi-Ya Chang, National Center for High-Performance Computing, Taiwan
Jian Chang, Bournemouth University, UK
Shuai Che, Advanced Micro Devices, USA
Albert M. K. Cheng, University of Houston, USA
Almadena Chtchelkanova, National Science Foundation, USA
Noelia Correia, University of Algarve | CEOT (Center for Electronics, Optoelectronics and Telecommunications), Portugal

Kei Davis, Los Alamos National Laboratory, USA
Amine Dhraief, ESEN/HANA Research Lab - University of Manouba, Tunisia
Vanessa End, GWDG, Germany
Iman Faraji, Queen's University, Canada
Ian Flood, Rinker School, College of Design, Construction and Planning - University of Florida, USA
Munehiro Fukuda, University of Washington, Bothell, USA
Alfred Geiger, T-Systems Solutions for Research GmbH, Germany
Birgit Gersbeck-Schierholz, Leibniz Universität Hannover, Germany
Franca Giannini, IMATI-CNR, Italy
Vincenzo Gulisano, Chalmers University of Technology, Sweden
Shakhmametova Gyuzel, Ufa State Aviation Technical University, Russia
Huong Ha, UON Singapore and University of Newcastle, Australia
Thomas Heller, Friedrich-Alexander-Universität Erlangen-Nürnberg, Germany
Enrique Hernández Orallo, Universidad Politécnica de Valencia, Spain
Daniel Holmes, EPCC | The University of Edinburgh, Scotland, UK
Friedrich Hülsmann, Gottfried Wilhelm Leibniz Bibliothek, Hannover, Germany
Haziq Jeelani, Galgotias University, India
Seifedine Kadry, American University of the Middle East, Kuwait
Larry Kaplan, Cray Inc., USA
Izabela Karsznia, University of Warsaw, Poland
Jinoh Kim, Texas A&M University-Commerce, USA
Alexander Kipp, Robert Bosch GmbH, Germany
Philipp Kremer, German Aerospace Center (DLR), Institute of Robotics and Mechatronics, Oberpfaffenhofen, Germany
Zlatinka Kovacheva, Department of Mathematics and Applied Sciences, Middle East College - Muscat, Oman
Manfred Krafczyk, Institute for Computational Modeling in Civil Engineering (iRMB) – TU Braunschweig, Germany
Bettina Krammer, MoRitS, Bielefeld University & Bielefeld University of Applied Sciences, Germany
Rolf Krause, Università della Svizzera italiana, Switzerland
Herbert Kuchen, Westfälische Wilhelms-Universität | Institut für Wirtschaftsinformatik, Germany
Kalyan Kumaran, Argonne Leadership Computing Facility, USA
Robert S. Laramee, Swansea University, UK
Edgar A. Leon, Lawrence Livermore National Laboratory, USA
Elżbieta Lewańska, Poznan University of Economics and Business, Poland
Yanting Li, City University of HongKong, China
Walter Lioen, SURFsara, Netherlands
Iryna Lishchuk, Institut für Rechtsinformatik | Leibniz Universität Hannover, Germany
Maciej Liskiewicz, Universität zu Lübeck, Germany
Xing Liu, IBM T. J. Watson Research Center, USA
Piotr Luszczek, University of Tennessee, USA

António Manuel Duarte Nogueira, University of Aveiro - Instituto de Telecomunicações, Portugal
Antonio Martí-Campoy, Universitat Politècnica de València, Spain
Nikolaos Matsatsinis, Technical University of Crete, Greece
Artis Mednis, Akero Systems, Latvia
Roderick Melnik, MS2Discovery Interdisciplinary Research Institute | Wilfrid Laurier University (WLU), Canada
Sangman Moh, Chosun University, Korea
Hans-Guenther Mueller, Cray, Germany
Marian Mureșan, Babes-Bolyai University, Cluj-Napoca, Romania
Syed Naqvi, Birmingham City University, UK
Christoph Niethammer, High Performance Computing Center Stuttgart (HLRS), Stuttgart, Germany
Lena Noack, Royal Observatory of Belgium (ROB), Belgium
Ulrich Norbisrath, University of Applied Sciences Upper Austria (FH UA) Linz, Austria / George Mason University, USA
Krzysztof Okarma, West Pomeranian University of Technology, Szczecin, Poland
Aida Omerovic, SINTEF ICT, Norway
Malgorzata Pankowska, University of Economics in Katowice, Poland
Giuseppe Patane', CNR-IMATI, Italy
Ron Perrott, Oxford e-Research Centre | University of Oxford, UK
Daniela Pöhn, Fraunhofer AISEC, Germany
Simon Portegies Zwart, Leiden University, Netherlands
Guillaume Puigt, CERFACS, France
Giovanni Puglisi, University of Cagliari, Italy
Francesco Quaglia, DIAG - Sapienza Universita' di Roma, Italy
Elena Ravve, ORT Braude College, Israel
Ustijana Rechkoska Shikoska, University for Information Science and Technology "St. Paul the Apostle" - Ohrid, Republic of Macedonia
Yenumula B. Reddy, Grambling State University, USA
Theresa-Marie Rhyne, Visualization Consultant, Durham, USA
Claus-Peter Rückemann, Westfälische Wilhelms-Universität Münster / Leibniz Universität Hannover / North-German Supercomputing Alliance, Germany
Hakizumwami Birali Runesha, Research Computing Center | University of *Chicago*, USA
Subhash Saini, NASA, USA
Sebastiano Fabio Schifano, University of Ferrara / INFN, Italy
Lutz Schubert, Institute of Information Resource Management, University of Ulm, Germany
Isabel Schwerdtfeger, IBM Deutschland GmbH, Germany
Tapan K. Sengupta, IIT Kanpur, India
Theodore Simos, Ural Federal University - Ekaterinburg, Russian Federation | University of Peloponnese - Tripolis, Greece
Rolf Sperber, Consultant, Huawei European Research Centre Munich, Germany
Mu-Chun Su, National Central University, Taiwan
Hongyang Sun, Vanderbilt University, USA

Mahmut Taylan Kandemir, Pennsylvania State University, USA
Rengan Xu, Dell EMC, USA
Qimin Yang, Harvey Mudd College, USA
Sotirios Ziavras, New Jersey Institute of Technology, USA
Jason Zurawski, Lawrence Berkley National Laboratory / Energy Sciences Network (ESnet), USA

**MODOPT Advisory Committee**

Ian Flood, Rinker School, College of Design, Construction and Planning | University of Florida, USA
Mauro Iacono, Seconda Università degli Studi di Napoli, Caserta, Italy
Jay Lofstead, Sandia National Laboratories, USA
Robert Wille, Johannes Kepler University Linz, Austria
Laura Carrington, PMaC Lab/SDSC/UCSD, USA
Frank Herrmann, Ostbayerische Technische Hochschule - Regensburg, Germany

**MODOPT 2017 Program Committee Members**

Jinbo Bi, University of Connecticut, USA
Laura Carrington, PMaC Lab/SDSC/UCSD, USA
Qiang (Shawn) Cheng, Southern Illinois University, USA
Ian Flood, Rinker School, College of Design, Construction and Planning | University of Florida, USA
Rachel Harrison, Oxford Brookes University, UK
Frank Herrmann, Ostbayerische Technische Hochschule Regensburg, Germany
Mauro Iacono, Seconda Università degli Studi di Napoli, Caserta, Italy
SangHyun Lee, University of Michigan, USA
Yaliang Li, SUNY Buffalo, USA
Jay Lofstead, Sandia National Laboratories, USA
Qi Mao, HERE, Chicago, USA
Roderick Melnik, Wilfrid Laurier University, Canada
Haralambos Mouratidis, University of Brighton, UK
Claus-Peter Rückemann, Westfälische Wilhelms-Universität Münster / Leibniz Universität Hannover / North-German Supercomputing Alliance, Germany
Junming Shao, University of Electronic Science and Technology of China, China
Vassilios Verykios, Hellenic Open University, Greece
Robert Wille, Johannes Kepler University Linz, Austria
Dietmar Winkler, Vienna University of Technology, Austria
Feng Yan, University of Nevada, Reno, USA
Yan Zheng, University of Utah, USA

**Copyright Information**

# Data Visualization of Agent-Based Simulation of an Infectious Spread

Jingyi Gan
Tepper School of Business
Carnegie Mellon University
Pittsburgh, PA 15213
Email: kyragan@cmu.edu

Dominique Thiebaut
Dept. Computer Science
Smith College
Northampton, MA 01063
Email: dthiebaut@smith.edu

***Abstract*—We present a novel data visualization approach to display the contact trace of the spread of an infection between individuals. This visualization presents the spread as a radial organizational chart, where each node is an infected person, and the distance from the root to a node is proportional to time. We use real registration information for a population of students at a small college to generate a social network that is fed to an agent-based simulator. The simulation implements the Susceptible-Infected-Recovered (SIR) model to control how the infection moves from one individual to another. Contrarily to other models that generate expected quantities, our tool displays scenarios of a typical outbreak, where individuals involved in the spread are identified, along with the trace of their infection. The usefulness of our tool is in illustrating at the micro level phenomena such as the appearance of super-spreaders, or the influence of interventions such as quarantine or vaccination. We present several visualizations corresponding to different SIR parameters, and also illustrating the effect of vaccination.**

***Keywords–data visualization; agent-based modeling; discrete event simulation; social network; contract graph; intervention strategies; contact-tracin; SIR model***

## I. Introduction

In this paper we present a novel approach for visualizing the *contact-trace* or *contact-map* [1] resulting from the spread of an infectious disease in a population whose *social network* [2], [3] is known a-priori. The contact map is generated from the data output by an *agent-based* simulator that uses the SIR model [4] to control agents representing the students enrolled at Smith College (2,625 students) during the fall semester of 2012, and for whom we have obtained the complete individual course registration (487 different courses), as well as their lodging information for that semester (49 different dorms). Because students at Smith College live on-campus, we can simulate their every-day contacts during class, during meals, and during study periods. The fine-grain simulation evolves on a one-hour scale, and lasts the 14 weeks of a semester, or shorter if the whole population gets infected.

Our contact-map is a variant of *radial organizational charts* [5], where a tree is displayed with its root in the middle of the graph, and all its descendants organized in a 360-degree fanout. In our implementation, each node of the tree is a student, and the root is the first infected student. Edges link students who directly infect other students, with the infecter closer to the root than the infected. New for this type of visualization, we set the length of an edge to be directly proportional to the time it takes for an infected student to infect another student. In the SIR model, individuals are infected only if they are susceptible, after which point they incubate the virus, and then become contagious for a given period of time, after which they recover and are not contagious any longer. Using time as the scale of the graph helps better understand how quickly the outbreak expands, and how long it lasts.

Different visualization attributes, such as node size and color, as well as edge width are available to enhance various properties of the infectius spread. We set the size of a node to vary proportionally to the number of other students directly and indirectly infected by the student associated with that node (number of tree descendants).

The advantage of such a map is that it can help the contact-tracing process at the beginning of an outbreak when a few individuals in a real population are found to be infected. If the social network of the whole population is known, then possible scenarios for the spread of the infectious disease can be plotted, and the efficacy of various preventive measures, e.g. vaccination, or quarantine, can be evaluated through simulation. The opportunity to assess visually the most probable path taken by an infectious disease as it spreads through a population is a beneficial complement to standard contact investigative techniques.

The population used in our simulation is a closed population, which we assume has no contact with the outside world. In a way we simulate a campus without staff or faculty. While it is a simplistic rendition of real life on campus, it does provide insights for important situations where the population is isolated from the rest of the world, such as in hospitals, on ships, or in small towns, as have been investigated in [6]–[8].

When studying an infectious outbreak, health researchers typically use stochastic models to assess the spread of a disease. Some tools use geographical information systems (see [9] for an example of a visualization of heat-maps of the spread of mosquito-based diseases), and others present statistical properties of the infected population over time. These tools provide a good understanding of the overall spread, but offer no knowledge of how the infection spreads from one individual to the next. The ability to trace a given individual and the spread of infection it creates, and to observe how key agents appear and affect the infection, such as *super-spreaders* [10], can help health professionals better control infection outbreaks.

In the next section, we review background information that puts our research in context. In Section II, we describe the real data we use to drive our agent-based model, which is presented in Section III. In Section IV, we present several data-visualizations illustrating how different SIR parameters or interventions affect the contact map, and we provide an analysis of the graphs in Section V. Section VI concludes this paper.

### A. Background

The major work that provides an overview of data visualization techniques in the health field is that of Carroll et al [11] who study a "myriad of new tools and algorithms [that] have been developed to help public health professionals analyse and visualize the complex data used in infectious disease control." Our visualization tool belongs in their *social network analysis* section, which they report as one of the most recent and growing fields of the health literature, accounting for approximately 10% of the total number of yearly health publications. While the general purpose of the tools surveyed is to address the identification of common characteristics, such as *risk stratification* of contacts, *identifying common characteristics* of those infected, *visually communicating* cases for improved understanding of outbreaks, and *identifying potential pathways of transmission*, they note that as network data becomes more available, new diverse methods of visualization will be needed [11]. We suggest our work fits in this arena.

Our work also parallels that of Hansen et al [6]. Their approach concentrates on visualizing possible scenarios of the spread of an infectious disease in a hospital, presenting the user with an interactive 3D graphic representation of the floors and rooms of a hospital, and how the infection spreads across the building. The data visualization is driven, as in our case, by an agent-based simulator which is fed the real-life records of the social contacts between health workers and patients. While their visualization has the added advantage of presenting the user with an interactive interface, it does not display a contact trace of the infection, although they very likely have access to the data needed to do so. We see our work as a logical extension, or addition to theirs.

Our data-visualization is also reminiscent of the *shortest-path tree* graph presented by Brokmann [12]. The nodes of Brokmann's tree are airports, and the edges are proportional to the geographical distance separating these airports. In contrast, the edges of our tree are proportional to time, and the nodes are infected individuals. In some ways Brokmann's edges represent an approximation of time, as well, since planes fly regularly from one airport to another, with approximately uniform speed. Our visualization allows an exploration on a much smaller scale than theirs, complementing their work as well.

In the next section, we present the social-network data used in our simulation.

## II. Social-Network Data

Our data is taken from a spreadsheet maintained by the Registrar's office at Smith College which catalogs all classes for which all 2,625 students registered during the Fall of 2012. Each student is identified by a unique Id number. For each student, we have a record of the dorm she resides in and the courses for which she is registered. Each course has a unique Id. A student typically takes four courses a semester, and for each one we have available the daily/weekly time block(s) in which a course meets. The name of the buildings and the classroom numbers where the courses take place are also available. In addition, the type of classroom meeting is also recorded, e.g. studio, performance, lecture, lab, colloquium, discussion, or seminar. We do not use this particular information, but note that it could be used in future work to refine the granularity of the simulation, for example in quarantine scenarios. We process this data and create lists of Ids of students located in each classroom on campus in each time block of the week. These lists of Ids associated to location and time-blocks form the base of our social network. For social connections outside the classroom, we extrapolate the spreadsheet data and assume that students will take their three daily meals in the dorm in which they reside, and that they also study in their dorm after dinner and on weekends. In the next section we describe the discrete-event simulation that processes the list of Ids and controls the state of each agent as the simulated time passes.

## III. The Agent-Based Model

The simulation keeps track of each student, or *agent*, during her weekly schedule, and maintains a status of her health according to the SIR model, where individuals evole through an epidemic by transitioning through different *states*. In the SIR model, somebody is initially assumed to be healthy and ***Susceptible***, then gets ***Infected***, which results in an incubation period $T_i$ during which the student is not contagious, followed by a period $T_c$ where she becomes contagious, which finally ends with the student healing and switching to a ***Recovered*** state. We assume that students maintain their regular activities while they are infected and contagious. In our model, we also allow for a (small) probability $p_r$ for recovered students to remain contagious.

When a susceptible student enters a location where contagious students are located, she experiences a probability $p$ to get infected by each one of them. Contagious students can be those who have recently been infected, or those who have recovered, but are still possibly lightly contagious (with probability $p_r$). In our SIR model, we assume that recovered students are imunized to future infection by the same virus.

The simulation lasts for a simulated time equivalent to a semester of 14 weeks, which matches exactly the duration of a Smith College semester. One student is picked at random (or not, if repeatable scenarios are of interest) at the beginning of the simulation, $T_0$, which coincides with the breakfast period of the first day of class. As the infected student goes about her daily schedule, she randomly infects the susceptible students who come in contact with her, in class, during meals, or during study periods.

The simulator is written in Java and takes an average of 7.8 seconds to run one simulation to completion on a 2.4 GHz Pentium Core i5 with 8 GB Ram. It generates a *contact-trace* of the spread of the infection as a collection of tuples of students Ids associated with a time. The time corresponds to the instant when the second student gets infected. These tuples form the edges of a tree data structure, which is recorded in *DOT* format [13], compatible with the *Graphviz* visualization package [14].

In the next section we present several data visualizations generated from the *dot* output of the simulator.

## IV. Data Visualization

The graphs presented below are generated using *dot* (not to be confused with the dot language), one of the applications

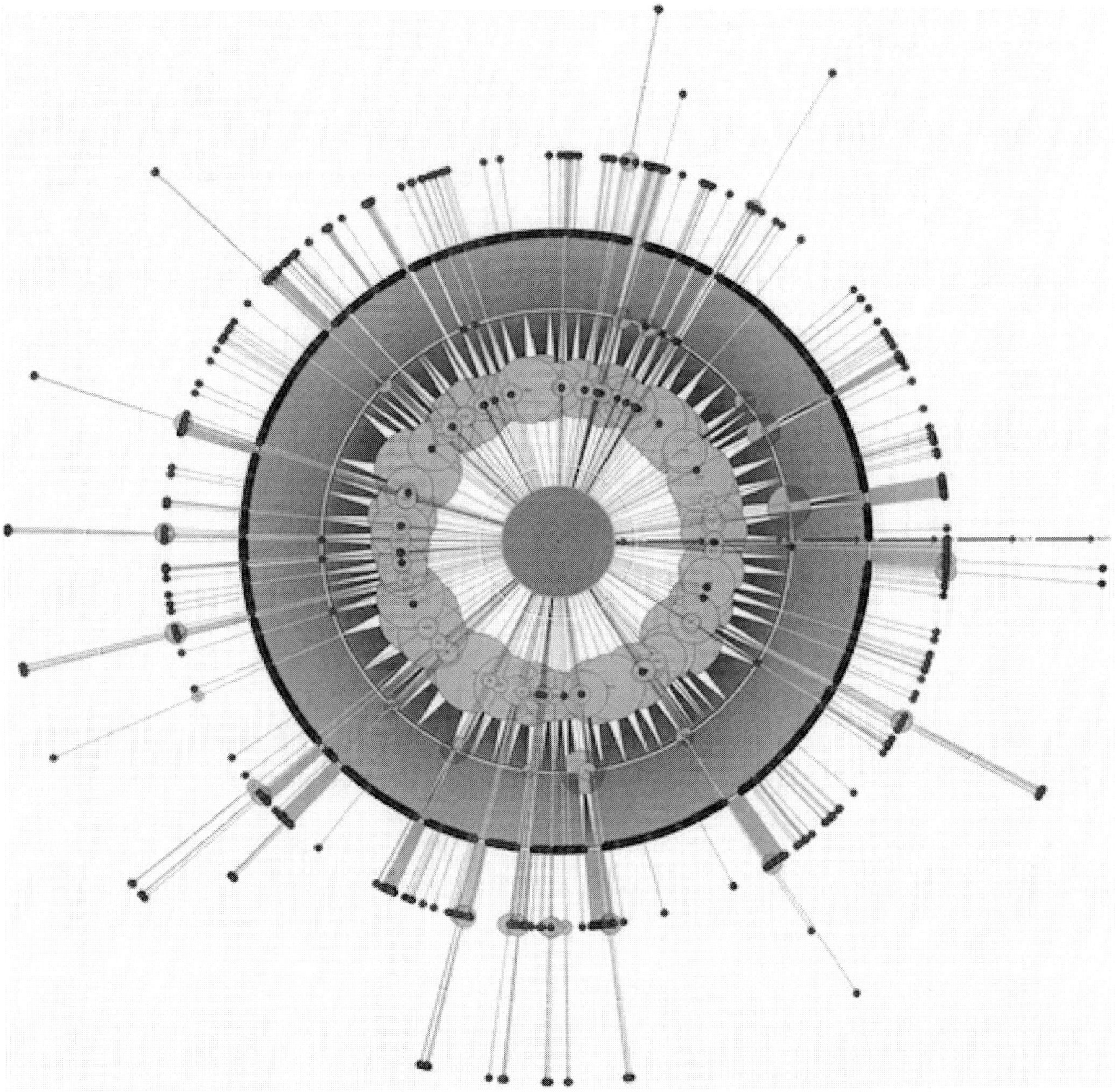

Figure 1. First infected is Student No. 82. $T_i$=6 days, $T_c$=8 days, no vaccination, no quarantine, $p$=1.0.

of the *Graphviz* package. Dot takes the dot-formatted file generated by the simulator and creates a graphic file of the resulting radial graph. We use the Scalable Vector Graphic [15] (SVG) format for the graphic output to fully capture the details of such a large number of tree nodes and levels. Generating the SVG file typically takes an average of 5.5 seconds on the same 2.4 GHz Pentium Core i5, and the resulting graphic file is 5 to 10 MBytes in size.

Figure 1 shows the contact-map resulting from a simulation where we set $p$=1.0, which ensures that if two students attend the same class, or share a meal in the same cafeteria, and one is infected, than the other automatically catches the infection. $p$=1 also ensures that the whole population gets infected (unless there exist subgroups of students who never interact with the larger population of students). While setting $p$ to 1 is not a realistic situation, it presents the interesting boundary-case scenario that would result from an extraordinarily virulent infection. The parameters used in Figure 1 are $p$=1, $p_r$=0, $T_c$=8 days, and $T_i$=6 days.

Each graph also bares a time axis organized as a series of

arrows going from the center of the graph to the East, and complements the graph. In Figure 1, the length of each arrow corresponds to 3 days. The largest concentric circle has a radius of 21 days, indicating that the whole student population is infected after 21 days.

The first infected student is at the center of the graph, and is shown in red. The size of a node is proportional to the number of people infected by the student associated with that node. The radius of a node is defined as $radius = \log(1 + number of descendants) * 0.35$. Nodes other than the root are either orange of purple, depending on whether they infect several people, or just one, respectively. We note that most of the orange nodes fall on the first concentric circle of the circular graph, and are the largest of the tree, indicating that these students will behave as super-spreaders, as they have more time than the others to infect students they'll come in contact with. Because the time periods $T_c$ and $T_i$ are constant, and not taken from a distribution, all the nodes fall exactly on a few concentric circles, relative to the root.

Note also that the locations where the tree nodes are placed are algorithmically picked for optimal use of the space by the *dot* application, and slight variations in the tree may result in significantly different looking graphs.

Figure 2 shows a close-up region of Figure 1, illustrating the numbering of the nodes with the student Id, and the detail of the time scale.

When $p$ is set to a more realistic value of 0.01, we obtain the graph depicted in Figure 3. It now takes 36 simulated days for the whole population to be infected, but the dynamics at the beginning of the infection is more complex than observed in Figure 1, with a distribution of differently sized super-spreaders who start their infectious path around Days 15 and 18.

In Figure4, we show how the visualization can help health officials understand the effect of various interventions. In this graph we assume that 50% of the initial population of students is vaccinated at the beginning of the semester, and that those vaccinated have a 0-probability of getting infected, or of becoming carriers of the infection. Since the visualization only shows infected students, Figure 4 contains only half of the population of students, namely those not vaccinated. The outbreak lasts 55 days, and a total of 15% of the total student population gets infected during this time, or 30% of the non-vaccinated students. Here again, we have very different dynamics at play, with a handful of super-spreaders who propagate most of the infection; they are the orange nodes appearing between the Day 24 and Day 36.

## V. ANALYSIS

Our model and visualization present new insights in the way an infectious disease spreads in a closed population for which the social network is well defined. Each figure represents one of many possible scenarios, and should not be seen as an average behavior; just a probable one. Unless the seed of the random number generated remains the same for different simulations, two different simulations with the same initial parameters and root student will yield two different trees. Whether the simulated growth of the infected population bears a chaotic component is open for research, however, it is helpful to see the trees generated by the agent-based simulator as

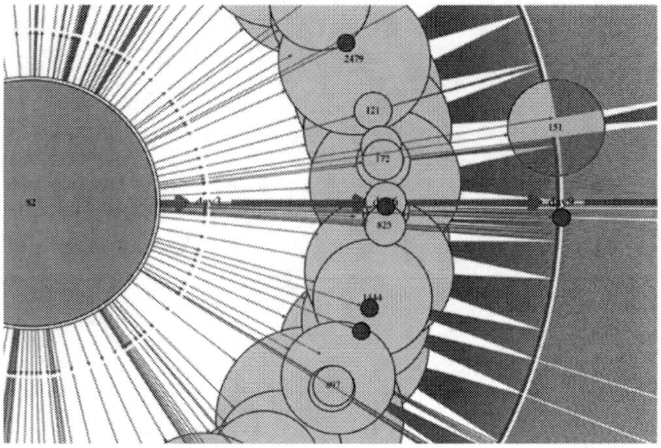

Figure 2. Close-up of Figure 1, showing details including node labeling and time scale.

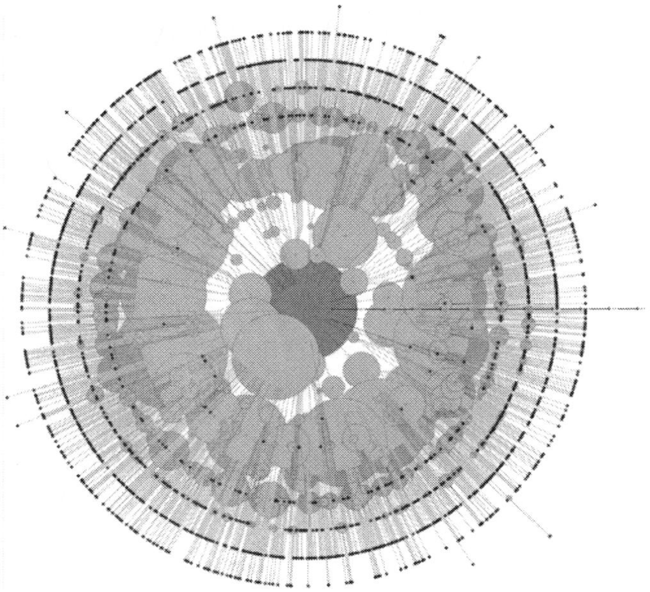

Figure 3. Contact map for $p$=0.01, $T_i$=6 days, and $T_c$=8 days.

different expressions of some dynamical system, all with the same *strange attractor* [16]. Our data visualizations present the micro-level dynamics of the infection, rather than an average variation of some quantity.

It is easy to see that given an infected student in the population, our model provides an exact trace of who infects her, and who she infects in turn. Moreover, the day and location of the infection from one student to the other is known exactly. Such information could easily be added to an interactive version of our visualizations.

Our visualizations also offer the ability for health officials to investigate an infectious spread in its early stage, when just a few students are found to be infected. Assuming the social network for the population is available, a modified data visualization can show the group of infected students in a collective multi-node root of the tree, and the trace of

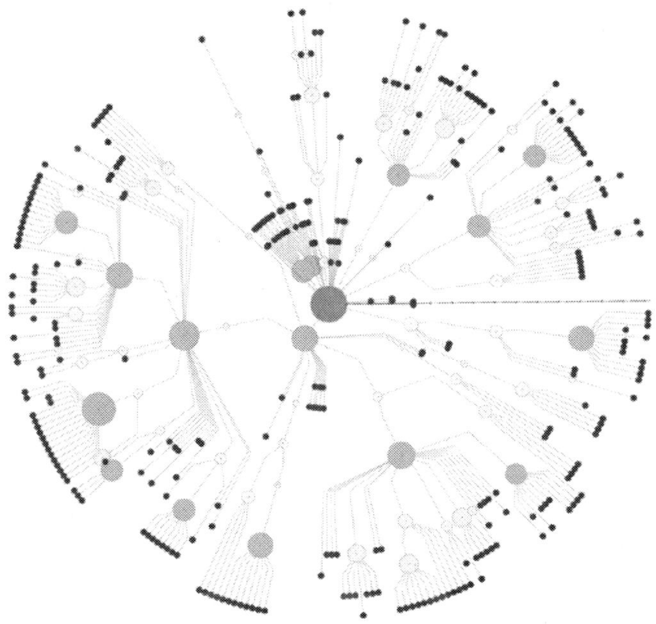

Figure 4. Contact-map for $p$=0.01, $T_i$=6 days, and $T_c$=8 days, with 50% of the initial population vaccinated. The probability that a vaccinated person is contagious is 0.

potential contacts emanating from it. Officials can then use this information to order local quarantines on buildings or dorms, or cancellation of meetings in particular locations or time blocks.

Different visualization attributes, such as node size and color, as well as edge width are available for enhancing various properties of the infectious spread. We decided to use the size of a node to grow proportionally to the number of other students directly and indirectly infected by its associated student. Interaction and animation could also enhance the visualization; time-lapse growth of the tree, or selection of particular branches or nodes, for example, could enhance the usefulness of our tool. We note, however that the size of the population makes it challenging to display the entirety of the tree with good resolution.

## VI. Conclusions

In [11], Carroll et al. review visualization and analytical tools for infectious disease, and state "visualization methods to help users understand network structures have not been widely employed in tools for public health." Our visualization tool answers this call and presents a novel approach for evaluating probable spreads of an infectious disease in a closed population with a known social network.

The radial organization provides a low-level understanding the dynamics of an infection, and how different parameters such as vaccination, or quarantine, can affect its spread, as illustrated in Figure 4.

Several improvements to the model are possible. For example, we could take $T_i$ and $T_c$ from a distribution other than the uniform distribution. We could also create super-spreaders by picking several agents before or during the simulation, and by giving them an a-priori probability distribution for the virulence with which they act. Both the population size of super-spreaders and their virulence can easily be coded in the model. The model can also be augmented so that various scenarios are triggered automatically when a particular threshold of infection is detected in the simulation. Such scenarios could involve the cancellation of classes taking place in amphitheatres, or forcing students to eat their meals in their dorm room.

We also noted earlier that an interactive visualization could provide additional information that is available but impossible to display on a static image. This include offering the user an interactive menu to modify key SIR and visual parameters, as is presented in [17]. Other improvements include generating a full contact path between selected students showing the identity of the students, the location and time of the contacts.

Finally, we note that our visualization tool could be used to evaluate various properties of key agents, such as super-spreaders, and compare simulation outputs to real data in an effort to find the model parameters best matching observed behavior. We have however to take Carroll's advice seriously, when he and his coauthors state [11] that visualization tools also risk misleading users due to misinterpretation or cognitive overload. Sometimes, simpler is better.

The code for the agent-based simulator can be found on this repository [18].

## Acknowledgments

We gratefully acknowledge the insightful comments and suggestions given to us by Professors Sarah Moore, of the engineering department, and Robert Dorit, of the department of biological sciences, both at Smith College.

## References

[1] S. Etkind, "Contact tracing. TB: a comprehensive international approach," in Lung Biology in Health and Disease, L. Reichman and E. Hershfield, Eds. New York, NY: Marcel Dekker, 1993, pp. 275 – 289.

[2] F. Viegas and J. Donath, "Social network visualization: Can we go beyond the graph," in Workshop on Social Networks, CSCW, vol. 4, 2004, pp. 6–10.

[3] P. McElroy, R. Rothenberg, R. Varghese, R. Woodruff, G. Minns, S. Muth, L. Lambert, and R. Ridzon, "A network-informed approach to investigating a tuberculosis outbreak: implications for enhancing contact investigations," The International Journal of Tuberculosis and Lung Disease, vol. 7, no. Supplement 3, 2003, pp. S486–S493.

[4] R. M. Anderson and R. M. May, Infectious Diseases of Humans: Dynamics and Control. Oxford University Press, 1992.

[5] R. L. Harris, Information Graphics: A Comprehensive Illustrated Reference. Oxford University Press, 2000.

[6] T. E. Hansen, J. P. Hourcade, A. Segre, C. Hlady, P. Polgreen, and C. Wyman, "Interactive visualization of hospital contact network data on multi-touch displays," in Proceedings of the 3rd Mexican Workshop on Human Computer Interaction, ser. MexIHC '10. San Luis Potosi, S.L.P. Mexico, Mexico: Universidad Politecnica de San Luis Potosi, 2010, pp. 15–22. [Online]. Available: http://dl.acm.org/citation.cfm?id=1978702.1978708

[7] B. Yu, J. Wang, M. McGowan, and G. Vaidyanathan, "Agent-based stochastic simulations of shipboard disease outbreaks," in Proceedings of the 2010 Spring Simulation Multiconference, ser. SpringSim '10. San Diego, CA, USA: Society for Computer Simulation International, 2010, pp. 123:1–123:8. [Online]. Available: http://dx.doi.org/10.1145/1878537.1878666

[8] J. B. B. C. D. Shamir, N. M. M. Laskowski, and M. F. R. D. McLeod, "Smartphone technologies for social network data generation and infectious disease modeling," Journal of Medical and Biological Engineering, vol. 32, no. 4, 2012, pp. 235–244.

[9] S. M. Mniszewski, C. A. Manore, C. Bryan, S. Y. Del Valle, and D. Roberts, "Towards a hybrid agent-based model for mosquito borne disease," in Proceedings of the 2014 Summer Simulation Multiconference, ser. SummerSim '14. San Diego, CA, USA: Society for Computer Simulation International, 2014, pp. 10:1–10:8. [Online]. Available: http://dl.acm.org/citation.cfm?id=2685617.2685627

[10] W. Duan, X. Qiu, Z. Cao, X. Zheng, K. Cui et al., "Heterogeneous and stochastic agent-based models for analyzing infectious diseases' super spreaders," IEEE Intelligent Systems, July/August 2013, pp. 18–25.

[11] L. N. Carroll, A. P. Au, L. T. Detwiler, T. chieh Fu, I. S. Painter, and N. F. Abernethy, "Visualization and analytics tools for infectious disease epidemiology: A systematic review," Journal of Biomedical Informatics, vol. 51, 2014, pp. 287 – 298. [Online]. Available: http://www.sciencedirect.com/science/article/pii/S1532046414000914

[12] D. Brockmann and D. Helbing, "The Hidden Geometry of Complex, Network-Driven Contagion Phenomena," Science, vol. 342, no. 6164, Dec. 2013, pp. 1337–1342. [Online]. Available: http://dx.doi.org/10.1126/science.1245200

[13] E. Gansner, E. Koutsofios, and S. North. Drawing graphs with dot. http://graphviz.org/Documentation/dotguide.pdf. (Accessed Nov. 1, 2006)

[14] A. Bilgin, J. Ellson, E. Gansner, Y. Hu, and S. North. Graphviz - graph visualization software. http://graphviz.org/Documentation/dotguide.pdf. (Accessed Nov. 1, 2016)

[15] O. Andersson, P. Armstrong et al. W3c working draft of scalable vector graphics 1.2. http://www.w3.org/TR/SVG12/. (Accessed Nov. 1, 2017)

[16] F. Takens, Detecting strange attractors in turbulence. Berlin, Heidelberg: Springer Berlin Heidelberg, 1981, pp. 366–381. [Online]. Available: http://dx.doi.org/10.1007/BFb0091924

[17] W. V. d. Broeck, C. Gioannini, B. Gonçalves, M. Quaggiotto, V. Colizza, and A. Vespignani, "The gleamviz computational tool, a publicly available software to explore realistic epidemic spreading scenarios at the global scale," BMC Infectious Diseases, vol. 11, no. 1, 2011, p. 37. [Online]. Available: http://dx.doi.org/10.1186/1471-2334-11-37

[18] J. Gan. Visualizing the transit map of the spread of an infectious disease. http://tinyurl.com/kyra-is. (Accessed Nov. 1, 2016)

# Virtual Reality Assessment of Usability and Ergonomics in Hand Vein Biometric Systems

Septimiu Crisan, Bogdan Tebrean
Faculty of Electrical Engineering
Technical University of Cluj-Napoca
Cluj-Napoca, Romania
email: septimiu.crisan@ethm.utcluj.ro
email: bogdan.tebrean@ethm.utcluj.ro

Simina Emerich
Faculty of Electronics, Telecommunications and Information Technology
Technical University of Cluj-Napoca
Cluj-Napoca, Romania
email: simina.emerich@com.utcluj.ro

***Abstract*—Vein pattern recognition is a relatively new biometric technique that has gained recognition and traction in the last years. Still, for active researchers of this domain, one of the problems that can be identified is the lack of end-user feedback regarding the usability and ergonomics of proposed biometric scanners. In addition, touch-free scanners introduce more issues regarding the pose and postures of users interacting with a biometric device. With the recent advent of virtual reality devices and motion capture systems, large scale tests can be conducted with commercially available packages at a fraction of the price and resource allocation of a real-life usability study. This paper aims to give an insight into the practical implementation of a virtual reality study applied to biometric usability and attempts to offer a possible roadmap where these technologies are complementing behavioral experiments in biometrics.**

***Keywords-vein patterns; biometric recognition; virtual reality; motion capture; inertial sensors.***

## I. INTRODUCTION

Vein pattern recognition is a biometric technique that has gained significant traction in the last decade. Mostly employed on the hand area, common blood vessels for visual extraction are the veins in the back of the hand, palm, forearm or fingers [1][2]. While the underlying science is thoroughly understood, the technology has rarely left the confines of academic research and there are few mainstream applications, usually from large industrial players [3][4].

As a long time research interest of the authors, vein biometrics, especially the veins in the back of the hand, have been analyzed and described in various scientific papers [5-9]. As a direct result of the research, several hardware devices and software algorithms have been devised by the authors for this biometric parameter. New sensing topics, such as unconstrained hand acquisition scenarios; posture, pose and angle of attack for users presenting biometric data and general ergonomics have also been recently discussed [10][11].

The underlying problem is represented by the lack of information regarding user preference -posture and ergonomics- and the degree of usability that a biometric system might have. There is little feedback in the creation of new hardware devices except for the intrinsic technical prowess of a newer prototype. A full-scale experiment involving several tangible mockup devices, where subjects are filmed on location interacting with the biometric systems is difficult to implement due to higher cost and required post-analysis. In addition, changes to real devices in order to account for the ongoing experimental data is difficult to achieve. Even small scale adjustments such as angle of positioning or distance between sensing elements and hand position are challenges for a real hardware device.

Virtual reality has advanced significantly in the last 5 years and commercially available headsets exhibit sufficient resolution and tracking speed for such an experiment. The participants' movements are tracked in real time while using virtual assets and exploring false environments. This technology transposes easily to behavioral data, biometric systems' assessment being a valid use case with no significant prior work being identified by the authors during the state of the art research.

Since the procedure used to acquire the veins of the hand in biometric systems is most often contactless [3]10], there are palpable advantages when using a virtual reality device. In an unconstrained hand scenario, the lack of physical objects to interact with increases immersion since there is no disconnect between what the user sees and feels. In addition, most users unconsciously refuse to walk through solid objects or touch objects that are undesirable to be touched in the real world [12].

With the help of a secondary inertial system, experiments have been carried out related to biometric presentation using free hand rotation with sub-millimeter tracking accuracy on various hand angles on all axes. Also, ergonomic data has been recorded and analyzed for future hardware implementations.

After the introduction in Section 1, Section 2 presents the experimental setup mentioned earlier and Section 3 unveils the experiments that were perform for the virtual reality usability study. The conclusions of the article are depicted in Section 3.

## II. EXPERIMENTAL SETUP

The experimental setup consists of a combination of several consumer level technologies. The general availability of these systems and devices, together with the reduced pricing, allows for reproducible virtual reality research due to early standardization efforts.

The Virtual Reality System chosen for this research is an Oculus Rift CV1 comprised of a headset, hand controllers and external reference cameras for position tracking [13][14]. Orientation tracking is performed using the integrated inertial sensors and the drift is corrected every 20ms by the reference infrared cameras providing a tracking accuracy of 0.5mm and a display refresh rate of 90Hz. The experimental setup involved the placement of four cameras in opposing corners denoting a movable testing space of 3.5 x 3.5m.

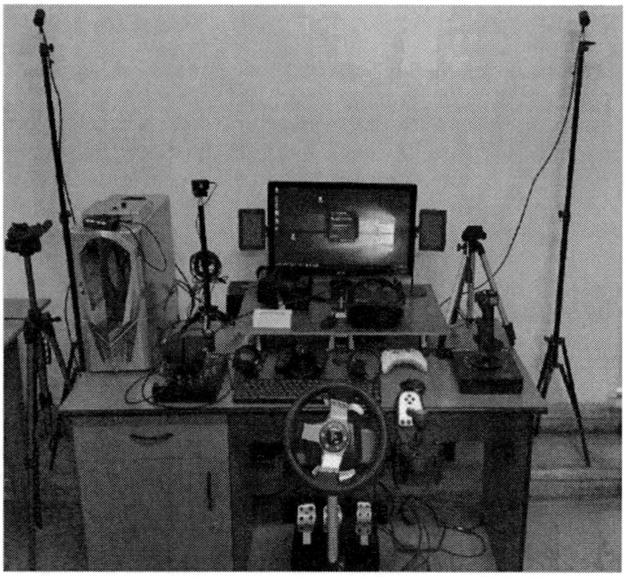

Figure 1. Virtual Reality station and reference sensors. The steering wheel and throttle and stick levers are not used in this particular set of experiments but they are employed for other behavioral studies using virtual reality in biomedical applications.

The Virtual Reality station can be observed in Figure 1 and the tracking area in Figure 2. Figure 1 also reveals other hardware devices used to monitor behavior and posture in multiple biomedical use-cases (intoxicated driving, day – night cycles for workers etc.)

The users of the system can move freely in the designated area; the only inconvenience is the headset cord (carrying video and sensor data) that can get tangled around the user.

A complete untethered package has also been created with the use of an older Oculus headset, the Developer Kit 2. Due to the reduced computational requirements, the headset has been paired with a laptop carried by the user for the duration of the experiments. While this technique has provided substantial data regarding user behavior, the reduced resolution and diminished moving space have been detrimental to the immersion level. The decision has been made to use the powerful but tethered modern system.

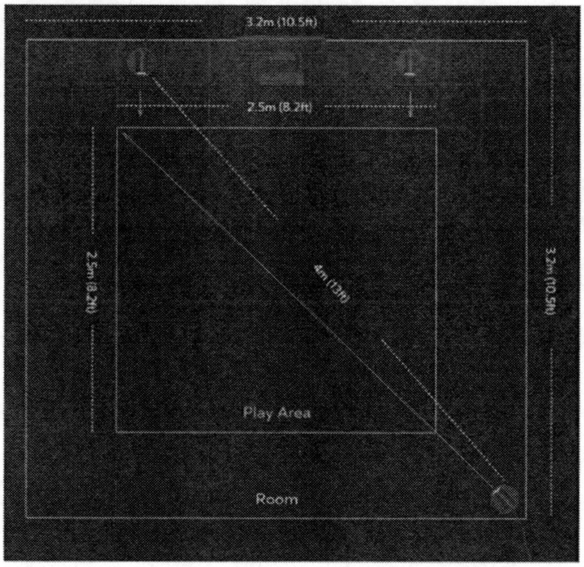


Figure 2. Area trackable by the Oculus Rift headset. [15].

Since the system is only able to distinguish position and orientation of the head and the hands, an extra hardware package has been employed for full body orientation acquisition. The secondary system is a Perception Neuron motion capture suit with 32 individual nodes called "neurons" [16]. Each node is a 9 Degree of Freedom (DoF) sensor (tri-axis accelerometer, gyroscope and magnetometer) that relays the orientation data to a central hub for further processing. Using inverse kinematics and considering the rigid model of the human body, fine movements of the limbs and body can be sensed. Due to the placement of nodes on the fingers of the hand, accurate orientation and position of the user's hand can be inferred, allowing the system to gather sensor data for the main battery of experiments related to usability in hand vein biometrics.

The conforming elastic glove, the active sensing elements and the connections to the central hub are shown in Figure 3.

The glove has 9 sensors capable of detecting minute movements of the hand and fingers in all axes and, due to the inclusion of two extra sensors on the wrist and forearm, the relative angles between the torso and the hands are correctly measured.

The stream of data is very stable if the user has the feet planted on the ground, as the system has a robust detection algorithm based on the fixed position of two neurons on the upper plantar area if the user is not moving. However, being an inertial system with no frame of reference, it is very susceptible to drift if the user displaces the feet from the ground either by walking or jumping.

In order to accurately track body stances and dynamic behavior -while allowing the subjects to move freely- both systems are needed. The difficulty in processing the data from two separate tracking entities arises from the mismatch between the coordinate systems. In addition, the Oculus Rift headset is tracked at the head level while the center node for the Perception Neuron Suit is situated in the middle of the body.

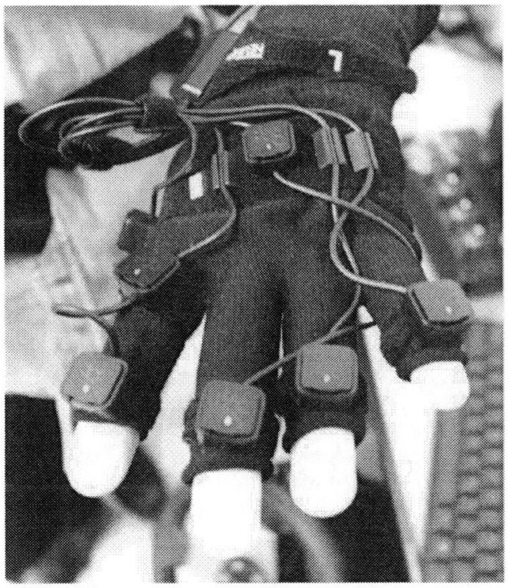

Figure 3. Perception Neuron inertial glove, sensing elements and connections.

Two approaches have been identified and implemented during the experimental phase:

- Fusing the sensor data from the Oculus Rift CV1 with the orientation information gathered from the Perception Neuron suit -using the head as a base node in the kinematics chain.
- Using the Oculus Rift hand controllers- since they are not needed on the hands if the motion capture gloves are employed- rigidly attached to the back and front of the body at the height of the original primary node of the suit.

While both solutions allow the data to be unified for further processing, using the head as a primary node creates additional tracking inaccuracies. This is in part due to the increased number of joints from the head node to the feet and several user poses will allow excessive drift to accumulate over short periods of time.

Using the touch controllers preserves the original point of reference for the inertial suit while offering the same level of accuracy provided by the Rift headset. Employing both hand controllers – while slightly adding difficulty to the pose estimation- offers a higher degree of resistance against optical occlusion, a four-sensor setup detects the position of one or both of the controllers at all positions inside the testing area.

This provides one complete solution for full body tracking in a virtual world with added emphasis on the hand and fingers.

Simulations have been created using Epic Unreal Engine, a photorealistic graphics engine. Asset geometry data has been devised and rendered in Autodesk 3dStudio Max including all the virtual objects, biometric scanners and environments, subsequently being imported in Unreal Engine.

Creating a virtual asset is significantly less expensive and time consuming than creating a real asset. In addition, the use of virtual reality provides multiple scenarios, difficult or impossible to recreate in real life. For the usability experiments, indoor and outdoor scenarios have been employed where the user position and relation to the virtual biometric scanner have been assessed. Initial tests and reactions allowed for a rapid evolution of the virtual prototypes in order to identify a suitable ergonomic and appealable biometric device that offers the highest usability score from the test group.

Data arriving from the Perception Neuron motion capture suit have been processed in real time using the Axis Neuron Pro application and relayed as a BVH stream (Biovision Hierarchical Data) of skeleton hierarchy and motion data to the simulation using the Unreal plugin of the Axis application. The motion to photon latency measured in the full pipeline is 27ms resulting in an adequate dynamic response of the virtual reality system while decreasing the risk of simulator sickness for the participants of the usability study.

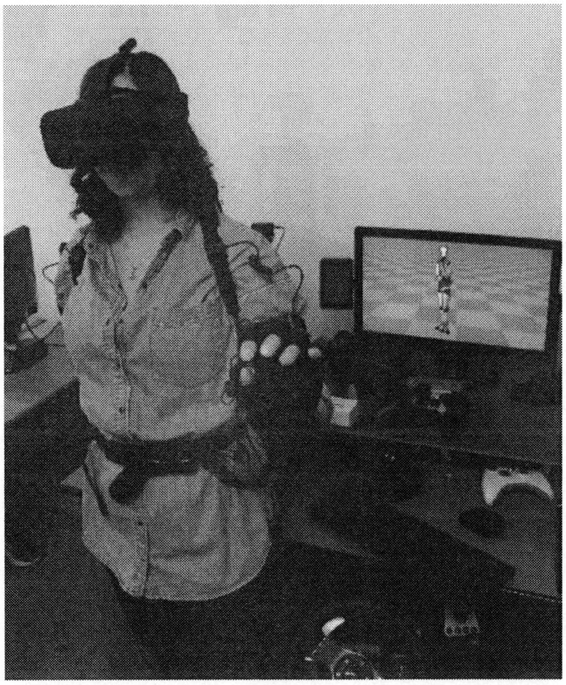

Figure 4. Experimental setup and sensor fusion results. Test-person in front of VR station wearing Oculus Rift headset with Neuron Perception suit.

Figure 4 shows the experimental setup in the post calibration stage.

## III. TESTING PROCEDURE AND RESULTS

A group of 37 people has been enrolled in the experiments. The experiments were detailed and an informed consent was obtained from all participants. The age interval is intentionally reduced and spans from 20 to 26 years. For this particular testing, the age constraint has been put in place to avoid potential false results due to different understanding and acceptance of cutting edge technology at different stages in life. The age group will be widened to be statistically relevant in future experiments after determining optimum positions and hand placement from users accustomed with the technology. All users have had a previous encounter with the same variant of a biometric vein scanner and have used the virtual reality device used in the experiments. In order to minimize external influences on the perception of the virtual system – nausea or dizziness associated with some applications of VR systems, excessive arm fatigue or altered proprioception due to sensory mismatch- several rules have been devised:

- Each user is presented with only 6 different virtual vein scanners starting from the known one. The goal is to avoid arm fatigue due to the position of the hand in the virtual scanner, a condition very similar to the "gorilla arm syndrome" exhibited by users of vertical touch screens [17].
- Movement is performed on a 1 to 1 scale and there is no vection and therefore no vestibular mismatch [18]. The user is free to roam the play area and the edges of the virtual space are marked with a subtle but easy to understand virtual grid that appears when the user is touching the borders of the play space.
- For each user, the Intra-Pupillary Distance (IPD) is measured and the height of the individual is also entered in the simulation thus preventing eye fatigue and disorientation.
- The virtual wall of the simulation is complemented by a real separator shifted 40cm outside the experiment area to increase immersion and in the same time to avoid users bumping into real walls since the virtual grid acts as an early alert system.
- There are no movable parts in the simulations or objects that might entice the user to lean on or touch, in part to avoid sensory disconnections and to prevent potential injuries.
- Generic, low feature avatars are used for the virtual bodies of the users involved in the usability experiments – setup does not elicit additional behavioral impulses [18].

For each individual user, a configuration file has been created based on their biometric data (height, IPD, vision correction parameters). In addition, every participant in the test received a 10-minute accommodation period in the testing area using the Oculus Rift headset and the Perception Neuron suit- with no biometric hardware setups shown at this stage.

Three sets of experiments have been performed using the virtual reality setup.

For experiment 1, each virtual scanner has a working area that has not been previously disclosed to the participants. Using a modified variant of the tests performed in [20], the users were asked to scan their vein patterns on a "contactless" device. The number of tries has been recorded as well as the distance of the user's hand to the biometric scanner. In addition, the ability of a user to quickly find the optimum position has been recorded as the total time between the start of the simulation and the successful scan.

Experiment 2 has been necessitated by current research of the authors in orientation and position invariant scanning algorithms. Calibration of the algorithms for hard angles (users inserting their hands in the scanning area at angles above 15°) is difficult to achieve in part due to the occlusion of veins when the hand is tilted too much. Experiments have determined that the overwhelming majority of users are below these limits and several steps can be introduced in the creation of biometric scanners to visually guide the user's hand placement.

For the last experiment, in order to verify the perceived accuracy and immersion of the experimental setup, a biometric system using a physical support handle for the hand has been modeled in the CAD software used previously. The part of the system that the user interacts with has also been physically created in Polylactic Acid (PLA) with the use of a general purpose Ultimaker 3D printer - employing the Cura software package for toolpath generation. The printed handle and support have been placed in a precise manner in the experimental area in order to match the position of the virtual handle module. This allows a level of interaction more common to an AR (Augmented Reality) setup and reveals both physical and behavioral user information.

Table 1 shows the results for the first virtual scanner-resembling the real device previously presented to the test participants.

TABLE I. USABILITY RESULTS FOR SCANNER 1

| Scanner 1 | Contactless scanner usability | | |
|---|---|---|---|
| | *Parameters* | *Number* | *Obs.* |
| Exp. 1 | Number of succesful first tries | 31 | |
| | Total number of tries (all users) | 44 | 5 double tries and one triple attempt |
| | Average distance of hovering hand to scanner | 12cm | 86 % of test-users in optimum range of 10-15cm |
| | Average time from simulation start to successful scan | 9.2 s | 37 people sample size |
| | Lower back angle compensation for scanner height | >11° for 15% of users | Consistent with height |
| Exp. 2 | Average angle of attack for vertical axis (roll on horizontal axis) | 6° | 96% of users between -15°...+15° |
| | Average angle of attack for horizontal axis (yaw on vertical axis) | 4° | 90% users between -10°...+8° |
| | Average angle of attack for horizontal axis (pitch on horizontal axis) | 11° | 68% users between -10°...+9° |
| | Percentage of clenched fist vs. open hand | 94% | Previously instructed to |

| Scanner 1 | Contactless scanner usability | | |
|---|---|---|---|
| | ***Parameters*** | ***Number*** | ***Obs.*** |
| | | | use clenched fist posture |
| Exp. 3 | Number of succesful first tries (reaching and touching real handle) | 35 | 2 users required multiple tries- eye conditions |
| | Willingness to retouch – number of users | 32 | 5 users expressed anxiety over retouching sensor 1 -either due to different feel of the texture or slight miscalibration of the visual cues. The general consensus was "lack of realism" |

Complete experimental results have been gathered for all six virtual biometric scanners and the designs have been updated to take into account the usability impact assessed in the tests. In order to aim for a standardization proposal for a modular vein pattern biometric scanner, usability and ergonomics data gathered in this research will allow an academic device to gain commercial attributes difficult to quantify in a real-life experiment.

## IV. Conclusions

As part of an ongoing research into the involvement of virtual reality in biometrics, this paper has attempted to depict the general hardware and software implementation of a virtual reality usability study concerning vein pattern recognition systems. Using the combination of a precise position acquisition from a virtual reality setup with the full body pose assessment of an inertial motion capture system, a complete real time user tracking system has been implemented.

The general workflow of the communication between these heterogenous systems has also been presented in the experimental setup description.

The participants in the experiments have been virtually placed in a false environment with various designs of hand vein biometric systems present in the simulation. Starting from a known, real biometric scanner, users have been asked to place their hands above or below 5 proposed scanner designs.

Several pieces of information have been successfully extracted from the experiments that add in the design of real-life biometric scanners. The paper has presented results concerning height variance and comfort rating for different scanner position and geometry. In addition, a battery of tests dealing with angle of attack measurement for unconstrained hand position has led directly to a simplification of algorithms for an orientation invariant hand vein biometric scanner. These results are relevant in both pure biometric studies and real security applications.

In order to cement the presence of virtual reality in the world of biometrics, a new experiment is underway where users are instructed to enroll in a multimodal biometric setup using five technologies (retina scan, iris recognition, finger vein, voice and fingerprints). A real setup with access to these scanning methods would be extremely difficult to construct.

By using virtual reality, small changes in the user position and behavior, coupled with the willingness to provide the biometric parameter (retinal scans perceived as intrusive and dangerous, face scanners easy to comply or fingerprint scanners -simple but carrying a "crime stigma") offer valuable data regarding user perception of different scanning technologies.

## Acknowledgment

This work was supported by a grant of the Romanian National Authority for Scientific Research and Innovation, CNCS-UEFISCDI, project number PN-II-RU-TE-2014-4-2196

## References

[1] A. K. Jain, A. Ross, S. Prabhakar, "An Introduction to Biometric Recognition", Invited paper in IEEE Transactions on circuits and systems for video technology, Vol. 14, No. 1. 2004.

[2] C. Wilson, "Vein pattern recognition: a privacy-enhancing biometric", Taylor & Francis, ISBN 978-1-4398-2137-4I, 2010.

[3] Fujitsu Develops Technology for World's First Contactless Palm Vein Pattern Biometric Authentication System , Fujitsu Laboratories Limited, Tokyo Japan Available from http://www.fujitsu.com/global/news/pr/archives/month/2003/20030331-05.html, 2014.09.02

[4] Introducing Hitachi Finger Vein Authentication (2005). Hitachi Corporation Japan. Available from http://www.hitachi.co.jp/Prod/comp/fingervein/global, 2015.12.13

[5] S. Crisan, I. G. Tarnovan, T. E. Crisan, "A Low Cost Vein Detection System Using Near Infrared Radiation", IEEE SAS, San Diego, USA, 2007

[6] S. Crisan, I. G. Tarnovan, T. E. Crisan, "Radiation optimization and image processing algorithms in the identification of hand vein patterns", Computer Standards and Interfaces, Volume 32, Issue 3, pp 130, Elsevier, 2010

[7] S. Crisan, "Researches concerning the development of biometric applications using infrared radiation", PhD Thesis, Technical University of Cluj-Napoca, 2008

[8] S. Crisan, I. G. Tarnovan, B. Tebrean, T. E Crisan, "Corellation of near and far infrared vein recognition for unified processing and simulation", XIX IMEKO World Congress Fundamental and Applied Metrology, Lisbon, Portugal. 2009

[9] S. Crisan, I. G. Tarnovan, B. Tebrean, T. E. Crisan, "Hand Vein Biometric Authentication in Optical Multi-touch Systems" In International Conference on Advancements of Medicine and Health Care through Technology (pp. 124-127). Springer Berlin Heidelberg, 2011

[10] S. Crisan, B. Tebrean, S. Emerich, "Optimized Vein Pattern Recognition for Biometric Applications, a Modern Approach" 14th IMEKO TC10 Workshop Technical Diagnostics New Perspectives in Measurements, Tools and Techniques for

system's reliability, maintainability and safety Milan, Italy, June 27-28, 2016

[11] S. Crisan "A Novel Perspective on Hand Vein Patterns for Biometric Recognition. Problems, Challenges and Implementations". Chapter in Biometric Security and Privacy. Opportunities & Challenges in The Big Data Era. Signal Processing for Security Technologies series. Jiang, R., Al-Madeed, S., Bouridane, A., Crookes, D., Beghdadi, A. (Eds.) 2017

[12] S. M. Lavalle, Virtual Reality, Cambridge University Press, 2017

[13] P. R. Desai, P. N. Desai, K. D. Ajmera, K. Mehta, "A review paper on oculus rift-a virtual reality headset". arXiv preprint arXiv:1408.1173, 2014

[14] D. Sharma, "A Review Paper On Virtual Reality Oculus Rift And Augment Reality", International Journal of Current Research, Vol. 8, Issue 9, pp. 37941-37945, 2016

[15] Oculus 3-Sensor 360° Experimental Setup, Upload VR, Available from https://uploadvr.com/oculus-guides-show-smaller-multi-sensor-tracked-spaces-htc-vive/, 2017.02.04

[16] W. Mason "Perception Neuron Review: In-Depth With The $1,500 Motion Capture Suit", Available from http://uploadvr.com/perception-neuron-review/, 2015.11.04

[17] S. Boring, J. Marko , A. Butz. "Scroll, tilt or move it: using mobile phones to continuously control pointers on large public displays." Proceedings of the 21st Annual Conference of the Australian Computer-Human Interaction Special Interest Group: Design: Open 24/7. ACM, 2009.

[18] A. I. Mallinson, "Visual Vestibular Mismatch." PhD diss., Université Henri Poincaré, 2011.

[19] J. Blascovich, J. Bailenson, "Infinite reality: Avatars, eternal life, new worlds, and the dawn of the virtual revolution", William Morrow & Co, 2011

[20] M. Jokisch, T. Bartoschek, A. Schwering, "Usability testing of the interaction of novices with a multi-touch-table in semi public space", Institute for Geoinformatics, University of Münster, 2010

# HPC Services and Big Data Challenges

Isabel Schwerdtfeger
Systems Services, IBM Global Technology Services
IBM Germany
Hamburg, Germany
schwerdtfeger@de.ibm.com

*Abstract*— **High performance computing (HPC) systems rely more on a service- based environment than on a strong hardware or technology-related environment, as more challenges arise for large scale HPC systems of the Exascale era. Naturally, the selection of a distinct HPC hardware technology is very important as the future of the HPC applications and Big Data workloads rely on it. However, the deployment concept including the long term operational aspects need to be considered, as they tend to be the next higher cost driver. Due to high digitization needs, large data growth, and new disruptive business models from organizations and businesses, all face a change and challenge to address these new deployment concepts for their future HPC needs. This paper highlights new possible approaches.**

***Keywords- HPC; HPCaaS; Data Center; Cloud; Hyperscale data center; Big Data; Exascale; energy efficiency.***

## I. Introduction

For a new large-scale supercomputing system ranging from the higher petaflop to pre-exaflop era, the technical design and the deployment solution are a vital purchase criteria, as there is the need for more efficiency while achieving faster time to market. The high amount of power consumption and its costs are limiting factors for a high capital-intensive investment in a supercomputer. After a successful implementation, the operational services concept needs to ensure high availability and cost efficiency of the various technical components for computing, network and storage, that create the overall system. A typical lifetime of a HPC system is five years and consultations about the new systems begin usually at least a year ahead [1]. But, due to shorter timelines of innovative technologies being available, and the pressure for businesses to foster their research and development (R&D) efforts within shorter timeframes to please their stakeholders, more flexible and adaptive HPC services need to be available.

At current, HPC deployment models are differentiated by so-called "on-premise" or "off-premise" implementations, while "on premise" resemble the traditional on-site hardware (HW) installation in a self-owned data center (DC), usually where the rest of IT of an organization or business resides. As more cloud services and Hyperscale DCs become available, there is increased interests to add HPC capacity "off-premise", as there is the perception that ideal parameters already exist there for this distinctive computing environment.

A standard HPC deployment for an on-premise installation, where the new supercomputing system is placed in an on-site DC center is characterized by best price purchasing of hardware and software (price per performance). The system selection comes together with the technology solution that demonstrates the lowest energy consumption to reduce power costs, i.e. with direct water cooling, and involving an innovative DC concept. In addition, the reliability of standard hardware and software maintenance support by the HPC vendor for the on-site system is critical and needs to be provided over the lifetime of the system.

HPC is custom built that includes writing software to solve cutting-edge problems and is not an IT function but a competitive business advantage for innovation [2]. HPC is now the technology to solve complex mathematical, scientific or engineering problems to foster research and development activities to drive innovation at companies. Therefore, HPC elevates beyond scientific teams to build footprints in enterprises of all industries.

HPC applications, such as for complex product simulations and optimizations, 3D rendering, complex weather prediction, and deep learning, need custom multiprocessor architectures to solve state of the art problems which comes along with a high capital intensive invest.

This paper is structured as follows: Section II describes the development of HPC in the market and its implications for large scale infrastructures. Section III describes a "Private HPC Cloud" deployment model outlining one of the largest DCs in Europe and its containerized solution for the industrialization of HPC as IT as a Service (IaaS). Section IV discusses the possible conjunction of Big Data with HPC and possible outcomes. The acknowledgement and conclusions close the article.

## II. HPC Market Development

Today, a high commoditization of hardware components, and a wider acceptance and usage of common software development tools exists. This leads to a high adoption rate from commercial firms and is not limited to existing research organizations: the democratization of HPC happens. However, the key aspects remain unchanged: the need for high energy efficiency for rising petaflop and future exaflop systems; scalable software that is power and failure aware, and data management software that can handle at minimum the "3Vs" of data: volume, velocity, and variety [3]. Thus, overall efficiency at low costs needs to be achieved.

Industrial HPC is the driving engine of the market growing at 6.8 percent over the forecast period, while education/government remain flat at ca. 3 percent until 2020 [4]. The HPC service market is ca. $4 billion in 2015 and is expected to grow to $5.5 billion by 2020, growing at a Compound Annual Growth Rate (CAGR) of 6.25 percent during the forecast period [5]. The HPC market in total was approximately $28 billion in 2016 and is to grow to over $35 billion globally until 2020 [6]. New era of Exascale computing and cloud-based HPC will offer lucrative opportunities for the market players in coming five years [7]. Emerging economies in regions such as Asia Pacific, and Latin America offer several untapped and unexplored opportunities. North America accounts for more than 45 percent of the total HPC market, followed by Europe with 26 percent market share [5].

The current landscape of large HPC deployments shows mostly "on- premise" installations, custom built in a DC with a range of 1 to 5 Megawatt (MW) power capabilities, in a CAPEX model, with limited adaption capability to a constantly changing IT market. A solution based on a price per core per hour or per Teraflop per Month in an "Infrastructure-as-a-Service" (IaaS) for HPC would remove the high CAPEX investment hurdle to enable HPC for small and medium enterprises (SMEs) and for industrial HPC applications. This accompanied with scalable services with a low consulting cliff, and either fully managed or self-serviced, would spur research and development efforts off.

A new discussion evolves in the HPC market among the existing Hyperscale DCs that are used by large internet companies such as Google, Facebook, and major cloud vendors. One might think that those facilities should be ideal places to host large scale HPC applications. However, when looked at it in detail, the following issues emerge: Servers and direct attached storage are the basic unit and data is widely spread. The hardware is not built with redundant components: if a failure occurs, the workload moves simply to another server [6]. Therefore, usually no or very little custom architecture design is available for applicable HPC requirements. In general, a Hyperscale facilities offers usually no given performance guarantee, nor provide benchmark capabilities. The HPC Cloud is today 3 percent of the total HPC market [4]. Thus, Hyperscale DCs fall short in addressing this growing market.

## III. Private HPC Cloud Deployment Model

As the democratization of HPC is already underway, the same happens for the data centers. This is called "The industrialization of data centers". The goal of this initiative is to become Europe's number one in terms of cost-efficiency, security, flexibility and sustainability. To reach it, the Lefdal Mine Data Center (LMD) is using standardized DC infrastructure based on Rittal's modular and standardized "RiMatrix S" data center portfolio [7]. "The Norwegian Solution" has developed out of the Lefdal Mine in a unique data center concept. Low cost and modularity in a scalable, green and secure facility [8]. In fact, this DC is the largest of the world. It spans 120.000 square meter, is fueled by 100% renewable energy (only wind and water power), direct water-cooled from the local fjord, and a five-level installation in an old mineral mine near Måløy (550 kilometers north-east of Oslo) in Norway. Fig. 1 shows the picture and the dimensions of LMD in comparison to the New York Statue of Liberty, a commercial airplane, a truck and a car vehicle.

Figure 1. Lefdal Mine Datacenter [7]

The solution offering of IBM's Private Cloud Service for Petascale to Exascale infrastructures for HPC includes the use of LMD, maximizing lowest energy costs and highest expandability at the same time. LMD in Norway aims to exploit Norway's and the Lefdal Mine's nature given advantages in terms of location, green power, the low cost of power and cooling, and a stable political environment.

An optimal floor space for "HPC as a Service" (HPCaaS) and a co-location space to cover the extensive capacity requirements of HPC resources in a highly energy- and cost-efficient way. The mine is already there. Cost of land is limited and the investment to be made to secure redundant power and fiber infrastructure and to build out the cooling solution is extremely low. The mine gives natural EMP security and there is less need of perimeter fencing and other investments in physical security. The construction cost per MW is leading in Europe: 30-60% lower than standard DC build out, yet bringing a Tier 3 product to the market [9]. The mine as a IT facility started its operation in the third quarter of 2016.

The high standardization and leveraging economies of scale arise using the standardized modular container solution from Rittal. The modules are suitable to be transported directly into the mine and can be fitted for instance in either containers or secure rooms depending on the protection level needed by the customer [7].

As standard and local client DCs have limitations for the density of racks, many businesses and organizations are not able to fully stack the hardware as tight as possible per rack. Up to 50 KW/rack with leading low cost of power, cooling and space [8]. Hence, LMD is an ideal location for HPC environments using cold- water for cooling. In addition, standard commodity air-cooled server, storage and switches can be used in any custom designed architecture, as the overall energy costs for the operations is at least 30 percent lower than in any standard German IT facility. The key measurement parameter to compare this is the Power Usage Effectiveness (PUE) value: for LMD the PUE is under 1.15. In contrast, current IT operation centers, according to general market information, range from a PUE of 1.35 up to 1.80.

Most of the companies today are interested in using HPC technologies but not necessarily managing it [10]. The combination of IBM Global Services and the offering of the DC capabilities fulfils this desire. Fig. 3 illustrates the solution by IBM in an integrated way, making use of the overall efficiency at low cost which is essential to achieve benefits in terms of high energy efficiency for the need of future Exaflops systems in Europe [11].

## IV. BIG DATA AND HPC AS A SERVICE

The growth of substantial amounts of digital data, files, objects or any other digitized information, relate to the term "Big Data". All those types can be characterized by the "5 Vs of Data": Volume, Velocity, Variety, Value and Veracity [12]. Driving needs evolve among businesses and organization to seek more evidence and knowledge out of existing and newly generated data. Available analytics software enables applications to discover new insights of structures, behaviors, trends and relationships. Big Data is extremely complex to deal with via traditional approaches, and requires real-time or almost real-time analysis. [13].

For HPC, open-source software developments are vital to expand the usage and further democratization of its use. OpenStack is a free and open-source software platform for cloud computing, mostly deployed as IaaS [14]. Big Data has changed the way people understand and harness the power of data, both in the business and research domains [15]. When HPC and OpenStack marry, Big Data comes alive within Supercomputing.

Businesses and organizations that are not familiar with HPC, may ask if a big data job could be run on existing HPC infrastructures. The answer is yes, as it is just another type of job vs. a traditional MPI job. [15] The challenges lie within the design of big data systems for I/O libraries and communication. [15]. Many Big Data workloads are running nowadays their new applications on Apache Spark, achieving twice the performance of traditional systems [17], thus supporting the rising demands of real-time or near-real-time analytics.

HPC workloads have varying data, compute and latency requirements. They can have either light data, running smoothly and fast via conventional networking and communication networks. Or they can be heavy workloads requiring more detailed designed communication and high-bandwidth networks. The HPC architectures are either designed in a cluster or in a lightweight grid of a distributed computing system. Fig. 2 outlines the four dimensions of HPC and High Performance Data Analytics (HPDA), also interchangeably used as term for Big Data, of different workloads.

It is critical that data-intensive computing middleware (such as Hadoop and Spark) process such data and are diligently designed, with high performance and scalability to meet the growing demands of Big Data applications. Big Data applications are found in many industries, i.e., in healthcare, bio-medical research, Internet search, finance, and scientific computing. Therefore, mainly the same organizations and businesses that use HPC today have also Big Data requirements. These technologies and applications play a vital role to gain meaningful insights for society and economies.

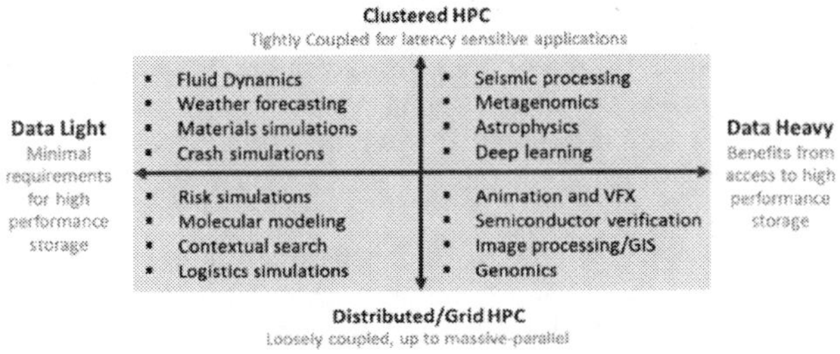


Figure 2. Dimensions of HPC Workloads [17]

Using Apache Spark as a key technology in Big Data leads to certain benefits:

- In-memory large-scale distributed processing;
- Uses distributed file system such as Hadoop Distributed File System (HDFS), which supports automatic data distribution across computing resources;
- Language supports the operations needed to implement the algorithm;
- Good for similar repeated analysis performed on the same large data sets [18].

It can be argued that the combination of Big Data and HPC brings together best of both worlds or it becomes a threat of a takeover to each other, as the demand for Big Data might overwhelm the distinctive HPC market. As a turnkey solution, HPCaaS should demonstrate the high value while delivering this at low costs. Natural benefits come along with the newest available technologies as in the computing processor units (CPUs), either from Intel's x86- or IBM Power-based processors, from many-core or accelerators (GPGPUs), such as from Nvidia P100 or Intel Xeon Phi x200, high performance Infiniband networks, and file-systems such as Spectrum Scale, Lustre, or CEPH based storage.

## V. CONCLUSION

This short paper summarized the current state of the HPC market and trend for the next five years. In parallel, as the democratization of HPC occur, the industrialization of DCs evolve, utilizing from the Earth the nature capabilities in a better way for IT demands; thus, being at the same time a novum to standard deployments of traditional DCs sites, matching the new requirements for the era of exaflop systems. As many Big Data applications need more computing capabilities (and more power consumption) to achieve real-time accessibility and more ease-of-use, HPC technologies can be found as the underlying infrastructure. However, the overall operational model must be considered so that further benefits are achieved to reduce increasing costs of those very large systems.

The outlook remains stable for HPC:

- The vendors in this market are continuously focusing on developing innovative technologies and solutions to boost performance and reduce the overall utility cost.
- The major focusing areas are Exascale computing, hot water cooling, networking technologies and embedded GPU and processors.
- The HPC market is no longer limited to the on-premise.
- The battle for HPC is between Intel and NVIDIA for the massive number crunching and data moving work that is the hallmark of HPC.

## ACKNOWLEDGMENT

To Martin Kipping, Director International IT-Projects from Rittal, Friedhelm Loh Group and Dr. Sebastian Ritz, CEO of iNNOVO Cloud GmbH, for their inspiration and solution competence.

## REFERENCES

[1] R. Blake, F. Robin and M. Sbrighi, PRACE 1IP Work Package 8: HPC Systems Procurement Best Practice, [Online]. Available from: http://www.prace-ri.eu.

[2] S. Conway, "10 Things CIOs Need to Know About High-Performance Computing", IDC Opinion, Mar. 2016.

[3] D. Soubra, "The 3V´s that define Big Data", Data Science Central, Jul., 2012, URL: http://www.datasciencecentral.com/forum/topics/the-3vs-that-define-big-data [accessed: 2017-04-15].

[4] M. Feldman, 2016, "Intersect360 Publishes New Five-Year HPC Market Forecast", Intersect360 Inc., URL: https://www.top500.org/news/intersect360-publishes-new-five-year-hpc-market-forecast/ [accessed: 2016-11-25].

[5] MarketsandMarkets, "High Performance Computing Market, Global Forecast to 2020", 2016.

[6] F. Moore, 2016, "Storage Outlook", Horison Information Strategies, URL: https://indico.bnl.gov/conferenceOtherViews.py?view=standard&confId=1955#20160828 [accessed: 2016-10-15].

[7] Rittal GmbH & Co. KG Press release, 2015, The industrialisation of data centre starts with Rittal, URL: https://www.rittal.com/com-en/content/en/unternehmen/presse/pressemeldungen/pressemeldung_detail_49856.jsp, [accessed: 2015-08-25].

[8] Lefdal Mine Data Center Company Website, 2016, URL: http://www.lefdalmine.com, [accessed: 2017-01-02].

[9] M. Andersson, "Lefdal Mine Data Center, Concept Description", Aug. 2015, unpublished.

[10] K. Elamrawi, 2016, "Brightskies Technologies: Shaping the Computing Industry of Tomorrow", URL: http://high-performancecomputing.cioreview.com/vendor/2016/brightskies_technologies, [accessed: 2016-11-25].

[11] I. Schwerdtfeger, "HPC Innovation Services", IBM Deutschland GmbH, Mar. 2017, unpublished.

[12] B. Marr, 2014, "Big Data: The 5 Vs Everyone Must Know", URL: https://www.linkedin.com/pulse/20140306073407-64875646-big-data-the-5-vs-everyone-must-know [accessed: 2016-05-12].

[13] S. Yin, O. Kaynak, 2015, "Big Data for Modern Industry: Challenges and Trends", in Proceedings of the IEEE Volume: 103 Issue: 2, Print ISSN: 0018-9219, Mar. 2015, URL: http://ieeexplore.ieee.org/document/7067026/?reload=true&arnumber=7067026 [accessed 2017-04-30].

[14] Wikipedia, 2016, URL: https://en.wikipedia.org/wiki/OpenStack [accessed: 2016-12-15].

[15] D. K. (DK) Panda, 2017, "Big Data Meets HPC: Exploiting HPC Technologies for Accelerating Big Data Processing", http://www.cse.ohio-state.edu/~panda, Talk at HPC Advisory Council -Switzerland, Apr. 2017.

[16] M. Christensen, 2017, "OpenPower Foundation Overview", Talk at HPC Advisory Council -Switzerland, Apr. 2017.

[17] S. Ritz, 2017, "HPC as a Service", iNNOVO Cloud GmbH Presentation, May 2017, unpublished.

[18] S. Saba, J. Kowalkowski, and M. Paterno, 2016, "Exploring the Performance of Spark for a Scientific Use Case, Saba Sehrish (Fermi National Accelerator Laboratory), HPBDC 2016, The 2nd IEEE International Workshop on High-Performance Big Data Computing, May 2016, URL: http://web.cse.ohio-state.edu/~lu.932/hpbdc2016/slides/hpbdc16-saba.pdf [accessed: 2017-04-12].

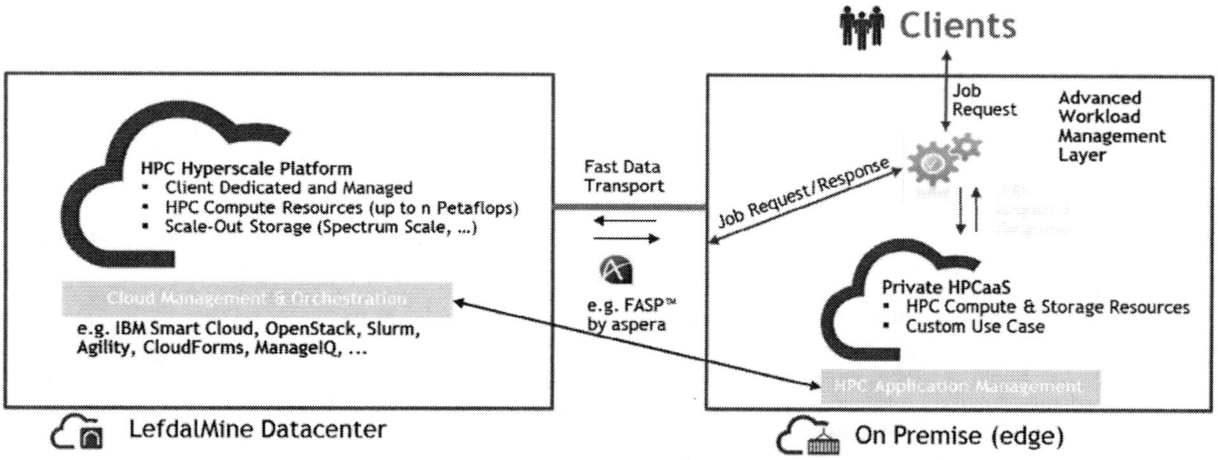


Figure 3. Private Cloud solution for HPCaaS, IBM Deutschland GmbH [11].

# Comparative Analysis of Data Entities: Knowledge Mining Objects

Claus-Peter Rückemann
Westfälische Wilhelms-Universität Münster (WWU),
Leibniz Universität Hannover,
North-German Supercomputing Alliance (HLRN), Germany
Email: ruckema@uni-muenster.de

*Abstract*—**This paper presents the research and results on creating means for a comparative analysis of data entities from knowledge resources. The research was started in order to tackle the challenges of data analysis with increasing and complex resources. Comparing data entities is a most ambitious task for increasingly complex data objects, integrated resources, and relations – from the knowledge resources, as well as from the computational perspective. The implementation utilises complementary components, which enable to structure and describe complex knowledge and support an advanced analysis. The paper presents practical examples and discusses the high level view of an implementation and case study. For practical reasons with the comparative analysis, the knowledge resources utilise references to publicly available data resources. The goal of this research is an advanced methodology and modular means for comparative analysis and knowledge mining with information systems and long-term multi-disciplinary knowledge resources.**

***Keywords–Knowledge Mining; Comparative Analysis; Content Factor; Universal Decimal Classification; Advanced Data-centric Computing.***

## I. Introduction

Advanced methods of knowledge mining with information systems and knowledge resources are becoming increasingly important. With that, improving knowledge mining and at the same time integrating larger amounts of data increases the challenges. The core of challenges is the data analysis. Within data analysis, comparing "data" is a central task. Comparing data entities is an even more ambitious task when data objects and relations are becoming more and more complex.

The term data entity in context with knowledge resources refers to any data representing objects of any kind like digital or realia objects, including references, e.g., to objects or conceptual knowledge.

Within this research, special application components were created and implemented in order to provide modular means to be integrated for a comparative analysis, e.g., knowledge resources referring to structured and unstructured data, conceptual data, especially knowledge classification, and methodologies specialised on the before mentioned means, e.g., the Content Factor method (CONTFACT) [1]. The multi-disciplinary knowledge resources and the application of the Content Factor method have enabled new flexible workflows and the creation of new complementary means for both the enhancement of multi-disciplinary knowledge resources and for data-centric knowledge discovery processes [2]. Some of the most widely required means with data entities of knowledge resources are components for a comparative analysis. Comparative Analysis (CA) is defined as an item-by-item comparison of two or more comparable entities.

This paper is organised as follows. Section II summarises the state-of-the-art, motivation, and frame of reference to the ground of comparison. Section III introduces the object and data entities integration with different resources, and implemented for this case study. Section IV provides the computation and analysis results based on the selected resources. Section V discusses the main results and evaluates them in context of the application. Section VI summarises the results and lessons learned, conclusions, and future work.

## II. State-of-the-art, motivation, and frame

The elementary way of knowledge mining, practised by the vast majority of approaches and services ignores content quality, document types, and cognitive knowledge. That means, content is handled independently from the creation process and expertise, content from databases, Web pages, and scanned books are not differentiated, and classification of content is disregarded.

CA modules can be used for arbitrary purposes with knowledge mining workflows, e.g., for selecting complementary resources as well as selecting objects supporting decision making processes. The methodology is used with knowledge mining workflows, integrating dedicated knowledge resources and publicly available content, e.g., text documents and books, because of their complementary nature regarding content, structure, and quality. The following sections describe the motivation and the base of the conducted CA.

### A. *Frame of reference*

The significance of integrating different data entities results from the context, in which they are placed. This research presents a methodology of comparing different data entities as referred from objects in advanced knowledge resources.

Objects with higher quality are mostly more complex. Advanced knowledge mining and decision making requires more than one methodology or algorithm for analysis of available objects and their references, data entities, and attributes. A major challenge is the difference of entities, e.g., regarding entity type, original purpose of the entity, and source but also content and structure.

Different types of entities cannot be ignored from advanced workflows because they contain unique knowledge and information. In most cases, the knowledge and information can even only be provided by different entities and referred sources. Methodologies should be provided, which are beneficial to be integrated in advanced workflows, especially for analysis, quantisation, and qualification of different entities. The deployed means should allow long-term data-centric applications and intrinsically foster the seamless integration with existing workflows. In addition, the methodologies and architecture of integration should allow the implementation of modular and least invasive components.

### B. *Grounds for comparison*

Besides the complexity, a combination of data entities from different sources and different types was choosen for the following reasons. The rationale behind the choice for knowledge resources and entities from referred objects results from complementary content and context. There is an arbitrary high quality of multi-disciplinary content in the knowledge resources, which are in continuous development [3]. In addition, the knowledge resources can provide an extremely high knowledge and information density. The Gutenberg resources [4] can provide a large number of fully publicly available standard text documents and elaborations for a wide multi-disciplinary context. Both types of resources contain essential amounts of textual content and are continuously extended and improved. The relationship between different entities is the addressed knowledge content with its unique nature. The thesis is, that different entities should neither be left out from advanced workflows nor should their content, the unique knowledge and information, be ignored. The following lens comparison discusses the most important aspects text-by-text, focussing on advanced knowledge resources and referred resources.

## III. Integration of Resources

The following sections describe how an integration was achieved and which results were gained with the analysis.

### A. *Data entities*

Data entities can be created from many resources. With this research, knowledge objects and data entities were automatically created from 'Gutenberg documents'. At the time of the case study (January 2017) Project Gutenberg [4] offered 53,855 free ebooks for download. The document files include the text in a version of the respective edition, which can be a revised edition or translation. The text editions are linked as different document files, e.g., plain text files, which can be converted into data entities and integrated with different data entities. Regarding conceptual knowledge, the Gutenberg documents use a flat implementation of the Library of Congress (LoC) classification outline [5]. The ebook links contain some relevant information, too, e.g., the bibliographic record, EBook-No. 25062, a link the LoC Class entries, and the release date of the edition. The original publication date of the source text is contained in the document files.

Data entities from knowledge resources' collections and containers [1] are used with many knowledge mining applications [3]. Knowledge resources contain multi-disciplinary knowledge objects, which can be used in arbitrary ways for providing factual, conceptual, procedural, and meta-cognitive knowledge. The objects can contain any content and context as well as references, e.g., translations, transliterations, synonyms, associations, references, conceptual knowledge (e.g., UDC), concordances, links, keywords, and Content Factors (of elements). The objects can be based on records, e.g., characters, words, lines, and complex records. Any content and context can be used for analysis and evaluation of an object.

With the created modules the data entities from the Gutenberg resources can be handled in the same way as knowledge resources' objects, e.g., of different origin. The following case study starts with a knowledge mining request for "Vesuvius" in the context of "volcanology". The primary Gutenberg result matrix contains a number of documents [6]-[12] provided with the precomputation.

### B. *Object and data entity integration*

Objects and data entities can be integrated with knowledge resources in arbitrary ways, e.g., as a referred object or by creating an instance of an object. The integration allows an analysis and evaluation, e.g., with knowledge resources' objects. The following excerpt (Figure 1) shows a knowledge resources' object automatically created from an entity of Gutenberg document 33483 [7] with LoC classification [13].

```
33483-0.txt [Document]:
               ...
               THE
               ERUPTION OF VESUVIUS
               IN 1872, ...
               BY
               PROFESSOR LUIGI PALMIERI,
               _Of the University of Naples; Director of the Vesuvian Observatory._
               ...
               WITH NOTES, AND AN
               _INTRODUCTORY SKETCH OF THE PRESENT STATE OF KNOWLEDGE_
               OF
               TERRESTRIAL VULCANICITY,
               _The Cosmical Nature and Relations of
               Volcanoes and Earthquakes._
               ...
               BY
               ROBERT MALLET,
               _Mem. Inst. C.E., F.R.S., F.G.S., M.R.I.A., &c., &c._
               ...
               WITH ILLUSTRATIONS. ...
               LONDON: ...
               _ASHER & CO._,
               13, BEDFORD STREET, COVENT GARDEN, W.C. ...
               1873.  ...
               W. S. Johnson, Nassau Steam Press, 60, St. Martin's Lane,
               Charing Cross, W.C.
               ...
```

Figure 1. Automatically created Gutenberg knowledge resources object for document 33483 (geosciences collection, LX, excerpt).

As an example, an object excerpt of an object instance "Vesuvius" from a knowledge resources' collection, resulting from a knowledge mining process, is shown in Figure 2. The objects can contain any knowledge, e.g., factual and conceptual knowledge. Here, the object carries names and synonyms in different languages, dynamically usable geocoordinates, Universal Decimal Classification (UDC) and so on, including geoclassification (UDC:(37), Italia. Ancient Rome and Italy). The data used here is based on the content and context from the knowledge resources, provided by the LX Foundation Scientific Resources (LX not an acronym) [3].

```
Vesuvius [Volcanology, Geology, Archaeology]:
         (lat.) Mons Vesuvius.
         (ital.) Vesuvio.
         Volcano, Gulf of Naples, Italy.
         Complex volcano (compound volcano).
         Stratovolcano, large cone (Gran Cono).
         Volcano Type: Somma volcano,
         VNUM: 0101-02=,
         Summit Elevation: 1281\UD{m}. ...
         ...
         Syn.: Vesaevus, Vesevus, Vesbius, Vesvius
         s. volcano, super volcano, compound volcano
         s. also Pompeji, Herculaneum, seismology
         ...
         compare La Soufrière, Mt. Scenery, Soufriere
         ...
         %%IML: UDC:[911.2+55]:[57+930.85]:[902]"63"(4+37+23+24)=12=14
         %%IML: GoogleMapsLocation: http://maps.google.de/maps?hl=de&gl=de&vpsrc
          =0&ie=UTF8&ll=40.821961,14.428868&spn=0.018804,0.028238&t=h&z=15
         ...
         ...
         ...
         ...
         ...
         ...
```

Figure 2. Knowledge resources collection object "Vesuvius" (LX resources, geoscientific collection, excerpt).

The LX knowledge resources' structure and the classification references [14] based on UDC [15] are essential means for the processing workflows and evaluation of the knowledge objects and containers. Both provide strong multi-disciplinary and multi-lingual support. For this part of the research all small unsorted excerpts of the knowledge resources objects only refer to main UDC-based classes, which for this part of the publication are taken from the Multilingual Universal Decimal Classification Summary (UDCC Publication No. 088) [16] released by the UDC Consortium under the Creative Commons Attribution Share Alike 3.0 license [17] (first release 2009, subsequent update 2012).

## IV. COMPUTATION AND ANALYSIS

### A. Content Factor computation for data entities

Objects of any kind can be integrated with knowledge resources. Objects can contain instances of data entities and refer to associated knowledge. For an analysis, a number of common information regarding the objects and data entities is required. The following excerpt (Figure 3) illustrates the creation of Content Factor definition sets [1] for the use with data entities. Definition sets are used for both Gutenberg resources and knowledge resources.

```
% (c) LX-Project, 2016, 2017
{Vol}:=[Vv][Oo][Ll][Cc][Aa][Nn]
{Vul}:=[Vv][Uu][Ll][Cc][Aa][Nn]
{Veu}:=[Vv][Ee][Ss][Uu][Vv]
{Vee}:=[Vv][Ee][Ss][Ee][Vv][Oo]
{Kom}:=[Kk][Oo][Mm][Ee][Tt]
{Com}:=[Cc][Oo][Mm][Ee][Tt]
{Met}:=[Mm][Ee][Tt][Ee][Oo][Rr]
{Erd}:=[Ee][Rr][Dd][Bb][Ee][Bb][Ee][Nn]
{Ear}:=[Ee][Aa][rr][Tt][Hh][Qq][Uu][Aa][Kk][Ee]
{Puz}:=[Pp][Uu][Zz][Zz][Oo][Ll]
{Poz}:=[Pp][Oo][Zz][Zz][Oo][Ll]
```

Figure 3. CONTFACT definition set for Gutenberg Project resources and knowledge resources, (LX, excerpt).

Figure 4 shows the Normed Basic Content Factor (NBCF, $\overline{\kappa}_{\mathrm{B}}$) [1] computed for a knowledge resources object reference to the Gutenberg Project document 33483.

```
CONTFACT:BEGIN
CONTFACT:20161227-234624:AU:{Veu}{Veu}{Vul}{Vol}{Ear}{Veu}{Met}{Veu}{Vol}{Met
 }...{Veu}{Veu}{Ear}{Veu}...{Veu}{Veu}{Veu}{Veu}...{Veu}{Ear}{Vol}{Ear}/39843
CONTFACT:20161227-234624:AS:{Ear}...{Veu}{Veu}{Vol}{Vol}...{Vul}{Vul}/39843
CONTFACT:20161227-234624:M:{Vol}:=[Vv][Oo][Ll][Cc][Aa][Nn]
CONTFACT:20161227-234624:M:{Vul}:=[Vv][Uu][Ll][Cc][Aa][Nn]
CONTFACT:20161227-234624:M:{Veu}:=[Vv][Ee][Ss][Uu][Vv]
CONTFACT:20161227-234624:M:{Vee}:=[Vv][Ee][Ss][Ee][Vv][Oo]
CONTFACT:20161227-234624:M:{Kom}:=[Kk][Oo][Mm][Ee][Tt]
CONTFACT:20161227-234624:M:{Com}:=[Cc][Oo][Mm][Ee][Tt]
CONTFACT:20161227-234624:M:{Met}:=[Mm][Ee][Tt][Ee][Oo][Rr]
CONTFACT:20161227-234624:M:{Erd}:=[Ee][Rr][Dd][Bb][Ee][Bb][Ee][Nn]
CONTFACT:20161227-234624:M:{Ear}:=[Ee][Aa][rr][Tt][Hh][Qq][Uu][Aa][Kk][Ee]
CONTFACT:20161227-234624:M:{Puz}:=[Pp][Uu][Zz][Zz][Oo][Ll]
CONTFACT:20161227-234624:M:{Poz}:=[Pp][Oo][Zz][Zz][Oo][Ll]
CONTFACT:20161227-234624:M:STAT:OBJECTELEMENTSDEF=11
CONTFACT:20161227-234624:M:STAT:OBJECTELEMENTSALL=39843
CONTFACT:20161227-234624:M:STAT:OBJECTELEMENTSMAT=356
CONTFACT:20161227-234624:M:STAT:OBJECTELEMENTSCFO=.00900324
CONTFACT:20161227-234624:M:STAT:OBJECTELEMENTSKWO=1
CONTFACT:20161227-234624:M:STAT:OBJECTELEMENTSLAN=0
CONTFACT:20161227-234624:M:INFO:OBJECTELEMENTSOBJ=33483-0.txt
CONTFACT:20161227-234624:M:INFO:OBJECTELEMENTSDCM=(c) LX-Project, 2016, 2017
CONTFACT:20161227-234624:M:INFO:OBJECTELEMENTSMTX=LX Foundation Scientific
 Resources; Object Collection
CONTFACT:20161227-234624:M:INFO:OBJECTELEMENTSAUT=Claus-Peter R\"uckemann
CONTFACT:END
```

Figure 4. NBCF $\overline{\kappa}_{\mathrm{B}}$ computed for knowledge resources object reference to Gutenberg Project document 33483 (LX Resources, excerpt).

Figure 5 shows the NBCF computed for a knowledge resources object reference to the object "Vesuvius".

```
CONTFACT:BEGIN
CONTFACT:20170205-161508:AU:{Veu}{Vol}{Veu}{Veu}{Vol}{Vol}{Vol}{Vol}{Vol}{Vol}{
 Vol}{Vol}{Vol}/71
CONTFACT:20170205-161508:AS:{Veu}{Veu}{Veu}{Vol}{Vol}{Vol}{Vol}{Vol}{Vol}{Vol}{
 Vol}{Vol}{Vol}/71
CONTFACT:20170205-161508:M:{Vol}:=[Vv][Oo][Ll][Cc][Aa][Nn]
CONTFACT:20170205-161508:M:{Vul}:=[Vv][Uu][Ll][Cc][Aa][Nn]
CONTFACT:20170205-161508:M:{Veu}:=[Vv][Ee][Ss][Uu][Vv]
CONTFACT:20170205-161508:M:{Vee}:=[Vv][Ee][Ss][Ee][Vv][Oo]
CONTFACT:20170205-161508:M:{Kom}:=[Kk][Oo][Mm][Ee][Tt]
CONTFACT:20170205-161508:M:{Com}:=[Cc][Oo][Mm][Ee][Tt]
CONTFACT:20170205-161508:M:{Met}:=[Mm][Ee][Tt][Ee][Oo][Rr]
CONTFACT:20170205-161508:M:{Erd}:=[Ee][Rr][Dd][Bb][Ee][Bb][Ee][Nn]
CONTFACT:20170205-161508:M:{Ear}:=[Ee][Aa][rr][Tt][Hh][Qq][Uu][Aa][Kk][Ee]
CONTFACT:20170205-161508:M:{Puz}:=[Pp][Uu][Zz][Zz][Oo][Ll]
CONTFACT:20170205-161508:M:{Poz}:=[Pp][Oo][Zz][Zz][Oo][Ll]
CONTFACT:20170205-161508:M:STAT:OBJECTELEMENTSDEF=11
CONTFACT:20170205-161508:M:STAT:OBJECTELEMENTSALL=71
CONTFACT:20170205-161508:M:STAT:OBJECTELEMENTSMAT=13
CONTFACT:20170205-161508:M:STAT:OBJECTELEMENTSCFO=.21311475
CONTFACT:20170205-161508:M:STAT:OBJECTELEMENTSKWO=2
CONTFACT:20170205-161508:M:STAT:OBJECTELEMENTSLAN=1
CONTFACT:20170205-161508:M:INFO:OBJECTELEMENTSOBJ=Vesuvius
CONTFACT:20170205-161508:M:INFO:OBJECTELEMENTSDCM=(c) LX-Project, 2016, 2017
CONTFACT:20170205-161508:M:INFO:OBJECTELEMENTSMTX=LX Foundation Scientific
 Resources; Object Collection
CONTFACT:20170205-161508:M:INFO:OBJECTELEMENTSAUT=Claus-Peter R\"uckemann
CONTFACT:END
```

Figure 5. NBCF $\overline{\kappa}_{\mathrm{B}}$ computed for knowledge resources object "Vesuvius" (LX Resources, excerpt).

Both NBCF were computed with the same definition set (Figure 3). The data entities from the referenced Gutenberg resources and knowledge resources both contain multiple matches. The resulting Content Factor for the knowledge resources object is higher due to the higher concentration of relevant elements in the object. The Gutenberg object shows a higher absolute number of matches and multiple hits.

### B. Procedures and modules

Two main modules were required with the assistance pre-computation for identifying and selecting objects and data entities from the Gutenberg resources before entering the CA workflow. The preparative assistance data was computed with a module `gutenberganalysis` and the classification was extracted with a module `gutenbergloc`. The implementation case study for the comparative analysis methodology required the creation of several major components and modules. Table I shows a sequence of modules, which allows to create the base for a CA workflow as created with this case study.

TABLE I. COMPARATIVE ANALYSIS WORKFLOW PROCEDURES AND IMPLEMENTED MODULES WITH GUTENBERG RESOURCES.

| *Procedure* | *Module* |
|---|---|
| **Gutenberg interface** | `textca_gutenberginterface` |
| Configuration | |
| Inconsistencies checker | |
| Data slicer | |
| **Analysis** | `textca_analysis` |
| Configuration | |
| **Data join** | `textca_join` |
| Configuration | |
| **Visualisation module** | `textca_visualisation` |
| Configuration | |
| Plotting generator | |
| Conditional visualisation | |
| **Statistics** | `textca_statistics` |
| Configuration | |
| **Visualisation plotting** | `textca_plotting` |
| Configuration | |

Practically, the modules can be implemented with any environment and frameworks. In the case study Perl, Shell, and Gnuplot have been used. In general this means any module could be replaced by a different implementation separately. Any module requires configuration options, which at least can be pre-configured options. In their application, the analysis up to visualisation modules for the Gutenberg resources are identical to the application for the knowledge resources. Therefore, the computations for all data entities were done with the `textca` group of modules.

### C. Comparison of data entities in collections

Figure 6 shows the computed CA module result for a case insensitive `vesuv` (`[Vv][Ee][Ss][Uu][Vv]`) target for the above Gutenberg object (Figure 1).

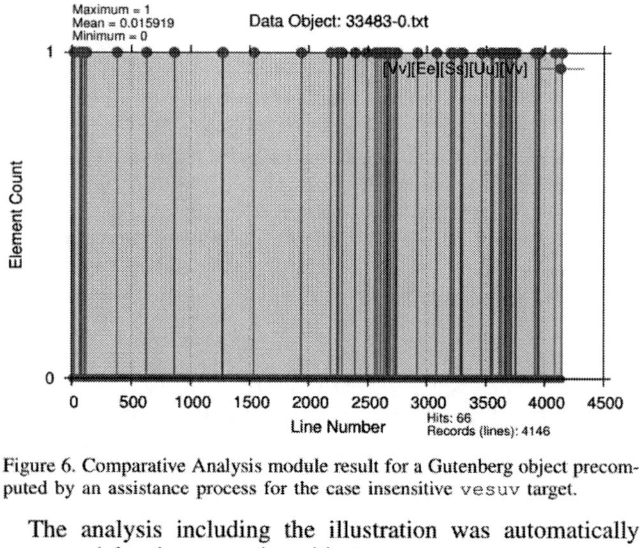


Figure 6. Comparative Analysis module result for a Gutenberg object precomputed by an assistance process for the case insensitive `vesuv` target.

The analysis including the illustration was automatically computed for the respective object.

Figure 7 shows the automatically computed CA module result with the respective target (pattern) for the resulting knowledge resources collection object "Vesuvius" (Figure 2).

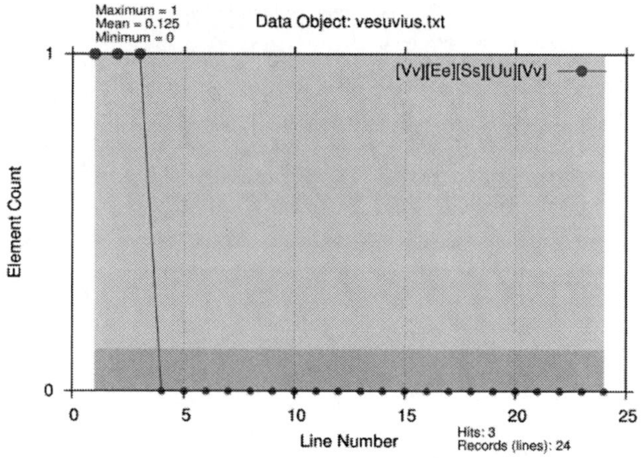


Figure 7. Comparative Analysis module result for the knowledge resources collection object "Vesuvius" (LX resources, geoscientific collection, excerpt).

The result shows some criteria of the object itself in context with the relevant mining pattern. The figure illustrates that the object contains a relevant mining result in the first and several consecutive records (here: lines) with a maximal occurance count of one in a record. The density of relevant occurances in the object is relatively high compared to common texts, even if from comparable special topic documents. Therefore, the mean value is quite high in that case. The computed background shading illustrates the space spanned by the available records (number of lines) and element counts. The mean value is illustrated by the border of the color change.

### D. Comparison of data entities in containers

Figure 8 shows the computed CA module result for a Gutenberg object for a case insensitive `vulc/volc` (`[Vv][UuOo][Ll][Cc]`) target.

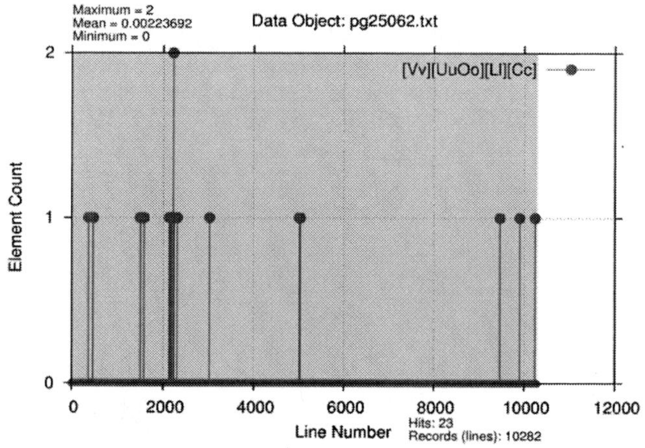


Figure 8. Comparative Analysis module result for a Gutenberg object precomputed by an assistance process for case insensitive `vulc/volc` target.

Figure 9 shows the automatically computed CA module result with the respective target (pattern) for the resulting knowledge resources collection object "Vesuvius" (Figure 2).

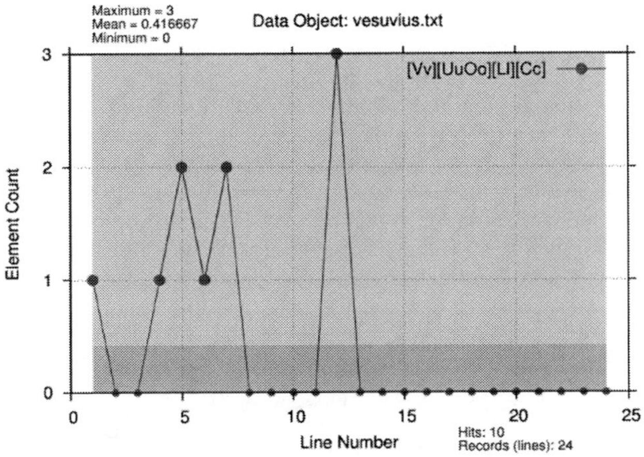


Figure 9. Comparative Analysis module result for the knowledge resources collection object "Vesuvius" (LX resources, geoscientific collection, excerpt).

There is more than one occurance in several lines each, with a maximal occurance count of three in a record. Figure 10 shows the computed CA module result for the volcanological features container for the same target.

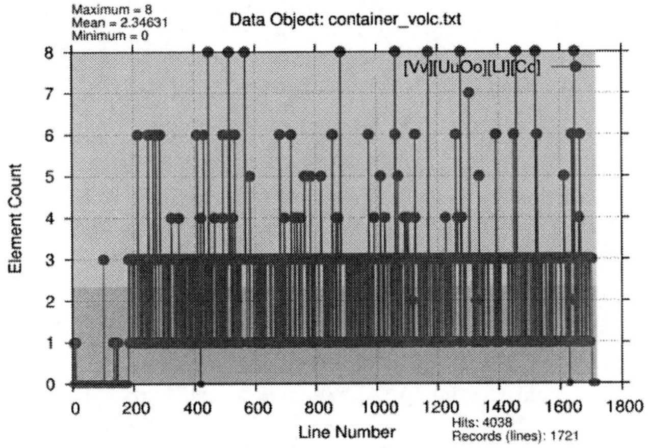


Figure 10. Comparative Analysis module result for the volcanological features container for case insensitive `vulc/volc` target (LX resources).

Both figures (Figures 10 and 8) illustrate the very high relevance of the objects. Nevertheless, the structure and density of hits is much higher in the container object than in the Gutenberg object. In addition, the mean value is extremely high for the container object. Also, the central part of the container object does not contain a line without the target. There are even more hits than records.

Even in a top hit Gutenberg object the number of records is much higher and the number of hits is lower. The comparison also reveals that both objects represent different object types, a knowledge resources object and a classical text object. The latter one mostly contains natural language. For any resources, many CA and Content Factor computations are done on a result matrix. With any workflow further information and decision making support can result from computing assistant views for the knowledge entities, e.g., based on their context. The results of the CA, the Content Factor, classification, and any results and attributes from assistant views can be included in an analysis, e.g., if a ranking of results is required for a specific knowledge mining workflow.

## V. Discussion

The case study integrates sources of different knowledge entities for knowledge mining workflows, selecting entities by computing advanced analysis criteria.

### *A. Integration and comparison*

The selected data compasses over 50,000 Gutenberg documents and more than 50,000 objects from knowledge resources. The selected sizes of objects range from hundreds of bytes to several megabytes.

The limitation for the case study was done for demonstration, due to the fact that the number of available overall knowledge resources objects may easily outnumber the number of Gutenberg documents. With the resources, the classification considers about fifty languages, summing up to about three million descriptions. Conceptual assistance is available for resource and object classification, which allows to automate integration workflows.

For the integration, instances of the objects containing the relevant data entities were automatically computed. It was possible to apply the provided means in the same way to the entities. The computation for the data entities from knowledge resources can be much more fine grained and systematic due to the complex structures and elements. The computation for the Gutenberg data entities can use the same means but some details and structure are not automatically available. The data sizes of the main Gutenberg data entities are most probably larger than these of the average knowledge resources' data entities.

### *B. CA mean values*

Table II compares CA mean values from the computation for selected objects and target groups for the integrated resources.

TABLE II. SELECTED COMPUTATION DATA ENTITIES: OBJECTS AND TARGET GROUPS SORTED BY THEIR CA MEAN VALUES.

| *Object* | *Target / Target-Group* | *CA Mean* |
|---|---|---|
| Knowledge res., Vesuvius | `[Vv][Ee][Ss][Uu][Vv]` | 0.125 |
| Gutenberg 33483-0 | `[Vv][Ee][Ss][Uu][Vv]` | 0.015919 |
| Know. res., volc. feat. cont. | `[Vv][Ee][Ss][Uu][Vv]` | 0.00291375 |
| Gutenberg 25062 | `[Vv][Ee][Ss][Uu][Vv]` | 0.000486287 |
| Know. res., volc. feat. cont. | `[Vv][UuOo][Ll][Cc]` | 2.34631 |
| Knowledge res., Vesuvius | `[Vv][UuOo][Ll][Cc]` | 0.416667 |
| Gutenberg 33483-0 | `[Vv][UuOo][Ll][Cc]` | 0.0356971 |
| Gutenberg 25062 | `[Vv][UuOo][Ll][Cc]` | 0.00223692 |

There are entities with higher and lower mean values, for the Gutenberg resources as well as for the knowledge resources. Higher values indicate a cumulation of relevant terms, e.g., as with the appearance in collections, tabulars, and listings.

Practice showed that for complementing knowledge in the volcanological features container with extended context, relevant entities from the Gutenberg resources with higher mean values can be a primary source for references. Relevant entities from the Gutenberg resources with lower mean values may primarily deliver reference information for collection objects.

### C. Ranking

For this scenario, a ranking was built from the rankings for the entities from the Gutenberg entities and from the knowledge resources.

The ranking considers the available information, e.g., classified targets, relevance of targets, references and context. The Gutenberg ranking especially considers the results from the CA, Content Factor and classification (LoC), based on the primary Gutenberg result matrix. The ranking of knowledge resources especially considers the CA, Content Factor, and classification, e.g., UDC and Universal Classified Classification (UCC). The integrated ranking considers the the CA, Content Factor values, and concordances of comparable entities.

An integration for a workflow ranking requires that the means need to be individually choosen for a certain application scenario. In this case, a records base (lines) was an appropriate choice for CA, Content Factor, and conceptual knowledge.

### D. Computational trace and context

A common knowledge discovery process integrates a sequence of decision making processes at different levels, e.g., from which resources to which single objects. Each step in a sequence can require to handle millions of objects and references. The access to the Gutenberg resources is not intended to be automated. Therefore, no performance data is available for the Gutenberg resources or for conducting the precomputation for its whole content. The precomputation assistance includes the cached Gutenberg content for the respective mining targets.

Table III shows the computation characteristics relevant with the workflow procedure for an example of the above integrated Gutenberg and knowledge resources case for two objects.

TABLE III. COMPUTATION CHARACTERISTICS WITH THE WORKFLOW PROCEDURE FOR TWO INTEGRATED OBJECTS, WALL TIMES PER CPU.

| *Workflow Procedure* | *Wall Time* |
|---|---|
| Precomputation assistance | 24.8 s |
| Analysis, resources classification | 1.2 s |
| Analysis, object classification | 14.7 s |
| Comparative Analysis | 3.2 s |
| (Integrative workflow step) | n s |

The table times refer to one Central Processing Unit (CPU) per mining process (Intel Xeon, at 2.9 GHz). Due to the complexity of the elementary workflows it is not desirable to have more than one CPU per process involved at the atomic level. Arbitrary practical application scenarios involving many processes with large data resources may be organised to fit the architecture of the available infrastructure. With certain scenarios, where an author wants to integrate complex references, the precomputation assistance can benefit a lot from using many-CPU infrastructures. The higher level workflow step, integrating the aforementioned procedures, will use a lot of intermediate results from procedures and content from resources. There is no general range for the time scale at the higher levels but at these levels the requirements on computation and communication can be extremely high, therefore, the higher level steps are candidates for parallelisation. Anyhow, workflow creators must always be aware that computing requirements can be non-linear, depending on the workflow created by an author for a choosen purpose.

## VI. CONCLUSION

The paper presented an advanced methodology for knowledge mining with multi-disciplinary knowledge resources and different data entities. Required modules and algorithms were successfully and efficiently implemented for supporting a Comparative Analysis, integrating different data entities in mining workflows.

This research showed that with the availability of appropriate methodologies different entities neither need to be left out from advanced knowledge mining workflows nor should their content be ignored. It was shown that in result, there is a complementary relationship between objects from knowledge resources and referred objects from external sources, including their data entities.

The Content Factor methodology for data description and analysis is used with all available resources. As was shown, CA methods cannot be replaced by other means like classification or Content Factor because they are based on completely different grounds but these complementary means can be integrated within more complex workflows. CA modules can help optimise the decision making, e.g., with supporting context-spanning Content Factor definition sets. CA modules can be used for delivering additional descriptive information, which can be used for documentation and knowledge mining purposes. CA is much beyond statistics. The significant part of the CA is the visualisation of pattern sequences in entities. The pattern sequences hold relevant parts of the entity characteristics and can also be used for documentation. The statistics are used in addition, for the analysis.

Objects from advanced knowledge resources can provide an excellent data base on knowledge. The knowledge resources can provide high quality object collections and containers with data entities of most reliable and unique content and qualities. Referred objects from external sources can extend the available data base regarding width and depth. Therefore, referred objects and external sources can extend the available data base and content. The best fit targets regarding volcanological features from the resources, including the Gutenberg resources, were automatically analysed.

On the side of the Gutenberg resources, a number of challenges have been found especially with the Gutenberg objects themselves. With the documents, workflow creators face a lot of inconsistencies in structure and marking even regarding major elements. Bibliographic data and versioning could also be improved. Better structured and more complete bibliographic data would be beneficial for any wider and systematic use. A common container format for the Gutenberg documents, handling any data files and associated data in a flexible and 'clean' way would be beneficial.

Besides the purpose laid out with this research, CA modules can be a complementary and supportive methodology applied with a wide range of advanced applications like document identification or plagiarism detection. Future work will be spent on further integrating different resources and creating methods and means for handling data entities and objects.

## ACKNOWLEDGEMENTS

We are grateful to the "Knowledge in Motion" (KiM) long-term project, Unabhängiges Deutsches Institut für Multidisziplinäre Forschung (DIMF), for partially funding this implementation, case study, and publication under grants D2014F1P04518, D2014F2P04518, D2016F1P04683, and to its senior scientific members, especially to Dr. Friedrich Hülsmann, Gottfried Wilhelm Leibniz Bibliothek (GWLB) Hannover, to Dipl.-Biol. Birgit Gersbeck-Schierholz, Leibniz Universität Hannover, and to Dipl.-Ing. Martin Hofmeister, Hannover, for fruitful discussion, inspiration, practical multi-disciplinary case studies, and the analysis of advanced concepts. We are grateful to Dipl.-Ing. Hans-Günther Müller, Cray, for his work on flexible practical solutions to architectural challenges and excellent technical support. We are grateful to all national and international partners in the Geo Exploration and Information cooperations for their constructive and trans-disciplinary support. We thank the Science and High Performance Supercomputing Centre (SHPSC) for long-term support of collaborative research since 1997, including the GEXI developments and case studies.

## REFERENCES

[1] C.-P. Rückemann, "Enhancement of Knowledge Resources and Discovery by Computation of Content Factors," in Proceedings of The Sixth International Conference on Advanced Communications and Computation (INFOCOMP 2016), May 22–26, 2016, Valencia, Spain. XPS Press, 2016, pages 24–31, ISSN: 2308-3484, ISBN-13: 978-1-61208-478-7, URL: http://www.thinkmind.org/download.php?articleid=infocomp_2016_2_30_60047 [accessed: 2017-01-22].

[2] C.-P. Rückemann, Z. Kovacheva, L. Schubert, I. Lishchuk, B. Gersbeck-Schierholz, and F. Hülsmann, Best Practice and Definitions of Data-centric and Big Data – Science, Society, Law, Industry, and Engineering. Post-Summit Results, Delegates' Summit: Best Practice and Definitions of Data-centric and Big Data – Science, Society, Law, Industry, and Engineering, Sep. 19, 2016, The Sixth Symp. on Advanced Computation and Information in Natural and Applied Sciences (SACINAS), The 14th Int. Conf. of Numerical Analysis and Applied Mathematics (ICNAAM), Sep. 19–25, 2016, Rhodes, Greece, 2016, URL: http://www.user.uni-hannover.de/cpr/x/publ/2016/delegatessummit2016/rueckemann_icnaam2016_summit_summary.pdf [accessed: 2017-01-22].

[3] "LX-Project," 2017, URL: http://www.user.uni-hannover.de/cpr/x/rprojs/en/#LX [accessed: 2017-02-05].

[4] "Project Gutenberg," 2017, URL: http://www.gutenberg.org [accessed: 2017-02-05].

[5] "Library of Congress Classification Outline," 2017, Library of Congress (LoC) Classification, URL: https://www.loc.gov/catdir/cpso/lcco/ [accessed: 2017-02-05].

[6] M. Saderra Masó, Catalogue of Violent and Destructive Earthquakes in the Philippines, 2006, Project Gutenberg, eBook, EBook-No.: 18556, Release Date: June 11, 2006, Digitised Version of the Original Publication from 1910, URL: http://www.gutenberg.org/ebooks/18556 [accessed: 2017-02-05], URL: http://www.gutenberg.org/cache/epub/18556/pg18556.txt [accessed: 2017-02-05].

[7] L. Palmieri, The Eruption of Vesuvius in 1872, 2010, Project Gutenberg, eBook, EBook-No.: 33483, Release Date: August 22, 2010, Digitised Version of the Original Publication from 1873, Translator: Mallet, Robert, (1810–1881), URL: http://www.gutenberg.org/ebooks/33483 [accessed: 2017-02-05], URL: http://www.gutenberg.org/files/33483/33483-0.txt [accessed: 2017-02-05].

[8] M. Serao, Sterminator Vesevo (English: Vesuvius the great exterminator), 2014, Project Gutenberg, eBook, EBook-No.: 46658, Release Date: August 22, 2014, Digitised Version of the Original Publication from 1907, Diary of the Eruption of April 1906, URL: http://www.gutenberg.org/ebooks/46658 [accessed: 2017-02-05], URL: http://www.gutenberg.org/cache/epub/46658/pg46685.txt [accessed: 2017-02-05].

[9] C. Davison, A Study of Recent Earthquakes, 2008, Project Gutenberg, eBook, EBook-No.: 25062, Release Date: April 12, 2008, Digitised Version of the Original Publication from 1905, URL: http://www.gutenberg.org/ebooks/25062 [accessed: 2017-02-05], URL: http://www.gutenberg.org/cache/epub/25062/pg25062.txt [accessed: 2017-02-05].

[10] W. Hamilton, Observations on Mount Vesuvius, Mount Etna, and Other Volcanos, 2011, Project Gutenberg, eBook, EBook-No.: 35433, Release Date: March 1, 2011, Digitised Version of the Original Publication from 1774, Editor: Cadell, T., (1742–1802), URL: http://www.gutenberg.org/ebooks/35433 [accessed: 2017-02-05], URL: http://www.gutenberg.org/cache/epub/35433/pg35433.txt [accessed: 2017-02-05].

[11] R. D'Awans, L'Ameublement de l'Hôtel de Pitsembourg au milieu du XVIIe siécle, 2004, Project Gutenberg, eBook, EBook-No.: 11586, Release Date: March 1, 2004, Digitised Version of the Original Publication from 1901, Communication faite en séance du 26 avril 1901, URL: http://www.gutenberg.org/ebooks/11586 [accessed: 2017-02-05], URL: http://www.gutenberg.org/cache/epub/11586/pg11586.txt [accessed: 2017-02-05].

[12] A. H. C. Gelpke, Ueber die schrecklichen Wirkungen des Aufsturzes eines Kometen auf die Erde und über die vor fünftausend Jahren gehabte Erscheinung dieser Art, 2006, Project Gutenberg, eBook, EBook-No.: 18471, Release Date: May 29, 2006, Digitised Version of the Original Publication from 1835, URL: http://www.gutenberg.org/ebooks/18471 [accessed: 2017-02-05], URL: http://www.gutenberg.org/cache/epub/18471/pg18471.txt [accessed: 2017-02-05].

[13] "QE: Science: Geology," 2016, Library of Congress (LoC) Classification, URL: https://www.loc.gov/aba/cataloging/classification/lcco/lcco_q.pdf [accessed: 2017-02-05].

[14] C.-P. Rückemann, "Enabling Dynamical Use of Integrated Systems and Scientific Supercomputing Resources for Archaeological Information Systems," in Proc. INFOCOMP 2012, Oct. 21–26, 2012, Venice, Italy, 2012, pp. 36–41, ISBN: 978-1-61208-226-4.

[15] "UDC Online," 2017, URL: http://www.udc-hub.com/ [accessed: 2017-02-05].

[16] "Multilingual Universal Decimal Classification Summary," 2012, UDC Consortium, 2012, Web resource, v. 1.1. The Hague: UDC Consortium (UDCC Publication No. 088), URL: http://www.udcc.org/udcsummary/php/index.php [accessed: 2017-02-05].

[17] "Creative Commons Attribution Share Alike 3.0 license," 2012, URL: http://creativecommons.org/licenses/by-sa/3.0/ [accessed: 2017-02-05].

# Mathematical Aspects of Application of Neural Networks to Processes with Delays

Zlatinka Kovacheva
Department of Mathematics and Applied Sciences
Middle East College
Muscat, Oman
e-mail: zlatinka@mec.edu.om

Valéry Covachev
Institute of Mathematics and Informatics
Bulgarian Academy of Sciences
Sofia, Bulgaria
e-mail: vcovachev@hotmail.com

***Abstract*—Neural networks are used to solve different kinds of problems from a wide range of disciplines. A brief overview of the history and performance of neural networks is given. Some neural network models are presented. Additionally, we summarize our results concerning the existence and global exponential stability of an equilibrium point or periodic solution of these models.**

***Keywords-neuron; artificial neural network; processes with delay.***

## I. INTRODUCTION

Artificial Neural Networks (ANN) are computational paradigms, which implement simplified models of their biological counterparts, biological neural networks.

Although the initial intent of ANN was to explore and reproduce human information processing tasks, such as speech, vision, and knowledge processing, ANN also demonstrated their superior capability for classification and function approximation problems. This has great potential for solving complex problems, such as systems control, data compression, optimization problems, pattern recognition, and system identification.

Neural networks have wide applicability to real world business problems. In fact, they have already been successfully applied in many industries. Since neural networks are best at identifying patterns or trends in data, they are well suited for prediction or forecasting needs including: sales forecasting, industrial process control, customer research, data validation, risk management, target marketing and so on.

ANN are also used in the following specific paradigms: recognition of speakers in communications; diagnosis of hepatitis; recovery of telecommunications from faulty software; interpretation of multi-meaning Chinese words; undersea mine detection; texture analysis; three-dimensional object recognition; hand-written word recognition; and facial recognition [1], [2], [3].

In this paper, we are focusing on the application of neural networks to processes with delay. The rest of this paper is organized as follows: In Section II, we give some information on the history and action of artificial neurons. In Section III, we consider some neural network models, namely, continuous-time neural networks of Hopfield- and Cohen-Grossberg-type and their discrete-time counterparts. We conclude the paper in Section IV.

## II. ARTIFICIAL NEURON

An artificial neuron is a device with many inputs and one output. The neuron has two modes of operation; the training mode and the using mode. In the training mode, the neuron can be trained to fire (or not), for particular input patterns. In the using mode, when a taught input pattern is detected at the input, its associated output becomes the current output. If the input pattern does not belong in the taught list of input patterns, the firing rule is used to determine whether to fire or not.

The first artificial neuron was produced in 1943 by the neurophysiologist Warren McCulloch and the logician Walter Pitts [4]. But the technology available at that time did not allow them to do too much. Neural networks process information in a similar way the human brain does. The network is composed of a large number of highly interconnected processing elements (neurons) working in parallel to solve a specific problem. Neural networks learn by example.

In the human brain, a typical neuron collects signals from others through a host of fine structures called dendrites. The neuron sends out spikes of electrical activity through a long, thin stand known as an axon, which splits into thousands of branches. At the end of each branch, a structure called a synapse converts the activity from the axon into electrical effects that inhibit or excite activity from the axon into electrical effects that inhibit or excite activity in the connected neurons.

A more sophisticated neuron is the McCulloch and Pitts model (MCP) [4]. The difference from the previous model is that the inputs are "weighted", the effect that each input has at decision making is dependent on the weight of the particular input. The weight of an input is a number which, when multiplied by the input, gives the weighted input. These weighted inputs are then added together and, if they exceed a pre-set threshold value, the neuron fires. In any other case, the neuron does not fire. In mathematical terms, the neuron fires if and only if

$$\sum_{i=1}^{m} X_i W_i > T,$$

where $W_i$, $i = \overline{1,m}$, are weights, $X_i$, $i = \overline{1,m}$, inputs, and $T$ a threshold. The addition of input weights and of the threshold makes this neuron a very flexible and powerful one. The MCP neuron has the ability to adapt to a particular situation by changing its weights and/or threshold. Various algorithms exist that cause the neuron to "adapt"; the most used ones are the Delta rule and the back error propagation [2],[3]. The former is used in feed-forward networks and the latter in feedback networks.

An important application of neural networks is pattern recognition. Pattern recognition can be implemented by using a feed-forward neural network that has been trained accordingly. During training, the network is trained to associate outputs with input patterns. When the network is used, it identifies the input pattern and tries to output the associated output pattern. The power of neural networks comes to life when a pattern that has no output associated with it, is given as an input. In this case, the network gives the output that corresponds to a taught input pattern that is least different from the given pattern.

## III. NEURAL NETWORK MODELS

### A. *Hopfield-Type Neural Networks*

Hopfield-type (additive) networks have been studied intensively during the last two decades and have been applied to optimization problems. The original model [5] used two-state threshold "neurons" that followed a stochastic algorithm: each model neuron $i$ had two states, characterized by the values $V_i^0$ or $V_i^1$ (which may often be taken as 0 and 1, respectively). The input of each neuron came from two sources, external inputs $I_i$ and inputs from other neurons. The total input to neuron $i$ is then

$$\text{Input to } i = H_i = \sum_{i \neq j} T_{ij} V_j + I_i,$$

where $T_{ij}$ can be viewed as a description of the synaptic interconnection strength from neuron $j$ to neuron $i$. The motion of the state of a system of $N$ neurons in the state space describes the computation that the set of neurons is performing. A model, therefore, must describe how the state evolves in time, and the original model describes this in terms of a stochastic evolution. Each neuron samples its input at random times. It changes the value of its output or leaves it fixed according to a threshold rule with thresholds $U_i$:

$$V_i \to V_i^0 \quad \text{if} \quad \sum_{i \neq j} T_{ij} V_j + I_i < U_i,$$

$$V_i \to V_i^1 \quad \text{if} \quad \sum_{i \neq j} T_{ij} V_j + I_i > U_i.$$

A simple Hopfield-type neural network is the following one:

$$C_i \frac{dx_i(t)}{dt} = -\frac{x_i(t)}{R_i} + \sum_{j=1}^{m} a_{ij} f_j\left(x_j(t)\right) + I_i, \quad i = \overline{1,m},$$

where $m$ denotes the number of units (neurons) in the network, $x_i(t)$ denotes the state of the $i$-th unit at time $t$, the positive constants $C_i$ and $R_i$ are the neuron amplifier input capacitance and resistance, respectively, $I_i$ is the constant input from outside the network, $f_j\left(x_j(t)\right)$ denotes the output of the $j$-th unit on the $i$-th unit at time $t$, $a_{ij}$ is the weight (strength) of the synaptic connection between the $j$-th unit and the $i$-th unit.

In the formulation of the above system, it is implicitly assumed that the neurons process input, produce output and communicate with each other instantaneously. But this is usually not true and there can be significant time delays both in neural processing and axonal transmission. Such delays can be concentrated (discrete), or continuously distributed over a certain duration of time, finite or infinite.

Most widely studied and used neural networks can be classified as either continuous or discrete. Recently, there has been a somewhat new category of neural networks which are neither purely continuous-time nor purely discrete-time. This third category of neural networks, called impulsive neural networks, displays a combination of characteristics of both the continuous and discrete systems. To the best of our knowledge, impulsive neural networks first appeared in 1999 [6], yet we would mention that after the publication of our paper [7] in 2004 hundreds or maybe thousands of papers devoted to impulsive neural networks appear each year.

In order to solve problems in the fields of optimization, neural control and signal processing, neural networks have to be designed such that there is only one equilibrium point and this equilibrium point is globally asymptotically stable so as to avoid the risk of having spurious equilibria and local minima. In the case of global stability, there is no need to be specific about the initial conditions for the neural circuits since all trajectories starting from anywhere settle down at the same unique equilibrium. If the equilibrium is exponentially asymptotically stable, the convergence is fast for real-time computations.

In our paper [7], we considered several Hopfield-type systems incorporating the aforementioned features. All of them can be put together as the following:

$$\frac{dx_i(t)}{dt} = -a_i x_i(t) + \sum_{j=1}^{m} b_{ij} f_j\left(x_j(t)\right) \tag{1}$$

$$+ \sum_{j=1}^{m} c_{ij} g_j\left(x_j\left(t - \tau_{ij}\right)\right)$$

$$+ \sum_{j=1}^{m} d_{ij} h_j\left(\int_0^{\infty} K_{ij}(s) x_j(t-s)\, ds\right) + I_i, \quad t > 0, \quad t \neq t_k,$$

$$\Delta x_i(t_k) = -B_{ik} x_i(t_k) \tag{2}$$

$$+ \int_{t_{k-1}}^{t_k} \psi_{ik}(s) x_i(s)\, ds + \gamma_{ik}, \quad i = \overline{1,m}, \quad k \in \mathbb{N},$$

with initial values prescribed by piecewise-continuous functions $x_i(s) = \phi_i(s)$ which are bounded for $s \in$

$(-\infty, 0]$. The coefficient $a_i > 0$ is the rate with which the $i$-th unit self-regulates or resets its potential when isolated from other units and inputs; $f_j(\cdot)$, $g_j(\cdot)$, $h_j(\cdot)$ denote activation functions; the parameters $b_{ij}$, $c_{ij}$, $d_{ij}$ represent the weights (or strengths) of the synaptic connections between the $j$-th unit and the $i$-th unit; the constant $I_i$ represents an input signal introduced from outside the network to the $i$-th unit; $\tau_{ij}$ are nonnegative numbers whose presence indicates the delayed transmission of signals at time $t - \tau_{ij}$ from the $j$-th unit to the $i$-th unit; the delay kernels $K_{ij}(s)$ incorporate the fading past effects (or fading memories) of the $j$-th unit on the $i$-th unit; $\Delta x_i(t_k) = x_i(t_k + 0) - x_i(t_k - 0)$ denote impulsive state displacements at fixed instants of time $t_k$ ($k \in \mathbb{N}$) involving integral terms whose kernels $\psi_{ik}(s): [t_{k-1}, t_k] \to \mathbb{R}$ are measurable functions, essentially bounded on the respective interval. Here, it is assumed that the sequence of times $\{t_k\}_{k=1}^{\infty}$ satisfies $0 = t_0 < t_1 < t_2 < \cdots < t_k \to \infty$ as $k \to \infty$; $B_{ik}$ and $\gamma_{ik}$ are some constants.

Using the Contraction Mapping Principle (Banach's Fixed Point Theorem), we found sufficient conditions for the existence of a unique equilibrium point of the above system. Further, using a suitable Lyapunov functional we found sufficient conditions for the global exponential stability of the equilibrium (that is, each solution of the system tends exponentially to the equilibrium point).

Recently, we considered a class of Hopfield neural networks with integral impulsive conditions and finite distributed delays, formulated in the form of an $\omega$-periodic system of impulsive delay differential equations

$$\frac{dx_i(t)}{dt} = -a_i(t)x_i(t) + \sum_{j=1}^{m} b_{ij} f_j\left(\int_0^{\omega} K_{ij}(s) x_j(t-s)\, ds\right) + I_i(t), \quad t \neq t_k,$$

$$\Delta x_i(t_k) = -\alpha_{ik} x_i(t_k) + \sum_{j=1}^{m} B_{ijk} \Phi_j\left(\int_{t_{k-1}}^{t_k} c_{ijk}(s) x_j(s)\, ds\right) + \gamma_{ik},$$

$$i = \overline{1, m}, \quad k \in \mathbb{Z}.$$

Using the Contraction Mapping Principle, we found sufficient conditions for the existence of a unique $\omega$-periodic solution. Moreover, if an $\omega$-periodic solution exists, using an appropriate Lyapunov functional we found sufficient conditions for its global exponential stability. We noted that the above-mentioned $\omega$-periodic solution can be found approximately by the method of successive approximations.

### *B. Cohen-Grossberg Neural Networks*

We have also studied continuous-time impulsive neural networks more general than the Hopfield-type neural networks, such as the Cohen-Grossberg neural networks. Thus, in [8] we considered the impulsive Cohen-Grossberg neural network with S-type delays

$$\frac{dx_i(t)}{dt} = a_i(x_i(t))\left[-b_i(x_i(t)) + \sum_{j=1}^{m} c_{ij} f_j(x_j(t)) + \sum_{j=1}^{m} d_{ij} \int_{-\tau}^{0} g_j(x_j(t+\theta))\, d\eta_{ij}(\theta) + I_i\right], t > 0, t \neq t_k,$$

$$\Delta x_i(t_k) = -B_{ik} x_i(t_k) + \int_{-\tau}^{0} x_i(t_k + \theta)\, d\zeta_k(\theta) + \gamma_{ik},$$

$$i = \overline{1, m}, \quad k \in \mathbb{N},$$

with initial values prescribed by piecewise-continuous functions $x_i(s) = \Phi_i(s)$ with discontinuities of the first kind for $s \in [-\tau, 0]$. Here $a_i(x_i)$ denotes an amplification function; $b_i(x_i)$ denotes an appropriate function which supports the stabilizing (or negative) feedback term $a_i(x_i)b_i(x_i)$ of the unit $i$; the past effect of the $j$-th unit on the $i$-th unit is given by a Lebesgue-Stieltjes integral; the impulsive state displacements at fixed moments of time $t_k$, $k \in \mathbb{N}$, also involve Lebesgue-Stieltjes integrals. This type of delays in the presence of impulses is more general than the usual types of delays studied in the literature. In fact, concentrated delays correspond to the points of discontinuity of the bounded variation functions.

For the above system, sufficient conditions are found for the existence of a unique equilibrium point and its global exponential stability. Examples of impulsive systems satisfying the sufficient conditions obtained are given, namely, the differential system with S-type delays

$$\dot{x}_1(t) = (2 + \sin x_1(t))[-2x_1(t) + 0.1 \arctan x_1(t) + 0.15 \arctan x_2(t) + 0.1 \int_{-1}^{0} x_1(t+\theta)\, de^{\theta} + 0.15 \int_{-1}^{0} x_2(t+\theta)\, de^{\theta}],$$

$$\dot{x}_2(t) = (3 + \sin x_2(t))[-3x_2(t) + 0.15 \arctan x_1(t) - 0.2 \arctan x_2(t) + 0.1 \int_{-1}^{0} x_1(t+\theta)\, de^{\theta} - 0.2 \int_{-1}^{0} x_2(t+\theta)\, de^{\theta}],$$

provided with one of the following three sets of impulse conditions:

$$\Delta x_1(t_k) = -\frac{1}{2}x_1(t_k) + \frac{1}{4}\int_{-1}^{0} x_1(t_k+\theta)\, de^{\theta},$$
$$\Delta x_2(t_k) = -\frac{1}{4}x_2(t_k) + \frac{1}{4}\int_{-1}^{0} x_2(t_k+\theta)\, de^{\theta};$$

$$\Delta x_1(t_k) = -100x_1(t_k) + \int_{-1}^{0} x_1(t_k+\theta)\, de^{\theta},$$
$$\Delta x_2(t_k) = -50x_2(t_k) + \int_{-1}^{0} x_2(t_k+\theta)\, de^{\theta},$$
$$t_k = 10k, \quad k \in \mathbb{N};$$

$$\Delta x_1(t_k) = -(k+1)x_1(t_k) + k\int_{-1}^{0} x_1(t_k+\theta)\, de^{\theta},$$
$$\Delta x_2(t_k) = -(k^2+1)x_2(t_k) + k^2\int_{-1}^{0} x_2(t_k+\theta)\, de^{\theta},$$
$$t_k = k^2, \quad k \in \mathbb{N}.$$

In all three cases, the equilibrium point $(0,0)^T$ is globally exponentially stable with Lyapunov exponent respectively: 1 in the first case, 0.039 in the second case, and any $\lambda \in (0,0.5)$ in the third case.

### C. *Discrete-Time Neural Networks*

For different Hopfield-type and Cohen-Grossberg neural networks, we have found their discrete-time counterparts and found sufficient conditions for existence and global exponential stability of equilibria and periodic solutions.

Here, we recall just the results of our paper [9], where we obtain a discrete-time counterpart of system (1), (2). Let $h > 0$ denote a uniform discretization step size and $[t/h]$ denote the greatest integer in $t/h$. For convenience, we denote $[t/h]$, $n \in \{0\} \cup \mathbb{N}$, and, by an abuse of notation, write $x_i(n)$ instead of $x_i(nh)$. Further on, we denote $\kappa_{ij} = [\tau_{ij}/h]$, $i,j = \overline{1,m}$. Finally, we replace the integral terms $\int_0^\infty K_{ij}(s)x_j(t-s)\,ds$, $i,j = \overline{1,m}$, by sums of the form $\sum_{p=1}^{\infty}\mathcal{K}_{ij}(p)x_j(n-p)$, where $p = [s/h]$, $\mathcal{K}_{ij}(p)$ stands for $\mathcal{K}_{ij}(ph)$ and $x_j(n-p)$ for $x_j((n-p)h)$.

Now, on the interval $[nh,(n+1)h)$ $(n \in \{0\} \cup \mathbb{N})$ we approximate system (1) by

$$\frac{dx_i(s)}{ds} = -a_i x_i(s) + \sum_{j-1}^{m} b_{ij} f_j\left(x_j(n)\right) + \sum_{j-1}^{m} c_{ij} g_j\left(x_j(n-\kappa_{ij})\right) + \sum_{j-1}^{m} d_{ij} h_j\left(\sum_{p=1}^{\infty}\mathcal{K}_{ij}(p)x_j(n-p)\right) + I_i. \tag{3}$$

We rewrite equation (3) in the form

$$\frac{d}{ds}\left(x_i(s)e^{a_i s}\right) = e^{a_i s}\left(\sum_{j-1}^{m} b_{ij} f_j\left(x_j(n)\right) + \sum_{j-1}^{m} c_{ij} g_j\left(x_j(n-\kappa_{ij})\right) + \sum_{j-1}^{m} d_{ij} h_j\left(\sum_{p=1}^{\infty}\mathcal{K}_{ij}(p)x_j(n-p)\right) + I_i\right), i = \overline{1,m},$$

and integrate it over the interval $[nh,(n+1)h]$ to obtain

$$x_i(n+1) = e^{-a_i h}x_i(n) + \frac{1-e^{-a_i h}}{a_i}\left(\sum_{j-1}^{m} b_{ij} f_j\left(x_j(n)\right) + \sum_{j-1}^{m} c_{ij} g_j\left(x_j(n-\kappa_{ij})\right) + \sum_{j-1}^{m} d_{ij} h_j\left(\sum_{p=1}^{\infty}\mathcal{K}_{ij}(p)x_j(n-p)\right) + I_i\right), i = \overline{1,m}, \tag{4}$$
$$n \in \{0\} \cup \mathbb{N},\ i = \overline{1,m}.$$

This system is the discrete-time analogue of the system without impulses (1). It is provided with initial values of the form $x_i(-\ell) = \varphi_i(-\ell)$ $(\ell \in \{0\} \cup \mathbb{N})$, where the sequences $\{\varphi_i(-\ell)\}_{\ell=0}^{\infty}$are bounded for all $i = \overline{1,m}$. The method used here is called *semi-discretization* [1]. It is easy to see that systems (1) and (4) have the same equilibria if any.

Further on, denote $n_k = [t_k/h]$ we approximate the impulsive conditions (2) by

$$x_i(n_k^+) - x_i(n_k^-) = \sum_{\ell=n_{k-1}+1}^{n_k} B_{ik\ell}x_i(\ell) + \gamma_{ik}, \tag{5}$$
$$i = \overline{1,m},\ k \in \mathbb{N}$$

where, for convenience, $n_0 = -1$ and $B_{ik\ell}$ are suitably chosen constants.

Finally, we find sufficient conditions for the global exponential stability of the unique equilibrium point of the system (4), (5).

## IV. CONCLUSION

In the present paper we gave a short overview of the history, performance and applications of neurons and neural networks. We presented several neural network models and our results concerning the existence and global exponential stability of an equilibrium point or periodic solution of these models.

## REFERENCES

[1] S. Mohamad and K. Gopalsamy, "Dynamics of a class of discrete-time neural networks and their continuous-time counterparts," Math. Comput. Simulat., vol. 53, pp. 1-39, 2000. ISSN: 03784754

[2] A. I. Galushkin, Neural Networks Theory. Berlin-Heidelberg: Springer-Verlag, 2007. ISBN: 9783540481249

[3] J. Heaton, Introduction to the Math of Neural Networks. Heaton Research. ISBN: 9781604390339

[4] W. McCulloch and W. Pitts, "A logical calculus of the ideas immanent in nervous activity," Bull. Math. Biophys., vol. 9, pp. 127-147, 1943. ISSN: 0007-4985

[5] J. J. Hopfield, "Neurons with graded response have collective computational properties like those of two-state neurons," Proc. Natl. Acad. Sci. USA, vol. 81, pp. 3088-3092, 1984. ISSN: 1091-6490

[6] Z.-H. Guan and G. Chen, "On delayed impulsive Hopfield neural networks," Neural Netw., vol. 12, pp. 273-280, 1999. ISSN: 0893-6080

[7] H. Akça, R. Alassar, V. Covachev, Z. Covacheva, and E. Al-Zahrani, "Continuous-time additive Hopfield-type neural networks with impulses," J. Math. Anal. Appl., vol. 290, pp. 436-451, 2004. ISSN: 0022-247X, 1096-0813

[8] H. Akça and V. Covachev, "Impulsive Cohen-Grossberg neural networks with S-type distributed delays," Tatra Mt. Math. Publ., vol. 48, pp. 1-13, 2011. ISSN: 1210-3195

[9] H. Akça, R. Alassar, V. Covachev, and Z. Covacheva, "Discrete counterparts of continuous-time additive Hopfield-type neural networks with impulses," Dyn. Syst. Appl., vol. 13, pp. 77-92, 2004. ISSN: 1056-2176

# Challenges for Advanced Applications in Archaeology

## What IT can still learn from humanities

Lutz Schubert
IOMI, University of Ulm
Ulm, Germany
email: lutz.schubert@uni-ulm.de

Keith Jeffery
Keith G Jeffery Consultants
Faringdon, UK
email: keith.jeffery@keithgjefferyconsultants.co.uk

Gill Hunt
Hunt Lancaster
Lancaster, UK
email: ghunt@huntlancaster.co.uk

*Abstract*—**Computer science frequently considers much of humanities and in particular archaeology "trivial". The "hard challenges" were defined by sciences, such as physics. Yet these "soft" domains have been and are struggling with challenges that still exceed computational capabilities and that cannot be solved with current approaches. On the other hand, climatological models, remote sensing, agent modelling etc. all can benefit from archaeological data and approaches. In this paper we review how current computer science is insufficient to address the challenges posed in an archaeological context.**

***Keywords – advanced applications; archaeology; high performance computing; physics; simulation; network analysis; social networks; agent systems; theoretical computer science.***

## I. Introduction

Archaeology developed into a complex science only in the last century. It brings together experts from numerous disciplines to preserve and unveil the (human) past. Though archaeology is typically associated with a pen and paper science (Figure 1), it may come as a surprise that it adopts modern technology fast, such as radiocarbon dating and remote sensing [1] [12].

Due to the nature of the field, namely working with (and "in") the past, the need for complex applications and simulations in archaeology is typically not apparent. Yet organisations such as the CAA (short for "Computer Applications and Quantitative Methods in Archaeology") exist since the 1970s, having identified the need for computational power in archaeology early on.

This paper examines some of the challenges arising from archaeology that necessitate complex and state-of-the-art computational methods. Existing approaches are frequently insufficient to address the requirements and challenges posed by this field. The main purpose of this paper is to raise awareness of these issues and elaborate how computer science methodologies could improve further by addressing them. Section 2 thus lists some of these challenges and elaborates why current methodologies are insufficient. The final section will examine how computer science could contribute to and benefit from addressing this field.

Figure 1. Archaeologist mapping the layout of a trench. Source: Wikipedia.

## II. The (Hidden) Complexity of Archaeolgy

Archaeology is no domain constrained to a single scientific area – as it deals with human behavior over a range of unknown factors, it incorporates aspects of social sciences, evolution theory and neuropsychology, but also of surrounding domains, such as weather and climate. The most important aspect however is that all data must necessarily be incomplete: not only is there scarce archaeological evidence in the first instance, but also such evidence consists only in what humans leave behind – and intentions and beliefs leave no visible trace. Imagine finding a watch somewhere in the street and try to derive what happened from what little evidence there is: did the owner lose it? This is unlikely if the strap is intact. Did the owner throw it away? Is there any sign of damage on the watch? If so, may it stem from being pushed around on the street? Was the wearer male or female? Form alone may indicate taste, not convention and so on.

Multiple factors have to be cross-examined when trying to reconstruct the potential events that led to the watch being on the street. Archaeology does this every day, very much similar to forensic criminology with the added complexity that assumptions about (modern) human thinking cannot be applied.

### A. Big Data, Data Mining etc.

The only way to approach the problem consists in gathering as much information – ideally hard evidence – about the situation as possible and then starting to make assumptions over potential relationships, causes and effects. In most cases this means that logical errors have to be eliminated first. The principle of Ockham's razor is equally important for archaeology as any other science, as e.g. the recent find of a Roman coin in Japan demonstrates [2]: an implausible explanation would be that ancient Japan by accident minted a coin that is absolutely identical to Roman coins, not only in shape and depiction, but also in metallurgic configuration. We can already note that comparison of type and metal plays an important role in identifying the coin's origin in the first instance.

Such analysis requires an in-depth knowledge about Roman coinage, which exceeds the capabilities of a single domain expert: metallurgists have to talk with Roman experts on coinage and on trading networks etc. Logical consistency across all these aspects is difficult to assess – for example the implications if some individual Romans may have indeed travelled as far as Japan. The amount of data involved in this analysis is not only vast and completely differently structured across domains, but in most cases only human (i.e. not machine) readable. Most importantly, however, it is incomplete, basing on scarce evidence and conjecture. Testing for logical implications is therefore difficult: not only because the data formalizes little of the logical constraints, but also because it is simply incomplete.

Statistical analysis is based on the assumption that sufficient sample and reference data exists. In the case of archaeological evidence, only little data exists and reference data is in most cases conjecture, e.g. when comparing ancient structures with modern ones. All data is therefore associated with a high error potential, which is insufficiently formalized, even though network analysis, sample clustering, typology etc. all are based on statistical methods.

The implicit error must therefore be formalized and taken into consideration in analytical methods – and, what is more, its implications discussed: a deviation propagated over multiple implications / relations not only carries forth but increases with all further associated errors.

*Approaches.* Modern data mining technologies are quintessential for archaeological analysis. Standard methods look for clusters in datasets to identify (potential) relationships – this essentially means that the analysis stays within one ontology. In cross-disciplinary analysis, however, the data belongs to different ontologies and their correlation is not obvious. Such relationships need to be explicitly defined and logically constrained by a metadata set that defines type, period, context, location etc. Notably, any find may be cross-referenced against any other find of same type and from a related period. Take the example of the Roman coin: would it be possible to travel the according distance given the means and conditions at the time? For each according assumption, the associated risk of error needs to be taken into account: how *likely* is such travel given the situation and what does that mean for all other assumptions made so far?

Due to the lacking structure of archaeological data, better data conversion techniques are needed, including natural language processing. As a first step, it would be sufficient to extract key words from the data that classify find types and context, including location, population, time frame etc. This would at least allow that finds and reports can be correlated according to their context – even if such information would be insufficient for (logical) reasoning. Metadata for scientific purposes is constantly being improved, but has not reached this level as yet [10].

To this end, logical relationships need to be encoded – notably, many of them take the form of complex simulations themselves (see below), whereas others can be simple constraints, such as that the context cannot be older than the find. New mechanisms for incomplete reasoning are needed that can perform statistical analysis and assumptions on insufficient data. By associating an error with the number of assumptions violated, Ockham's razor can be used as a qualitative assessment. Regarding our Roman coin in Japan, logical explanations include equally trading networks, individual travelers and chance reproduction. Given the time and circumstances, however, direct travel and trading are highly unlikely, as is chance reproduction. This does not mean that an indirect trading "chain" could not have existed along which route a coin happened to travel as an exotic gift. The likelihood of an individual traveler can be calculated by (a) the complexity and cost of such a travel, (b) the other evidence for exchange, i.e. frequency of similar finds, and (c) relative timing of the contexts, i.e. appearance of other finds in the same context etc.

Potential explanations (assumptions) must be encoded and their logic must be reproducible. As opposed to this, most modern AI focuses on statistical analysis of massive amount of (equally structured) data.

### B. Simulating Human Behaviour

Archaeology is about humans: how they lived, what they have done, when and why. However, in an illiterate society, ways of thinking leave no traces and even in literate societies, written evidence should not be confused with facts [1]. The challenge for archaeology therefore consists in relating finds to potential behaviour, intentions and way of thinking. Some of this behaviour is obvious and straight-forward: a ceramic pot indicates that (a) someone was there to leave the pot behind and (b) someone made the pot. However, was the pot used as a domestic item, was it an item of worship, was it just decorative, was it discarded right away? All this cannot be gathered from the pot alone.

As seen (data mining, above), a considerable amount of information has to be cross-linked. What is more, though, is that human behaviour, intentions and beliefs, capabilities and knowledge etc. stand at the middle of the explanation chain and form the basis for any conjecture. As indicated above, this can obviously take different levels:

1. Presence. At the most straight-forward level, the remains are just indicators for human presence and actions, such as that someone must have brought the

find to the location, must have made it etc. Notably, not always is a find clearly of human origin, as e.g. is the case with some Palaeolithic "tools" [3]. This is the level of direct archaeological evidence.

2. Capabilities. At an intermediate level of complexity, human capabilities must be taken into consideration. This defines whether it was e.g. possible to reach a location, build a structure etc. How humans reached the American continent is one unsolved question on this level. At this level we talk about the assumptions that can be substantiated by archaeological evidence (existence of boats), but not fully proven.
3. Belief and Intention. At the most complex level we need to argue over belief and actions that are behind the evidence. It is a frequent cliché that archaeologists classify any evidence without clear functionality as "ritualistic". Indeed, it is difficult to assess the intention of an object that has no comparison in modern context. At this level, all "evidence" is pure conjecture and may change on basis of new theories.

Whereas knowledge at level 1 and partially at level 2 falls clearly into big data management, i.e. cross-checking facts, most of level 2 and in particular level 3 are conjecture and base on logical possibilities alone. Aspects such as movement of peoples require that the behaviour is simulated and the likelihood assessed on basis of this simulation.

*Approaches.* Human behaviour can be simulated in many different ways. Standard approaches consist in agent based simulations, which model multiple entities and their interactions on a simplified level [4]. There is a considerable amount of criticism of these models, as they must naturally be incomplete and error prone – it is currently not even possible to appropriately simulate how a crowd walks on a street, let alone how a whole settlement would behave [5].

Human behaviour is complex and cannot be easily abstracted, so a major question relates to which human aspects have to be modelled in the first instance and how. Much can be learned from social network interactions, but care must be taken when applying modern contexts to ancient circumstances, as behaviour and mindset are in constant flux [1].

Statistical analyses can reduce the computational effort, even though they have a high error margin. They can help to eliminate *unlikely* situations, such as for the Roman "tourist" in Japan which would necessitate the according means of travel, communication etc. [6] suggest an analysis basing on throwing angles and strengths to assess the layout of shell middens. This is a highly simplified human behaviour model but already allows for some degree of feasibility assessment.

### C. Simulating Climate

Climate is constantly changing – not only due to human interference, but also due to the earth's rotation and movement, leading to glacial and hot periods. The implication of such weather changes is obvious and can already be observed today: different plants grow in different climatic zones, animals (and certainly humans) move to different areas, clothing changes etc. In times before Air Conditioning, this hit doubly strong and will have caused (and prevented) massive movement and settlement patterns, following game or reacting to environmental pressure.

Climate completely changes the face of the earth, from rising (and sinking) sea levels to landscapes covered in ice sheets or turned into steppes. These changes leave their marks and are sometimes directly measurable, such as in tree growth (dendrochronology) or remains of marine life in the dessert, respectively vice versa [1] [12].

In the archaeological context climate is only of interest insofar as it influences humans [7]. As such, it is only a contributing factor to Simulating Human Behaviour (see section II.B) and can serve equally as an explanation, as well as an obstacle. For example, the movement of Homo Sapiens to the American continent is frequently explained by the possibility of a connection between North America and Siberia (the Bering land bridge) [8]. This land bridge could have existed due to a massive amount of water being locked in ice, thus causing the sea-level to sink considerably. Similarly, the movement of hominins into central Europe from Africa may have been made possible by fluctuations (inter-pluvial arid periods) in the temperature of the Sahara [9].

Climate conditions apparently play a role in any discussion about behaviour influenced by weather, such as clothing, foodstuff etc. Therefore, modelling the weather and in particular the climatic changes over history is a relevant aspect of the argumentation chain related to Simulating Human Behaviour (see section II.B).

*Approaches.* It is well-known that weather simulation belongs to the most difficult tasks in advanced applications [11]. While meteorological simulations try to accurately predict local, minute changes in the weather, climate models can be more coarse-grained, identifying patterns of general weather trends over longer periods of time. However, already the overall climatic changes in the glacial and interglacial periods are difficult to predict and not all factors are known. Such models base more on observed factors, such as glacial movements and encapsulated $CO^2$, than on calculations [12].

Nonetheless, different models are under development (e.g. [13]) and particularly try to provide more local and fine-grained climatic conditions, so as to assess the size and distribution of ice sheets, but also just to predict shorelines, climatic zones etc. Such models can be validated partially against archaeobotanical finds, i.e. seeds that have been preserved under anaerobic conditions.

### D. Physics

Physics pervade all human life for obvious reasons and thus are relevant for interpreting any (archaeological) find – for example, when arguing why and how a find ended in a specific position. Complex physic simulations can (and do) contribute to various aspects in archaeology, of which only a few examples will be listed here:

Humans having been killed violently and / or moved after death will end up in certain positions and orientation. For example skeletons in the Tollense valley have been moved by water slides and thus ended up in a collective heap [14]. Knowing the shape of the land, the flow of water and intensity of rainfall allows reconstructing where the bodies originated from, and (to a degree) their original positions. As the process is irreversible, this is not entirely possible – but the order of skeletons already indicates how they must have been flooded down the hill. Notably, the state of decomposition makes a major difference with this respect.

Related to this, wounds in the body (skeleton) give an indicator for strength and direction of a blow or of the projectile. Arrowheads embedded in bones tell something about the position of the opponents relative to each other, but also about how the weapon was used and the force that the respective weapon can transmit. Obviously, human factors have to be taken into consideration, such as whether the force could be created by muscle strength (spear) or whether additional means would have been needed (bow). Given e.g. the Tollense layout, a reconstruction of the event can thus be attempted.

Other aspects related to physics simulation are e.g. how structures or burial mounds collapse and organic material decomposes over time. Just as in the Tollense case, the layout of the original structure can never be reconstructed from the final collapsed heap. Nonetheless, the shape and layout of the elements in the heap allow reasoning over the possible original structures. By comparing these with existing, similar structures (see section II.E), reasonable assumptions about the original layout can be made, as well as about the factors that led to the final distribution.

Human intervention is a factor in both scenarios. In the first case, humans define in particular the strength and way of usage. In the second case, they (may!) define the causes for collapse and potential rearrangement of the final structure, e.g. if stones were removed or shifted to make space for other structures.

*Approaches.* Rigid body physics belong to the oldest forms of computational simulations and in principle can already be employed in the fashion suggested – however, only for performing the "forward" calculation, i.e. from a given structure to the collapsed heap. Inverting this process is not possible, though, and thus the likelihood that a structure will lead to the observed distribution is highly unlikely.

New methods are needed that essentially invert physics, i.e. to reconstruct the original layout from the final distribution by taking different influencing factors into consideration. These include human intervention, which so far is still most difficult to model. Essentially, such a model would generate a likelihood assessment that a recorded heap relates to a specific structure, given the conditions specific to the context of the find.

### *E. Matching*

By nature, most archaeological finds are in fragments: destroyed, decomposed, collapsed etc. Next to the general layout of the finds, the actual material and shape of the fragments themselves provide indicators for their relationship. Consider the various forms of pottery that can be found in archaeology: shape, material and texture, respectively decoration are good indicators as to whether two sherds may have belonged to the same object. This also applies to (human) bones, larger sculptures etc.

Generally, parts are missing, scattered all over the place, or even archived in a completely different city / country due to different excavation processes, movement after excavation etc. Furthermore, due to the vast amount of similar fragments, identification of corresponding parts is close to impossible.

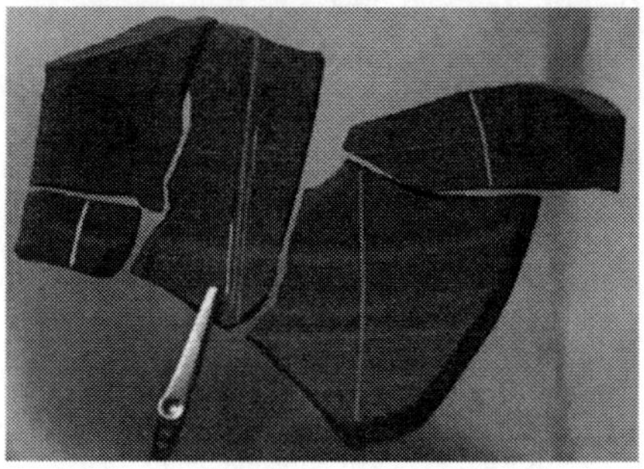

Figure 2. Matching sherds on basis of profile information [15].

In itself, this is a considerable big data process where multiple factors need to be compared and cross-correlated to identify potential matches. These in turn will have to be matched in shape and against types of objects. Ideally, the fragments touch and thus have a common breakage area. Though this may sound like "just" a fitting task, one needs to consider (a) the amount and size of fits and (b) that natural processes change the breakage area by smoothing and reducing it etc., so that no perfect fit can be achieved anymore. Such processes will have to be taken into consideration when asserting whether two fragments match [16].

In most cases, no 3d models are available, let alone provide sufficient details to attempt a match in the first instance. As the number of available models increases, so does the complexity to match all the available finds – but even just within a single excavation, the effort is considerable.

*Approaches.* Various approaches exist for automated shape matching, but they mostly assume that the fragments show near-perfect fits (Figure 2). Fewer approaches consider additional factors, such as general shape and continuation of patterns or pigments, which in both cases require additional knowledge about shapes and types of objects in the period and region. It is already helpful to use continuation aspects both for the overall shape and for the basic principles of the pattern, as discontinuity is comparatively rare.

As opposed to this, matches of the actual breakage surface must be similar, not identical. This means that fragments can be placed basing on continuation aspects of shape and breakage area: as distance between the sherds increases, the breakage surface will have been subject to other processes and thus similarity in the surfaces becomes increasingly irrelevant – up to the point where intermediate pieces are lacking (the distance at which this is the case is influenced by the type of material).

### *F. Geophysics*

Remote sensing is relevant for archaeology as it is generally non-intrusive and thus non-destructive [18]. It can provide essential information as to whether an excavation is justified in the first instance. Most remote sensing technologies base on the principle that differences in density or conductivity of the material can be measured up to a certain distance (Figure 3).

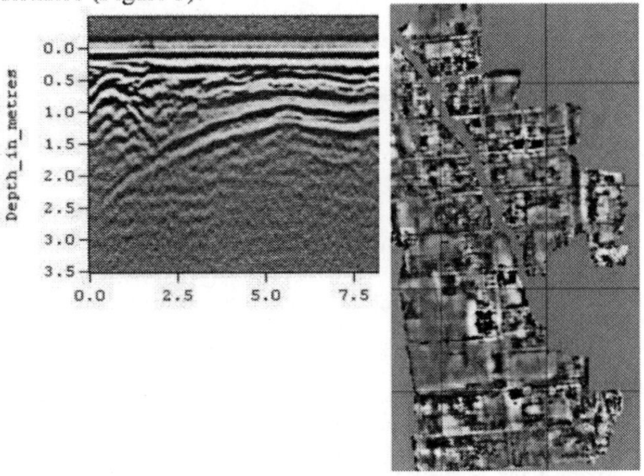


Figure 3. Ground Penetrating Radar (left) and map resulting from a resistance survey (right). Source: Wikipedia.

The resulting data is not meaningful on its own and only predicts a change in material within the ground. It does (currently) not allow any conjecture about the material, let alone about the structure itself. Even larger area scans can only indicate whether a regular structure (building) may be present at all.

Producing a visual depiction from the raw data takes considerable computational power – however, even more important is the assessment of the data against known structures and comparison of material distribution in surrounding ground (i.e. geological properties of the area). With such knowledge, the interpretation of the geophysical data could be improved considerably.

*Approaches.* The task is comparable to big data mining. Next to the obvious shape information, however, material properties of the objects / structures play an important role as they influence the details in the remote sensing data. As of now, most remote sensing data focus on larger structures, mostly due to the coarse granularity of the data in the first instance.

As with any human (or in fact animal) artefacts, non-regarding all past and present standardisation efforts, individual structures will differ from each, already just because of taste. In addition to this, local circumstances, as well as the differences in collapse and deterioration will lead to strong individual deviations.

These factors make direct data comparison, as is typically the case in other data mining tasks, difficult. Instead, the data must be considered indicative, in the sense that certain properties are correct rather than the whole structure – this includes an indirect match with the possible material properties, and a comparison to the rough layout. Layouts must be represented as key features with *likely* positioning, because, as noted, the individual layout will differ considerably. The likelihood of the layout may thereby be linked to the physics simulations discussed above.

### G. 3d images

3d scanning is a growing field of interest in general, but also more and more archaeologists are making use of photogrammetry to document the excavation [17]. There is a high risk here that this is considered sufficient documentation, though it cannot replace profile drawings or good maps, but we shall not follow this discussion in this paper.

Generating 3d models from pictures taken in the open field is still time consuming and error prone, where missing pictures can only be identified after generation of the point cloud, which can take days in itself. Since the excavation will have progressed by then, this can lead to considerable problems. Better methods are needed to assess quality and potential gaps right at the time of taking the pictures, and the process in general needs to become more flexible – both requires new algorithmic approaches that are highly related to performance optimisation in general.

One should also not ignore the fact that 3d scanning generates massive amount of data (i.e. the 3d points) that so far cannot be easily processed. Identifying an object in 3d space, i.e. which points belong to each other to form an artefact of its own, is still basically impossible. Similar challenges exist in 2d image analysis, where major progress has been made. So far most approaches simply generate a mesh of the whole scan, thus not allowing to (re)move individual objects, let alone perform an analysis on this level.

Since the advent of LIDAR scanning [18], processing of 3d images becomes an important factor for detecting hidden and obscured structures, very similar to identifying hidden structures in geophysical data (see section II.F).

*Approaches.* So far, most approaches rely on methods from 2d image processing, such as similarity of colour, identification of key features and of their relationship etc., but application in 3d is still very limited – not alone because the size of data is considerably larger (at least from $n^2$ to $n^3$).

Google and Microsoft already try to incorporate scans and 3d data from multiple (social) sources, but the sheer amount and computational complexity is still an unsolved challenge. Ideally, however, multiple sources are integrated in scanning, but notably, these will all have to be calibrated individually and the data then has to be cross-correlated first.

Some attempts also try to make use of additional data, such as arising from the accelerometer to pre-assess the quality and usability of the images, but there is no general good solution as yet and the amount of data will only increase.

### H. Others

Additional aspects include simulation of decomposition of organic material, such as wood and flesh, but also of inorganic material, i.e. rusting of metal etc. Similar to the collapse of structures, reproduction of the original shape or even just identifying conjoining pieces is a challenge in itself.

Reconstruction in general relies on reference material, which typically only indicates general layout, not concrete shape (such as in the typology of vases). Identifying the appropriate structures from fragments is still basically unsolved given the complexity of the domain.

Many more challenges such as this exist.

## III. Conclusions

The list of issues presented in this paper is far from exhaustive but already demonstrates the shortcoming of current computer science methodologies with respect to the needs of archaeology. Specifically, by addressing these challenges and incorporating knowledge from archaeology, the following improvements could be achieved:

- improved geological modelling: archaeology has knowledge about more short-term processes, such as soil deposition and collapse that can be exploited for engineering, city planning etc.;
- better human and agent models: anthropology and archaeology have information about human movement that is not reflected in simulation, thus leading to unrealistic movement and agency models;
- prospecting can benefit from prediction models and material knowledge gained from excavations;
- data mining and big data do not address complexities raised by such interdisciplinary fields as archaeology, which develops such methods for 100 years now;
- statistical analysis is an important field in archaeology and needs to be applied differently for network analysis, clustering etc. The feedback is rarely incorporated (see e.g. [20]);
- structure from motion is constantly being improved through landscape archaeology and field surveys [17] – new more robust methods and better object recognition are still being researched;
- most simulations model time forward from a given situation– in archaeology, time needs to be modelled backwards, i.e. leading from effect to cause which in turn improves simulation performance and analysis capabilities [6];
- dealing with incomplete data by adding assumption models: archaeology is using methods for this on a daily basis, yet big data still struggles with it;
- both fields need better methods to capture the probability and likelihood of complex data to be correct and to identify logical and improbable errors;
- reasoning needs to improve beyond stochastic data mapping and in particular needs to include the probability that two actions are related. Artificial Intelligence concepts from the 90ies already approach such issues on a limited scale.

Not only can computer science improve archaeology further, but also knowledge from archaeology can help advance computer science capabilities in particular for application in any human-centric simulation or modelling.

## References


[1] M. Sutton, "Archaeology: The Science of the Human Past," Routledge, July 2015

[2] E. Jozuka, "Ancient Roman coins found in ruined Japanese castle," CNN, 2017 [Online]. Available from: http://edition.cnn.com/2016/09/27/luxury/ancient-roman-coins-japan/ [retrieved: June 2017]

[3] K. Wong, "Wild Monkeys' Stone 'Tools' Force a Rethink of Human Uniqueness," Scientific American, 2016 [Online]. Available at: https://www.scientificamerican.com/article/wild-monkeys-stone-tools-force-a-rethink-of-human-uniqueness/ [retrieved: June 2017]

[4] G. Wurzer, K. Kowarik, and H. Reschreiter (eds.), "Agent-based Modeling and Simulation in Archaeology," Springer 2015.

[5] D. Thalmann and S.R. Musse, "Crowd Simulation," Springer 2012

[6] L. Schubert and K. Jeffery, "Modelling Physics in Shell Middens," Proceedings of the CAA 2017, in press

[7] M. Tallavaara et al., "Human population dynamics in Europe over the Last Glacial Maximum," PNAS, vol. 112, no. 27, pp. 8232-8237, July 2015

[8] S. Armstrong Elias, "First Americans Lived on Bering Land Bridge for Thousands of Years," Scientific American 2016 [Online]. Available at: https://www.scientificamerican.com/article/first-americans-lived-on-bering-land-bridge-for-thousands-of-years/ [retrieved: July 2017]

[9] W.J. Burroughs, "Climate Change in Prehistory: the end of the reign of chaos," Cambridge University Press, 2007.

[10] K. Jeffery and A. Asserson, "Why CERIF?" W3 2016. [Online] Available at: http://www.w3.org/2016/11/sdsvoc/SDSVoc16_paper_15 [retrieved: July 2017]

[11] U. Gähde et al., "Models, Simulations, and the Reduction of Complexity," de Gruyter, 2013

[12] M.J. Aitken, "Science-Based Dating in Archaeology," Routledge, February 2014

[13] J.d'A. Guedes et al., "21st-Century Approaches to Ancient Problems: Climate and Society," PNAS, vol. 113, no.51, pp. 14483-14491.

[14] A. Curry, "Slaughter at the bridge: Uncovering a colossal Bronze Age battle," Science Magazine 2016. [Online] Available at: http://www.sciencemag.org/news/2016/03/slaughter-bridge-uncovering-colossal-bronze-age-battle [retrieved: June 2017]

[15] M.I. Stamatopoulos and C.-N. Anagnostopoulos, "3D digital reassembling of archaeological ceramic pottery fragments based on their thickness profile," ResearchGate 2016. [Online] Available at: https://www.researchgate.net/publication/301873740_3D_digital_reassembling_of_archaeological_ceramic_pottery_fragments_based_on_their_thickness_profile [retrieved: July 2017]

[16] F. Stanco, S. Battiato, and G. Gallo, "Digital Imaging for Cultural Heritage Preservation: Analysis, Restoration, and Reconstruction of Ancient Artworks," CRC Press, 2011

[17] M. Llobera, "Archaeological Visualization: Towards an Archaeological Information Science (AISc)," J Archaeol Method Theory, vol. 18, no. 3, pp. 193-223, September 2011

[18] A.J. Clark, "Seeing Beneath the Soil, Prospecting Methods in Archaeology," Batsford London, 1990

[19] C. Hopkins, "Lidar archaeology shines a light on hidden sites" BBC 2014. [Online] Available at: http://www.bbc.com/future/story/20120827-the-laser-archaeologists [retrieved: May 2017]

[20] A. Collar et al., "Networks in Archaeology: Phenomena, Abstraction, Representation." J Archaeol Method Theory, vol. 22, no. 1, pp. 1–32. January 2015

# What Do Scientific Applications Need? An Empirical Study of Multirail Network Bandwidth

Edgar A. León, Chris Chambreau, and Matthew L. Leininger

Lawrence Livermore National Laboratory
Livermore, California, USA
Email: {leon,chambreau1,leininger4}@llnl.gov

*Abstract*—**High performance computing applications are commonly executed on large parallel machines composed of commodity components. These commodity clusters utilize high-speed interconnects that provide low latency and high bandwidth such as InfiniBand. Understanding the characteristics of scientific applications is important to properly configure and tune these machines and their software stacks. Are applications limited by network performance? Can they leverage increased network bandwidth? What type of network operations and message sizes do they use? This work provides a better understanding of the communication requirements of scientific applications by investigating the impact of multirail networking on their performance. We measure the performance of a suite of high performance computing mini-applications under different multirail configurations to determine their sensitivity to network bandwidth. The selected mini-applications provide simplified source code containing data access patterns and computational characteristics of larger production codes. The type of analysis presented in this paper can be applied to inform the procurement of future systems maximizing application productivity within a given capital budget.**

***Keywords–HPC; performance measurement; multirail networking; network characterization; scientific applications.***

## I. INTRODUCTION

Most scientific applications use the Message Passing Interface (MPI) to leverage parallelism across multiple nodes. As such, network performance is important for application and system developers and those responsible for hardware procurements. When procuring a supercomputing cluster, for example, there is a range of options in terms of processor, memory, and network capabilities. A question one may ask is whether doubling the network bandwidth is worth sacrificing upgrades in processor speed. The right balance depends on the suite of applications that will execute on such system. The more we understand the characteristics and requirements of our applications, the better decisions we can make to provide the best performance within a given capital or power budget.

In this work, we provide an empirical study of the network requirements of a suite of high performance computing (HPC) applications and the impact of network speed on their performance. The codes we employ are part of a suite of mini-applications that contain data access patterns and computational characteristics of larger production codes within the U.S. Department of Energy (DOE). These include sparse linear algebra, shock hydrodynamics, Monte Carlo particle transport, finite element, and radiation transport codes.

We start by characterizing the communication requirements of these applications in terms of their point-to-point (P2P) and collective operations and message sizes. Point-to-point operations, such as `Send` and `Receive`, require some form of synchronization between two processes and scale primarily in terms of message size. Collective operations, such as `Barrier` and `Allreduce`, require the synchronization of all tasks in a particular group (often all MPI processes) and scale with respect to the number of participating nodes and message size.

We leverage multirail networking (multiple network interfaces per node) as a vehicle to examine the impact of network speed on application performance. When using multirail we evaluate several policies to understand locality and affinity tradeoffs. Our sensitivity study includes two parts. In the first part, we evaluate the performance improvements of multirail on micro-benchmarks to determine the potential gains of this technology. Although micro-benchmark evaluations have been done in the past [1]–[4], we need information to assess how much of these gains is actually realized by applications. This is the focus of the second part, where we evaluate the sensitivity of our codes to network bandwidth. Our goal is to better understand how dependent these applications are to network performance, information that can be used by application and system developers and for system procurements.

The reminder of the paper is organized as follows. Section II describes the machine environment used for the empirical study. Sections III and IV describe the multirail policies and applications employed, respectively, while Section V characterizes the communication characteristics of the selected applications. We measure the impact of multirail on micro-benchmarks and applications in Sections VI and VII, respectively. The limitations of this study are presented in Section VIII and the related work presented in Section IX. Finally, Section X presents our conclusion and future work.

## II. MACHINE PARAMETERS

We employed the *Catalyst* machine at Lawrence Livermore National Laboratory (LLNL), a 324 node Linux cluster with two Intel IvyBridge (Xeon E5-2695 v2) processors and 128 GB of memory per node. Each processor has 12 cores at 2.4 GHz with 2 hardware threads per core (Intel Hyper-Threading). The nodes are connected via an InfiniBand dual-rail, Quad Data Rate network (Intel QDR-80) in a fully-provisioned Fat-Tree topology. It runs the Tri-Lab Operating System Software (TOSS) [5]. At the time the experiments were executed, Catalyst was running TOSS version 2.2, which is based on Red Hat Enterprise Linux Server release 6.5. Each processor has a theoretical peak memory bandwidth of 59.7 GB/s and uses DDR3 memory at 1866 MHz. The MPI library we used is MVAPICH2 version 1.9 with the GNU compiler.

## III. Multirail Networking Policies

Multirail networks consist of multiple network interface controllers (NICs) per compute node. Catalyst has two InfiniBand cards per node (4x10 Gb/s links per card) connected to a single plane. Each card is placed in proximity to a processor socket. The MPI library is implemented on top of a low-level network layer: Intel Performance Scaled Messaging (PSM). PSM provides options for binding network traffic from a given MPI task or process to a given card [6].

To understand the impact of the increased bandwidth provided by multirail and the affinity to a local NIC, we instrumented the policies shown in Table I.

TABLE I. Multirail network policies.

| | |
|---|---|
| *Default* | PSM default dual-rail policy. It allocates MPI processes to the NICs in an alternating or round robin fashion |
| *NIC-0* | Route all traffic through card 0 |
| *NIC-1* | Route all traffic through card 1 |
| *Local-NIC* | Route traffic from each socket through its local NIC |

We make the following observations about our policies and network configurations. First, we consider both policies NIC-0 and NIC-1 because even though the hardware configuration is symmetric, NIC 0 is used for system-level traffic. Depending on the application, this network *noise* may have an impact on performance. Second, the PSM driver version installed on Catalyst does not instrument striping of messages across NICs or using a local NIC at the PSM level (thus the need for our Local-NIC policy). And, third, even though MVAPICH provides dual-rail policies, they were not implemented for Intel fabrics at the time the experiments were executed.

Our goal is not to provide a comprehensive study of multirail policies but to understand the impact of the network on application performance.

## IV. Applications Suite

Our codes consist of five mini-applications from the CORAL benchmark suite [7], which represent DOE workloads and technical requirements [8]. CORAL is the result of a joint Collaboration between Oak Ridge, Argonne, and Lawrence Livermore National Laboratories, and provides simplified source code to emulate the data access patterns and computational characteristics of larger production codes. These codes were used in the procurement of LLNL's next advanced technology system, *Sierra*, which will provide over 100 petaflop/s and is expected to be operational in 2018.

The CORAL benchmarks are grouped into several categories including scalable science, throughput science, and data-centric benchmarks. In this paper, we use the throughput codes shown in Table II and will study the other two categories in future work. The throughput benchmarks represent particular subsets of codes used as part of the everyday workload of science applications frequently executed on commodity clusters.

**AMG2013** is a benchmark application derived directly from the BoomerAMG solver in the Hypre linear solvers library. AMG2013 is an algebraic multigrid solver for linear systems built from problems on unstructured grids. The default problem is a Laplace-type problem with various jumps and anisotropy in one part.

TABLE II. Our CORAL throughput benchmark suite.

| | |
|---|---|
| AMG2013 | Algebraic multi-grid linear system solver |
| LULESH | Shock hydrodynamics for unstructured meshes |
| MCB | Monte Carlo transport |
| miniFE | Finite element code |
| UMT2013 | Unstructured mesh deterministic radiation transport |

**LULESH** is an explicit hydrodynamics application performed on a staggered grid mesh. It solves the Sedov problem on one octant of a sphere using Lagrangian hydrodynamics. Originally developed as one of the five DARPA UHPC challenge problems, it is now used in DOE co-design activities and machine procurements.

**MCB** is a Monte Carlo particle transport proxy-application for multi-physics simulation codes. It is written in C and uses MPI+OpenMP for parallelism. MCB performs a significant number of integer operations as well as branches.

**miniFE** is designed to be the "best approximation to an unstructured implicit finite element or finite volume application, but in 8000 lines or fewer." The benchmark attempts to provide as much coverage of the implicit finite element application space as possible given its size constraints.

**UMT** is an unstructured-mesh deterministic radiation transport benchmark. It is a single physics package code that performs three-dimensional, non-linear, radiation transport calculations using deterministic methods. UMT exercises memory bandwidth and is compute intense.

## V. MPI Characteristics of Applications

We collect MPI statistics using mpiP, an MPI profiling library [9]. Figure 1 shows the percentage of execution time spent on communication (left) and the average message size exchanged by our applications (right). These metrics are itemized in terms of P2P and collective operations using two configurations: MPI-only—1 task per core—and MPI+OpenMP—1 task per socket with 12 threads per task. Given that each node has two sockets, each with 12 cores, the MPI-only configuration has 24 processes per node (PPN) while the MPI+OpenMP configuration has 2 PPN. The MPI performance characteristics were similar for these two configurations.

We observe that most applications spend more than half of their MPI execution time performing collective operations. The exceptions are AMG and MCB. AMG spends a large fraction of time on P2P calls. In addition, it spends by far the highest percentage of execution time on communication. Despite taking a large percentage of execution time, AMG sends mostly small P2P messages. Similarly, MCB uses small messages for P2P operations but larger messages for collectives.

With the exception of MCB, collective operations send significantly less data across the network than P2P operations in the same application. LULESH spends nearly all of its MPI time making calls to Allreduce with a message size of 8 bytes, while a number of `Isend` calls incur orders of magnitude more bandwidth while requiring roughly one tenth of the time compared to the Allreduce calls.

Based on the communication characteristics of applications, we expect their sensitivity to network bandwidth to be application-dependent. In AMG or UMT, we would expect increased bandwidth to be helpful. However, in LULESH or

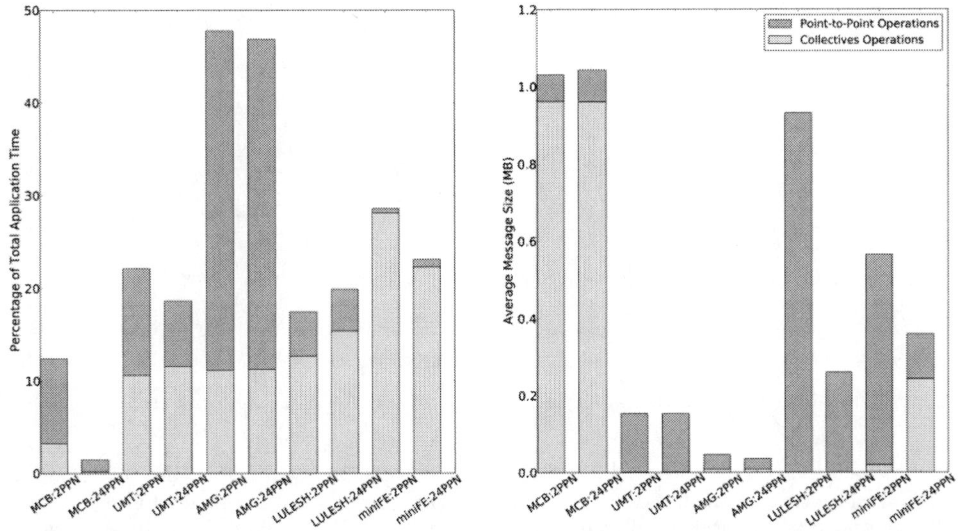


Figure 1. Collectives and P2P communication breakdown as a percentage of total execution time and their average message size. Experiments executed under two configurations, MPI-only (24 PPN) and MPI+OpenMP (2 PPN), on 256 nodes.

miniFE factors affecting latency, such as system noise and message injection rate, may impact their performance more than efforts to increase bandwidth.

## VI. Characterizing Multirail Bandwidth

To assess the potential benefits of multirail we employ the Phloem MPI Benchmarks [10]. They provide a collection of vendor-independent benchmarks that measure various aspects of MPI performance including aggregate bandwidth, interconnect messaging rate, collective latencies, and point-to-point latency. We focus on network bandwidth.

A significant advantage of dual-rail over single-rail is the potential for doubling the off-node communication bandwidth. Using the Phloem *Presta* aggregate bandwidth benchmark [10], we measured off-node aggregate bandwidth by exchanging messages between 24 tasks on one node and 24 tasks on a different node. Message sizes range between 32 bytes and 8 MB. As Figure 2 shows, for small message sizes, single and dual-rail performance is similar, with only a slight advantage for dual-rail. However, for message sizes greater than 256 bytes, the dual-rail aggregate bandwidth provides better performance reaching twice the bandwidth at around 1 KB. For message sizes of 32 KB and greater, the aggregate bandwidth for both single-rail and dual-rail plateaus with the dual-rail aggregate bandwidth essentially twice that of single rail.

Thus, using micro-benchmarks, dual-rail can double the off-node bandwidth when messages are sufficiently large. The next aspect to evaluate is whether the selected applications can benefit from this doubling of network bandwidth.

## VII. Impact on Applications

Each of the CORAL benchmarks reports a metric called *Figure of Merit (FOM)* indicative of application performance. The FOM is defined independently for each application and designed to scale linearly with performance [8]. We measured the FOM for each application with our network policies between 80 and 100 times because of nontrivial levels of

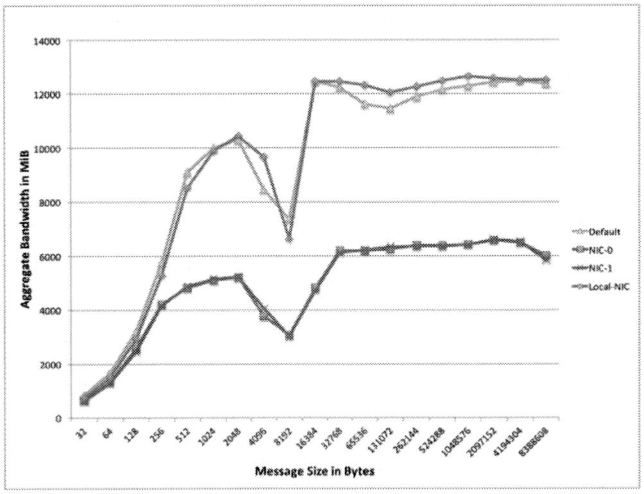


Figure 2. Network bandwidth between two nodes, each node uses 24 tasks.

runtime variations between runs. Using box-and-whisker plots, we show the first and third quartiles, median, minimum, maximum, and outliers. Figure 3 shows the MPI-only results for AMG, miniFE, and LULESH, where higher (FOM) is better. The MCB results are not shown because they are similar to miniFE and we discuss UMT separately (Figure 4) since this application demonstrated the most gains with dual-rail.

We observe negligible difference in application performance with the different network policies, except for slight improvements with the default dual-rail on AMG and UMT. Second, there is a significantly higher variability in execution time with NIC-0 compared to NIC-1 as shown by miniFE and MCB. As mentioned previously, system messages use NIC-0 for communication affecting the larger messages sent with collective operations of these two applications.

As shown in Figure 3c, despite significant time spent on P2P communications, AMG only benefits from the increased

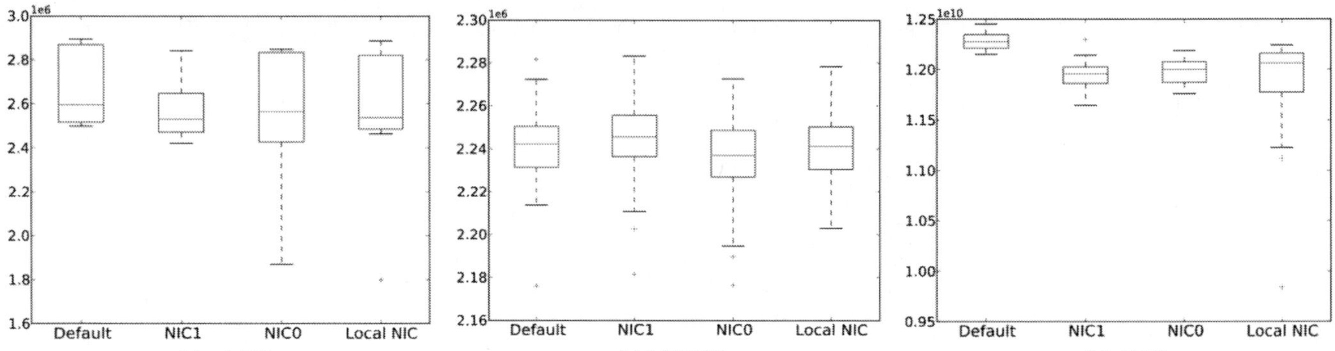


(a) miniFE (b) LULESH (c) AMG

Figure 3. Application performance, measured as Figure of Merit, as a function of different network configurations. Higher is better.

bandwidth provided by multirail on the order of 2%. This is due to the relatively small average P2P message size, which indicates that MPI performance for AMG is driven more by latency and synchronization overhead than bandwidth.

UMT exhibited the most gains from multirail but even here performance only increased by approximately 3.2%. To understand this result, we measure the percentage of execution time spent on MPI (vertical axis) as a function of P2P and collective operations over many runs (horizontal axis) and plot it in Figure 4. Most of the UMT gains with dual-rail are due to reductions in time spent on P2P operations (contrast solid lines at the top and bottom), which are as much as 18% faster overall, with collectives showing modest improvements but significant variations in performance.

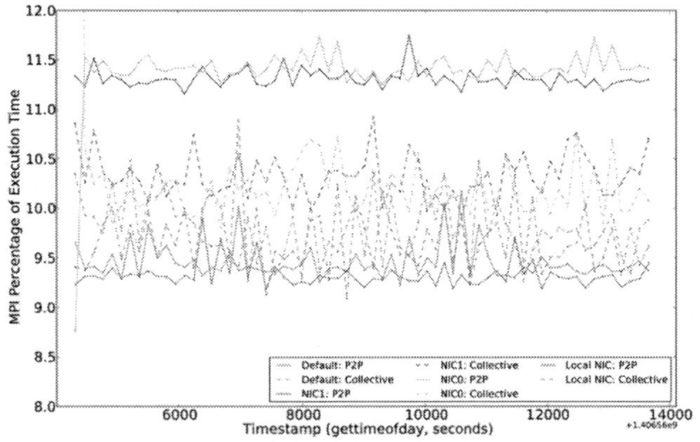


Figure 4. UMT percentage of execution time spent on MPI itemized by P2P (solid lines) and collective operations (dashed lines) over successive runs. Colors represent different network configurations.

While both AMG and UMT spend significant time on P2P operations, UMT's messages are larger on average, making it more sensitive to bandwidth increases. In contrast, miniFE and LULESH heavily rely on collective communications, where performance is dominated by issues of synchronization, communicator size, and latency. As Figure 4 also shows, collectives show significant variations in performance because of their sensitivity to system noise.

## VIII. Discussion and Limitations

In this work, we demonstrate that a suite of scientific HPC codes are, mostly, not sensitive to network bandwidth. The current bandwidth provided by a single rail is sufficient for our codes resulting in negligible improvements with an additional rail. In addition, these applications spend a significant percentage of communication time in collectives of small sizes, which are more sensitive to system noise rather than network speed. Furthermore, as scale increases so does the impact of noise and, thus, the amount of time spent on collectives.

The throughput benchmarks studied here represent important subsets of applications that are executed as part of the everyday workload of science applications on commodity clusters. This, however, does not mean that *all* scientific applications behave this way. In particular, other scalable science applications designed to run at the highest scale on the largest non-commodity machines may present a different sensitivity. Similarly, data-centric applications such as data analytics may impose more demanding network requirements. Furthermore, the differences between the mini-applications and the full-fledged applications from which they are derived may have an impact on their communication.

The scale of this study involves up to 6,144 MPI tasks over 256 nodes. Even though this scale is representative of workloads in commodity systems, it is likely that as scale increases to a few thousand nodes the ratio of compute to communication may change significantly resulting in different communication bottlenecks than what we observed here.

Finally, we want to emphasize that using realistic benchmarks such as the CORAL mini-applications and, ideally, full-fledged applications, provides a more accurate representation of the real impact of a proposed technique or approach. While micro-benchmarks are useful in the design of hardware and software components, ultimately, these are not the codes that are run on production systems. As we demonstrated, multirail can double network bandwidth on micro-benchmarks, but this improvement does not necessarily translate in a significant improvement in application performance. As shown in Section V, a medium-sized run with 6 K processes shows that codes are not necessarily bound by network bandwidth.

## IX. Related Work

Related work includes the evaluation of different approaches to leverage multiple rails including striping messages across two NICs [1]–[4]. These mechanisms have shown significant improvements in network bandwidth and latency. Communication libraries such as MPI have been instrumented accordingly to take advantage of multirail networks. Simulation approaches have also been useful in complementing empirical studies with added flexibility in terms of network topology, routing algorithms, etc. [11], [12]. Furthermore, multiple rails have been shown to address network congestion and network failures [13], [14]. For many of these studies, micro-benchmarks have been used to demonstrate the improvements in latency and bandwidth with multi-rail.

The investigations closer to ours include empirical studies that analyze the impact of multirail on the performance of applications. Choi et al. evaluates the AMBER and LAMMPS applications on a Torus network using 256 and 512 cores [15]. Schreiber et al. shows performance improvements of the LS-DYNA application on a Hypercube network on 256 cores [16]. Liu evaluates the performance of LAMMPS under different input tests on a Hypercube network on 1,536 cores [17]. Depending on the application and input test, performance improvements with multirail vary.

In this paper, we focus our multirail evaluation on several codes of interest to the DOE. The scale of our study involves 6,144 cores on a fully-provisioned Fat-Tree network. While there are multiple factors in multirail performance including topology, scale, and congestion, ultimately, its performance impact depends on the communication characteristics of the workloads of interest.

## X. Conclusion and Future Work

This work provides a better understanding of the network characteristics of a suite of scientific mini-applications representing data access patterns and computational characteristics of larger applications within the U.S. Department of Energy. Increased network bandwidth via multirail may be of limited benefit for many scientific codes running on commodity clusters. Despite substantial improvements on micro-benchmarks, the communication patterns of scientific workloads seem to benefit only slightly. These applications are not bandwidth bound sending mostly small messages, and many of the larger messages are performed asynchronously. These codes are more sensitive to network latency and load imbalance.

There are multiple avenues for future work. First, characterizing the selected codes at larger scales, particularly to identify any potential changes in compute to communication ratios. Second, analyzing other types of applications including scalable science and emerging data-centric codes. Third, comparing the effects of varying network bandwidth on application performance via other mechanisms including down clocking network links, say, from 50 Gb/s (HDR link speed) to 25 Gb/s (EDR link speed). Then, we can compare the tradeoffs of having one fast NIC per node vs. two slower NICs per node, e.g., HDR single rail vs. EDR dual rail.

## Acknowledgment

We would like to thank the anonymous reviewers for their useful feedback. Our appreciation to our colleagues Trent D'Hooge, Adam Moody, and Jim Foraker for their help and support with the Catalyst system.

Prepared by LLNL under Contract DE-AC52-07NA27344. LLNL-CONF-670475.

## References

[1] J. Cai, A. P. Rendell, and P. E. Strazdins, "Non-threaded and threaded approaches to multirail communication with uDAPL," in International Conference on Network and Parallel Computing, ser. NPC'09. Gold Coast, Australia: IEEE, Oct. 2009, pp. 233–239.

[2] V. Vishwanath, T. Shimizu, M. Takizawa, K. Obana, and J. Leigh, "Towards Terabit/s systems: Performance evaluation of multi-rail systems," in High Speed Networks Workshop. Anchorage, AK: IEEE, May 2007.

[3] A. Vishnu, G. Santhanaraman, W. Huang, H.-W. Jin, and D. K. Panda, "Supporting MPI-2 one sided communication on multi-rail InfiniBand clusters: Design challenges and performance benefits," in International Conference on High Performance Computing, ser. HiPC'05, Dec. 2005, pp. 137–147.

[4] J. Liu, A. Vishnu, and D. K. Panda, "Building multirail InfiniBand clusters: MPI-level design and performance evaluation," in Conference on Supercomputing, ser. SC'04. Pittsburgh, PA: IEEE, Nov. 2004, p. 33.

[5] "TOSS: Speeding up commodity cluster computing," Apr. 2016. [Online]. Available: https://computation.llnl.gov/projects/toss-speeding-commodity-cluster-computing

[6] True Scale Fabric OFED+ Host Software. User Guide., Intel Corporation, Sep. 2013.

[7] "CORAL benchmark codes," Dec. 2013. [Online]. Available: https://asc.llnl.gov/CORAL-benchmarks/

[8] CORAL: Collaboration of Oak Ridge, Argonne and Livermore National Laboratories, "Draft CORAL build statement of work," Office of Science and the National Nuclear Security Administrations Advanced Simulation and Computing (ASC) Program, U.S. Department of Energy, RFP No. B604142, LLNL-PROP-636244, Dec. 2013.

[9] "mpiP: Lightweight, scalable MPI profiling," Mar. 2014. [Online]. Available: http://mpip.sourceforge.net/

[10] "ASC Sequoia benchmark codes," Jun. 2013. [Online]. Available: https://asc.llnl.gov/sequoia/benchmarks/

[11] N. Wolfe, M. Mubarak, N. Jain, J. Domke, A. Bhatele, C. D. Carothers, and R. B. Ross, "Preliminary performance analysis of multi-rail fat-tree networks," in International Symposium on Cluster, Cloud and Grid Computing, ser. CCGrid'17. Madrid, Spain: IEEE/ACM, May 2017.

[12] S. Coll, E. Frachtenberg, F. Petrini, A. Hoisie, and L. Gurvits, "Using multirail networks in high-performance clusters," in International Conference on Cluster Computing. Newport Beach, CA: IEEE, Oct. 2001, pp. 15–24.

[13] S. P. Raikar, H. Subramoni, K. Kandalla, J. Vienne, and D. K. Panda, "Designing network failover and recovery in MPI for multi-rail InfiniBand clusters," in International Parallel and Distributed Processing Symposium Workshops & PhD Forum, ser. IPDPSW'12. IEEE, 2012, pp. 1160–1167.

[14] A. Nukada, K. Sato, and S. Matsuoka, "Scalable multi-GPU 3-D FFT for TSUBAME 2.0 supercomputer," in International Conference on High Performance Computing, Networking, Storage and Analysis, ser. SC'12. Salt Lake City, Utah: IEEE, 2012, pp. 44:1–44:10.

[15] D. J. Choi, G. K. Lockwood, R. S. Sinkovits, and M. Tatineni, "Performance of applications using dual-rail InfiniBand 3D Torus network on the Gordon supercomputer," in Conference on Extreme Science and Engineering Discovery Environment, ser. XSEDE'14. Atlanta, GA: ACM, 2014, pp. 43:1–43:6.

[16] O. Schreiber, M. Raymond, and S. Kodiyala, "LS-DYNA performance improvements with multi-rail MPI on SGI Altix ICE clusters," in International LS-DYNA Users Conference, Dearborn, MI, Jun. 2008, pp. 5:21–5:26.

[17] J. Liu, "LAMMPS on advanced SGI architectures," SGI, White Paper, 2011.

# A Parallel Nonzero CP Decomposition Algorithm for Higher Order Sparse Data Analysis

Oguz Kaya

Department of Computer Science
École Normale Superiéure de Lyon and INRIA, 46 Allée d'Italie 69007, Lyon, France
**e-mail:** oguz.kaya@ens-lyon.fr

***Abstract*—In the age of big data, tensor decomposition methods are increasingly being used due to their ability to naturally express and analyze high dimensional big data. Obtaining these decompositions gets very expensive both in terms of computational and memory requirements, particularly as the tensor's dimensionality increases. To efficiently handle such high dimensional tensors, we propose a parallel algorithm for computing a CP decomposition in which factor matrices are assumed to not contain any zero elements. This additional constraint enables a very efficient computation of the costliest step of the algorithms for computing CANDECOMP/PARAFAC (CP) decomposition for high dimensional tensors, and the performance gains increase with the dimensionality of tensor. For an $N$-dimensional tensor having $k$ nonzero entries, our method provides $O(\log k)$ and $O(\log N \log k)$ faster preprocessing times, and performs $O(N)$ and $O(\log N)$ less work in computing a CP decomposition over two efficient state-of-the-art libraries SPLATT and HYPERTENSOR, respectively. With these algorithmic contributions and a highly tuned parallel implementation, we achieve up to 16.7x speedup in sequential, and up to 10.5x speedup in parallel executions over these libraries on a 28-core workstation. In doing so, we incur with up to 24x less preprocessing time, and use up to $O(\log N)$ less memory for storing intermediate computations. We show using a real-world tensor that the accuracy of our method is comparable to the standard CP decomposition.**

***Keywords–parallel sparse tensor factorization; CP decomposition; higher order data analysis.***

## I. INTRODUCTION

In parallel with the overwhelming increase in the size of big data problems, the variety of data features also grows, which in turn raises the data dimensionality. Such high dimensional big data can be naturally modeled by tensors, or multi-dimensional arrays, and effectively analyzed using tensor decomposition methods. For this reason, tensors have been increasingly used in many application domains in the recent past, including the analysis of Web graphs [1], knowledge bases [2], recommender systems [3], signal processing [4], computer vision [5], health care [6], and many others [7]. In these applications, tensor decomposition algorithms are employed to perform a profound analysis of the high dimensional data to extract hidden information, or predict some missing data elements of interest. To this end, there have been considerable efforts in providing numerical algorithms for tensor decompositions [7], and in developing efficient computational methods and high performance software to render these algorithms amenable to use in real-world applications [8]–[13].

One of the most popular tensor decomposition methods is called the CANDECOMP/PARAFAC decomposition (CP, or CPD). The most common algorithm for computing the CP decomposition is an iterative method using alternating least squares (ALS), and is therefore called CP-ALS [14], [15]. At the core of the CP-ALS algorithm, each iteration involves a special operation called the matricized tensor-times Khatri-Rao product (MTTKRP). For a sparse $N$-dimensional tensor, this operation carries out the element-wise multiplication of $N-1$ matrix row vectors and accumulates their scaled sum, which is repeated for each nonzero element of the tensor. As the tensor gets higher dimensional, the cost of this operation dramatically increases, and efficiently carrying out this operation becomes crucial to be able to process such tensors. For this reason, there has been significant recent efforts in the literature towards efficiently computing this operation in particular, and CP-ALS in general, in different computational settings such as MATLAB [8], [16], MapReduce [17], shared memory [11], and distributed memory parallel environments [9], [13], [18], [19]. In this paper, we are interested in an efficient parallel computation of CP-ALS for high dimensional big sparse tensors in a shared memory environment, which is particularly motivated by emerging big data applications [6].

We summarize our contributions in this work as following:

- We introduce a method for efficiently computing MTTKRP for high dimensional sparse tensors. This scheme asymptotically reduces the computational cost of MTTKRP as well as the cost of a common precomputation step performed in the state-of-the-art.
- We provide an efficient parallelization of this computational scheme that runs up to 10.5 times faster than the state-of-the-art on a 28-core workstation.

The rest of the paper is organized as follows. In Section II, we provide our tensor notation and some tensor operations, then describe the CP-ALS algorithm and the MTTKRP operation. Next, in Section III, we provide an overview of existing methods for computing CP-ALS together with a summary of their computational and memory costs. Then, in Section IV we describe our method for computing MTTKRP and CP-ALS, which imposes a nonzero constraint on factor matrices to reduce the computational costs. We compare the complexity of our approach with the state of the art, and discuss a carefully tuned parallelization of this approach for a shared memory NUMA architecture. Finally, Section V provides a comparison of sequential and parallel executions of our method with two state-of-the-art implementations.

## II. BACKGROUND

### A. Notation

We mostly follow the tensor notation used in [7], [19]. We denote the set $\{1, \ldots, k\}$ of integers by $\mathbb{N}_k$ for $k \in \mathbb{Z}^+$. We denote vectors using bold lowercase Roman letters, as in $\mathbf{x}$. Similarly for matrices, we use bold uppercase Roman letters, e.g., $\mathbf{X}$. For tensors, we use bold calligraphic fonts, e.g., $\boldsymbol{\mathcal{X}}$. We define the *order* of a tensor as the number of its *dimensions* or *modes*, and denote it by $N$. We use italic lowercase letters with corresponding indices to represent vector, matrix, and tensor elements, e.g., $x_i$ for a vector $\mathbf{x}$, $x_{ij}$ for a matrix $\mathbf{X}$, and $x_{ijk}$ for a 3-dimensional tensor $\boldsymbol{\mathcal{X}}$. For column vectors of a matrix, we use the corresponding lowercase letters with a subscript corresponding to the column index, e.g., $\mathbf{x}_i$ to denote the $i$th column of $\mathbf{X}$. A *slice* of a tensor in the $n$th mode is a set of tensor elements obtained by fixing the index only along the $n$th mode. For matrix rows and columns as well as tensor slices, we use the MATLAB notation, e.g., $\mathbf{X}(i,:)$ and $\mathbf{X}(:,j)$ are the $i$th row and the $j$th column of $\mathbf{X}$, whereas $\boldsymbol{\mathcal{X}}(:,:,k)$ represents the $k$th slice of $\boldsymbol{\mathcal{X}}$ in the third dimension.

A tensor $\boldsymbol{\mathcal{X}} \in \mathbb{R}^{I_1 \times \cdots \times I_N}$ can be *matricized*; a matrix $\mathbf{X}$ can be associated with $\boldsymbol{\mathcal{X}}$ by identifying a subset of its modes to correspond to the rows of $\mathbf{X}$, and the rest of the modes to correspond to the columns of $\mathbf{X}$. This is done by mapping the corresponding elements of $\boldsymbol{\mathcal{X}}$ to those of $\mathbf{X}$. We will be exclusively dealing with the matricizations of tensors along a single mode, meaning that a single mode is mapped to the rows of the resulting matrix, and the rest of the modes correspond to its columns. We use $\mathbf{X}_{(d)}$ to denote matricization along the mode $d$, e.g., for $\boldsymbol{\mathcal{X}} \in \mathbb{R}^{I_1 \times \cdots \times I_N}$, the matrix $\mathbf{X}_{(1)} \in \mathbb{R}^{I_d \times I_1 \cdots I_{d-1} I_{d+1} \cdots I_N}$ denotes the mode-1 matricization of $\boldsymbol{\mathcal{X}}$. Specifically, in this matricization the tensor element $x_{i_1,\ldots,i_N}$ corresponds to the element of $\mathbf{X}_{(1)}$ with row and column indices $\left(i_1, i_2 + \sum_{j=3}^{N} \left[(i_j - 1) \prod_{k=2}^{j-1} I_k\right]\right)$. Matricizations in other modes are defined similarly.

The *Hadamard product* of two vectors $\mathbf{u}, \mathbf{v} \in \mathbb{R}^I$ is a vector $\mathbf{w} = \mathbf{u} * \mathbf{v}, \mathbf{w} \in \mathbb{R}^I$, where $w_i = u_i \cdot v_i$ for $i \in \mathbb{N}_I$. Similarly, *Hadamard division* of the two vectors is a vector $\mathbf{w} = \mathbf{u} \oslash \mathbf{v}$ with elements $w_i = u_i / v_i$, $v_i \neq 0$. Hadamard product and division of matrices of same size are defined similarly. The *Kronecker product* of vectors $\mathbf{u} \in \mathbb{R}^I$ and $\mathbf{v} \in \mathbb{R}^J$ results in the vector $\mathbf{w} = \mathbf{u} \otimes \mathbf{v}$ where $\mathbf{w} \in \mathbb{R}^{IJ}$ is defined as

$$\mathbf{w} = \mathbf{u} \otimes \mathbf{v} = \begin{bmatrix} u_1 \mathbf{v} \\ u_2 \mathbf{v} \\ \vdots \\ u_I \mathbf{v} \end{bmatrix}.$$

For matrices $\mathbf{U} \in \mathbb{R}^{I \times K}$ and $\mathbf{V} \in \mathbb{R}^{J \times K}$, their *Khatri-Rao product* corresponds to their column-wise Kronecker product

$$\mathbf{W} = \mathbf{U} \odot \mathbf{V} = [\mathbf{u}_1 \otimes \mathbf{v}_1, \ldots, \mathbf{u}_K \otimes \mathbf{v}_K], \quad (1)$$

where $\mathbf{W} \in \mathbb{R}^{IJ \times K}$. We use the shorthand notation $\circ_{i \neq n} \mathbf{U}^{(i)}$ to denote an associative operation $\mathbf{U}^{(1)} \circ \cdots \circ \mathbf{U}^{(n-1)} \circ \mathbf{U}^{(n+1)} \circ \cdots \circ \mathbf{U}^{(N)}$ over a set $\{\mathbf{U}^{(1)}, \ldots, \mathbf{U}^{(N)}\}$ of matrices (and similarly for vectors).

### B. CP decomposition

The rank-$R$ CP-decomposition of a tensor $\boldsymbol{\mathcal{X}}$ expresses $\boldsymbol{\mathcal{X}}$ as the sum of $R$ rank-1 tensors. For instance, for $\boldsymbol{\mathcal{X}} \in \mathbb{R}^{I \times J \times K}$, with CP decomposition we obtain $\boldsymbol{\mathcal{X}} \approx \sum_{r=1}^{R} \mathbf{a}_r \circ \mathbf{b}_r \circ \mathbf{c}_r$ where $\mathbf{a}_r \in \mathbb{R}^I$, $\mathbf{b}_r \in \mathbb{R}^J$, and $\mathbf{c}_r \in \mathbb{R}^K$. This decomposition gives an element-wise approximation (or equality) $x_{i,j,k} \approx \sum_{r=1}^{R} a_{ir} b_{jr} c_{kr}$. The minimum $R$ value rendering this approximation an equality for all tensor elements is called as the *rank* (or CP-rank) of the tensor $\boldsymbol{\mathcal{X}}$. Here, the matrices $\mathbf{A} = [\mathbf{a}_1, \ldots, \mathbf{a}_R]$, $\mathbf{B} = [\mathbf{b}_1, \ldots, \mathbf{b}_R]$, and $\mathbf{C} = [\mathbf{c}_1, \ldots, \mathbf{c}_R]$ are called the *factor matrices*, or *factors*. For an $N$-mode tensor $\boldsymbol{\mathcal{X}} \in \mathbb{R}^{I_1 \times \cdots \times I_N}$, we use $\mathbf{U}^{(1)}, \ldots, \mathbf{U}^{(N)}$ to refer to the factor matrices respectively having $I_1, \ldots, I_N$ rows and $R$ columns.

**Input:** $\boldsymbol{\mathcal{X}}$: An $N$-mode tensor, $\boldsymbol{\mathcal{X}} \in \mathbb{R}^{I_1,\ldots,I_N}$
$R$: The rank of CP decomposition
$\mathbf{U}^{(1)}, \ldots, \mathbf{U}^{(N)}$: Initial factor matrices
**Output:** $[\![\lambda; \mathbf{U}^{(1)}, \ldots, \mathbf{U}^{(N)}]\!]$: The rank-R CP decomposition of $\boldsymbol{\mathcal{X}}$
1: **for** $n = 1, \ldots, N$ **do** ▶ Initialization
2: $\quad \mathbf{W}^{(n)} \leftarrow \mathbf{U}^{(n)T} \mathbf{U}^{(n)}$
3: **repeat**
4: $\quad$ **for** $n = 1, \ldots, N$ **do**
5: $\quad\quad \mathbf{M}^{(n)} \leftarrow \mathbf{X}_{(n)} (\odot_{(i \neq n)} \mathbf{U}^{(i)})$ ▶ MTTKRP
6: $\quad\quad \mathbf{H}^{(n)} \leftarrow *_{(i \neq n)} \mathbf{W}^{(n)}$
7: $\quad\quad \mathbf{U}^{(n)} \leftarrow \mathbf{M}^{(n)} \mathbf{H}^{(n)\dagger}$
8: $\quad\quad \lambda \leftarrow$ COLUMN-NORMALIZE($\mathbf{U}^{(n)}$)
9: $\quad\quad \mathbf{W}^{(n)} \leftarrow \mathbf{U}^{(n)T} \mathbf{U}^{(n)}$
10: **until** convergence or the maximum number of iterations
11: **return** $[\![\lambda; \mathbf{U}^{(1)}, \ldots, \mathbf{U}^{(N)}]\!]$

Figure 1. CP-ALS: ALS algorithm for computing CPD.

**Input:** $\boldsymbol{\mathcal{X}}$: $N$-dimensional sparse tensor
$\mathbf{U}^{(1)} \ldots \mathbf{U}^{(N)}$: Factor matrices
$n$: The dimension of matricization for MTTKRP
**Output:** $\mathbf{M}^{(n)}$: MTTKRP result matrix of size $I_n \times R$
$\mathbf{M}^{(n)} \leftarrow 0$
**for** $x_{i_1,\ldots,i_n,\ldots,i_N} \in \boldsymbol{\mathcal{X}}$ **do**
$\quad \mathbf{M}^{(n)}(i_n,:) \mathrel{+}= x_{i_1,\ldots,i_n,\ldots,i_N} \left[ *_{(j \neq n)} \left( \mathbf{U}^{(j)}(i_j,:) \right) \right]$

Figure 2. Performing MTTKRP for a sparse tensor $\boldsymbol{\mathcal{X}}$ in a mode $n$.

The standard algorithm for computing the CP decomposition is CP-ALS, which establishes a good trade-off between convergence rate (number of iterations) and iteration cost [7]. It is an iterative algorithm, shown in Figure 1, that progressively updates the factors $\mathbf{U}^{(n)}$ in an alternating fashion starting from an initial guess, which can be randomly set or obtained from the truncated SVD of the matricizations of $\boldsymbol{\mathcal{X}}$ [7]. CP-ALS iterates until it can no longer improve the solution, or it reaches the allowed maximum number of iterations. Each iteration of CP-ALS consists of $N$ *subiterations*, and the $n$th subiteration updates $\mathbf{U}^{(n)}$ using $\boldsymbol{\mathcal{X}}$ as well as other factor matrices.

Computing the matrix $\mathbf{M}^{(n)} \in \mathbb{R}^{I_n \times R}$ at Line 5 of Figure 1 is the sole part involving the tensor $\boldsymbol{\mathcal{X}}$, and is the most expensive computational step of the CP-ALS algorithm, both for sparse and dense tensors. The operation $\mathbf{M}^{(n)} \leftarrow \boldsymbol{\mathcal{X}}_{(n)} (\odot_{(i \neq n)} \mathbf{U}^{(i)})$ is called the *matricized tensor-times Khatri-Rao product* (MTTKRP). The Khatri-Rao product of the involved $\mathbf{U}^{(n)}$s defines a matrix of size $(\prod_{i \neq n} I_i) \times R$ according to Equation (1), which can get very costly in terms of computational and memory requirements when $I_i$ or $N$ is large—which is indeed the case for many real-world sparse tensors. To alleviate this, various methods are proposed in the literature that enable performing MTTKRP without forming the Khatri-Rao product, which is made possible by exploiting the sparsity of the tensor. In Figure 2, we provide a such algorithm for computing MTTKRP in mode $n$ using a sparse tensor $\boldsymbol{\mathcal{X}}$. This computation amounts to performing Hadamard product of $N-1$ vectors of size $R$ and accumulating these products for each nonzero element of the tensor. The overall cost of the algorithm is $O(\text{nnz}(\boldsymbol{\mathcal{X}}) N R)$ as each nonzero induces an Hadamard product of $N-1$ row vectors followed by an addition of a row vector of size $R$.

## III. RELATED WORK

Computing the CP decomposition of a big sparse tensor can get very costly; for this reason, computing it efficiently by exploiting the sparsity of the tensor has attracted significant recent interest in the scientific community in various computational settings. In [20], Bader and Kolda demonstrate efficiently carrying out many sparse tensor operations, including MTTKRP, in MATLAB. Their approach for MTTKRP translates into Figure 2. In [21], Chi and Kolda present an alternative Alternating Poisson Regression (CP-APR) algorithm for computing the CP decomposition of large scale sparse datasets. GIGATENSOR [17] provides a distributed memory parallelization of CP-ALS using the Map-Reduce framework. DFACTO [18] is a distributed memory parallel implementation (C++, MPI) that formulates MTTKRP as a series of sparse matrix-vector multiplication. SPLATT [11]–[13] is an efficient parallelization of MTTKRP and CP-ALS both in shared [11], [12] and distributed memory environments [13] using OpenMP and MPI, and is implemented in C. DFACTO and SPLATT aim to reduce the cost of Figure 2 with the help of the following observation. For a 3-dimensional tensor $\mathcal{X}$ having nonzeros $x_{i,j,k_1}$ and $x_{i,j,k_2}$, one can first compute $x_{i,j,k_1}\mathbf{U}^{(3)}(k_1,:) + x_{i,j,k_2}\mathbf{U}^{(3)}(k_2,:)$, then multiply this result with $\mathbf{U}^{(2)}(j,:)$ to obtain the final contribution to $\mathbf{M}^{(1)}(i,:)$. In other words, multiplying all tensor nonzeros with a matrix in one dimension before proceeding to the other can potentially reduce the number of Hadamard multiplications performed, and this reduction is possible owing to overlapping nonzero indices. However, the worst-case complexity of this approach stays the same, i.e., $O(\text{nnz}(\mathcal{X})NR)$. HYPERTENSOR [10] is an efficient sparse tensor factorization library implemented in C++ using OpenMP and MPI for parallelism. It employs a data structure called dimension tree to reduce the MTTKRP cost by storing and reusing some intermediate results for MTTKRP in the course of CP-ALS iterations. MTTKRP is expressed as a series of $R$ tensor-times-vector multiply operations, whose amortized cost translates to $O(\text{nnz}(\mathcal{X}) \log NR)$ for each tensor dimension, which provides significant performance gains as the tensor's dimensionality increases.

## IV. Parallel CP Decomposition Using Nonzero Factors

Here, we first introduce our approach for efficiently performing MTTKRP with the assumption that factor matrices do not involve zeros or very small entries. When a such entry $\mathbf{U}^{(n)}(i,j)$ with $|\mathbf{U}^{(n)}(i,j)| < \epsilon$ is encountered in the course of CP-ALS, we slightly "perturb" the factor matrix by replacing it with $sign(\mathbf{U}^{(n)}(i,j))\epsilon$ where $sign(x)$ equals to -1 if $x$ is negative, and 1 otherwise. In practice such a perturbation is expected to have a negligible impact on the quality of solution for a sufficiently small $\epsilon$. Next, we introduce a shared memory parallelization of this scheme, and argue how to establish load balance among processes. Finally, we discuss optimization strategies for better parallel performance on a NUMA architecture.

### A. Computing CP decomposition with nonzero factors

The cost of the algorithm in Figure 1 is dominated by the MTTKRP step at Line 5 that involves the multiplication of the elements of the sparse tensor $\mathcal{X}$ with the rows of $N-1$ factor matrices at each subiteration. This amounts to performing $N-1$ vector Hadamard products and a vector addition for each nonzero element of the tensor, as pointed out at Line 3 of Figure 2. Here, we present a new technique for efficiently performing this costly step with the nonzero factor matrix assumption. In this case, for each nonzero $x_{i_1,\dots,i_N} \in \mathcal{X}$, instead of performing the Hadamard product of $N-1$ row vectors, one can precompute a vector $\mathbf{z}_{i_1,\dots,i_N} \in \mathbb{R}^R$ as $\mathbf{z}_{i_1,\dots,i_N} = *_{(n\in\mathbb{N}_N)}\mathbf{U}^{(n)}(i_n,:)$, then perform the MTTKRP update due to this nonzero as $\mathbf{M}^{(n)}(i_n,:) \mathrel{+}= \mathbf{z}_{i_1,\dots,i_N} \oslash \mathbf{U}^{(n)}(i_n,:)$. A similar idea is also employed in the CP-APR algorithm for handling sparse tensors [21]. Here, the cost per nonzero reduces to a single Hadamard division, which can always be performed since $\mathbf{U}^{(n)}(i_n,j) \neq 0$. Once new $\mathbf{U}^{(n)}$ is computed using $\mathbf{M}^{(n)}$ at Line 7, $\mathbf{z}_{i_1,\dots,i_N}$ needs to be updated accordingly with the new $\mathbf{U}^{(n)}(i_n,:)$. This can be done by dividing it with the old value of $\mathbf{U}^{(n)}(i_n,:)$, then multiplying by its new value, which amounts to a single Hadamard multiplication and division. This way, instead of $N-1$ vector Hadamard products, we perform a Hadamard multiplication and two Hadamard divisions for each tensor element, which effectively reduces the cost of MTTKRP to $O(\text{nnz}(\mathcal{X})R)$. In contrast, SPLATT and DFACTO require up to $N-1$ vector Hadamard products per tensor nonzero, yielding the worst-case complexity $O(\text{nnz}(\mathcal{X})NR)$, and HYPERTENSOR takes $O(\text{nnz}(\mathcal{X}) \log NR)$ time. Therefore, our approach provides significant computational gains over all these methods particularly as $\mathcal{X}$ gets higher dimensional. In doing so, we use only $\mathbf{U}^{(n)}$ for executing CP-ALS in dimension $n$, whereas SPLATT and DFACTO access all $N-1$ factor matrices except $\mathbf{U}^{(n)}$; hence, our method also yields a better memory footprint.

In our method, we need to store the matrix $\mathbf{Z}$ which takes $O(\text{nnz}(\mathcal{X})R)$ space. In contrast, HYPERTENSOR uses $O(\log N)$ buffers each taking up to $O(\text{nnz}(\mathcal{X})R)$ space. SPLATT uses only $O(PR)$ memory for intermediate results for an execution using $P$ threads, yet it incurs the highest computational cost.

### B. Parallelization

Performing MTTKRP in a mode $n$ amounts to performing a divide-add operation for each vector $z_{i_1,\dots,i_N}$ to eventually form the matrix row $\mathbf{M}^{(n)}(i_n,:)$. Similarly, after the new $\mathbf{U}^{(n)}(i_n,:)$ is computed, one needs to update the vector $z_{i_1,\dots,i_N}$ with a Hadamard multiplication and a division. Therefore, all nonzero elements of $\mathcal{X}$ whose $n$th index equals to $i_n$ contributes a summand to $\mathbf{M}^{(n)}(i_n,:)$, and the corresponding vectors in $\mathbf{Z}$ needs to be updated subsequently using the old and new values of $\mathbf{U}^{(n)}(i_n,:)$. To perform this, for each dimension $n \in \{1,\dots,N\}$ and for each matrix row $i_n \in I_n$ we compute a *reduction list* of tensor nonzeros whose $n$th index is $i_n$, which we denote as $rl^{(n)}(i_n)$. This way, each row $\mathbf{M}^{(n)}(i_n,:)$ can be computed in parallel by performing $|rl^{(n)}(i_n)|$ vector operations. Similarly, once $\mathbf{U}^{(n)}$ is computed, one can process each row $i_n$ in parallel to update the corresponding vectors $z_{i_1,\dots,i_N}$ for each contributing nonzero $x_{i_1,\dots,i_N}$.

The parallel algorithm for computing the CP decomposition is shown in Figure 3. In the main subiteration loop, we first compute the MTTKRP result $\mathbf{M}^{(n)}$ in parallel using $P$ processes at Lines 4–9. This step assumes a partition $\mathcal{I}_1^{(n)},\dots,\mathcal{I}_P^{(n)}$ of row indices $1,\dots,I_n$. Each process $p$ computes the set $\mathcal{I}_p^{(n)}$ of rows of the matrix $\mathbf{M}^{(n)}$ independently thanks to the precomputed reduction lists. Immediately after the process uses the entry $\mathbf{z}_{i_1,\dots,i_N}$ in MTTKRP, it divides it by the old value of $\mathbf{U}^{(n)}(i,:)$. Once $\mathbf{M}^{(n)}$ is formed, at Line 10 we compute $\mathbf{H}^{(n)}$ by performing the Hadamard

**Input:** $\mathcal{X}$: An $N$-mode tensor, $\mathcal{X} \in \mathbb{R}^{I_1,\dots,I_N}$
$R$: The rank of CP decomposition
$\mathbf{U}^{(1)}, \dots, \mathbf{U}^{(N)}$: Initial factor matrices with nonzero entries
**Output:** $[\![\lambda; \mathbf{U}^{(1)}, \dots, \mathbf{U}^{(N)}]\!]$: The rank-R CP decomposition of $\mathcal{X}$
1: Initialize $\mathbf{Z}$ and $\mathbf{W}^{(n)}$ for all $n \in \mathbb{N}_N$.
2: **repeat**
3: **for** $n = 1, \dots, N$ **do**
4: **parallel for** $p = 1 \dots P$ **do** ▶ Compute $\mathbf{M}^{(n)}(\mathcal{I}_p^{(n)}, :)$
5: **for** $i_n \in \mathcal{I}_p^{(n)}$ **do**
6: $\mathbf{M}^{(n)}(i_n, :) \leftarrow 0$
7: **for** $\mathbf{z}_{i_1,\dots,i_N} \in rl^{(n)}(i_n)$ **do**
8: $\mathbf{M}^{(n)}(i_n, :) \mathrel{+}= \mathbf{z}_{i_1,\dots,i_N} / \mathbf{U}^{(n)}(i_n, :)$
9: $\mathbf{z}_{i_1,\dots,i_N} = \mathbf{z}_{i_1,\dots,i_N} \oslash \mathbf{U}^{(n)}(i_n, :)$
10: $\mathbf{H}^{(n)} \leftarrow *_{(i \neq n)} \mathbf{W}^{(i)}$ ▶ Matrix Hadamard product
11: $\mathbf{U}^{(n)} \leftarrow \mathbf{M}^{(n)} \mathbf{H}^{(n)\dagger}$ ▶ Row-parallel GEMM
12: $\lambda \leftarrow$ NONZERO-COLUMN-NORMALIZE($\mathbf{U}^{(n)}$)
13: $\mathbf{W}^{(n)} \leftarrow \mathbf{U}^{(i)T} \mathbf{U}^{(i)}$ ▶ Row-parallel SYRK
14: **parallel for** $p = 1 \dots P$ **do** ▶ Update $\mathbf{Z}$
15: **for** $i_n \in \mathcal{I}_p^{(n)}$ **do**
16: **for** $\mathbf{z}_{i_1,\dots,i_N} \in rl^{(n)}(i_n)$ **do**
17: $\mathbf{z}_{i_1,\dots,i_N} = \mathbf{z}_{i_1,\dots,i_N} * \mathbf{U}^{(n)}(i_n, :)$
18: **until** convergence or reaching maximum number of iterations
19: **return** $[\![\lambda; \mathbf{U}^{(1)}, \dots, \mathbf{U}^{(N)}]\!]$

Figure 3. Parallel CP-ALS with nonzero factors.

product of $R \times R$ matrices $\mathbf{W}^{(k)}$ for $k \neq n$, whose cost is negligible as $R$ is a small constant in practice. Next, at Line 11 we update the factor $\mathbf{U}^{(n)}$ in a parallel dense matrix multiplication step, in which each process $p$ performs the multiplication $\mathbf{M}^{(n)}(\mathcal{I}_p^{(n)}, :)\mathbf{H}^{(n)\dagger}$. Once $\mathbf{U}^{(n)}$ is computed, we swap its small entries with $\epsilon$ or $-\epsilon$ and normalize its columns in a combined step at Line 12 in which each process $p$ works on the sub-matrix $\mathbf{U}^{(n)}(\mathcal{I}_p^{(n)}, :)$. Using the updated $\mathbf{U}^{(n)}$, we first compute the new $\mathbf{W}^{(n)}$ in another parallel dense matrix multiplication step at line Line 13, where the process $p$ similarly performs $\mathbf{U}^{(n)}(\mathcal{I}_p^{(n)}, :)^T \mathbf{U}^{(n)}(\mathcal{I}_p^{(n)}, :)$, then multiply the entries of $\mathbf{Z}$ with the corresponding rows of $\mathbf{U}^{(n)}$ using the same parallelization scheme as in Line 4. The initialization of matrices $\mathbf{Z}$ as well as $\mathbf{W}^{(n)}$ at Line 1 are done in parallel similar to the manner of updating these matrices in the iteration loop. At the end of each iteration, one has to check the convergence as well. This computation takes insignificant amount of time [19], hence we skip the details.

Reduction lists for a dimension $n$ can be computed by making two passes over the tensor nonzero indices in $n$th dimension to form a very efficient compressed data structure consisting of $rl^{(n)}$, which correspond to reduction list pointers, and $rli^{(n)}$, which correspond to the elements in the reduction list, in $O(\text{nnz}(\mathcal{X}))$ time. This yields $O(N\text{nnz}(\mathcal{X}))$ cost for all dimensions, and we can process each dimension in parallel. In contrast, existing methods in the literature require sorting the tensor indices which takes $O(N\text{nnz}(\mathcal{X}) \log(\text{nnz}(\mathcal{X})))$ time for SPLATT [12], and $O(N \log N \text{nnz}(\mathcal{X}) \log(\text{nnz}(\mathcal{X})))$ for HYPERTENSOR [19]. We show this data structure for a small tensor $\mathcal{X} \in \mathbb{R}^{5\times5\times5\times5}$ in Figure 4, and skip the computational details.

### C. Load balancing

For a $P$-way parallel execution of Figure 3, one needs to partition the row indices $1, \dots, I_n$ into $P$ sets $\mathcal{I}_1^{(n)}, \dots, \mathcal{I}_P^{(n)}$ for each dimension $n$. There are two types of computational costs imposed on each process $p$ by a such partition. First,

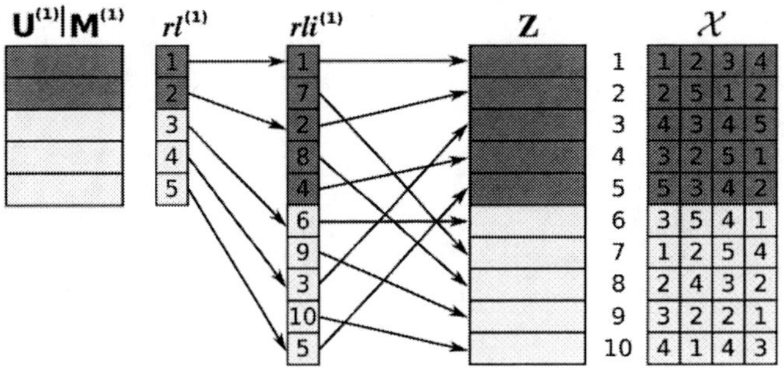


Figure 4. Performing MTTKRP for a 4-dimensional tensor $\mathcal{X} \in \mathbb{R}^{5\times5\times5\times5}$ in the first mode. Red (dark) and yellow (light) colors represent memory regions that are first touched by two different threads.

the process $p$ performs $O(\sum_{i \in \mathcal{I}_p^{(n)}} |rl^{(n)}(i)|)$ vector Hadamard operations at Lines 8, 9 and 17. Second, it performs the multiplication of matrices of size $|\mathcal{I}_p^{(n)}| \times R$ and $R \times R$ at Line 11, and of two matrices of size $|\mathcal{I}_p^{(n)}| \times R$ at Line 13. To balance the first cost pertaining to sparse tensor computations, one has to make sure that the associated cost $\sum_{i \in \mathcal{I}_p^{(n)}} |rl^{(n)}(i)|$ is partitioned equitably to processes. Regarding the second cost for dense matrix operations, each process should have equal number of rows, i.e., $|\mathcal{I}_p^{(n)}|$ should be balanced. Though these rows can be partitioned arbitrarily, in practice we desire to assign a contiguous set of rows to each thread to preserve the data locality. This not only helps improve the memory footprint of the MTTKRP step, but also increases the efficiency of BLAS routines used for dense matrix computations.

We define partitioning problem in this case as follows. For each row $i_n$, we have an associated pair $(|rl^{(n)}(i_n, :)|, 1)$ of costs that corresponds to sparse tensor and dense matrix computations, respectively. We aim to partition this "chain" of rows into $P$ contiguous parts so that both cost metrics are balanced across processes. The single-cost version of this problem corresponds to the chains-on-chains partitioning (CCP) problem in the literature for which many fast optimal algorithms and effective heuristics exist [22]. We employ CCP algorithms by using only the first cost metric $|rl^{(n)}(i, :)|$ for partitioning, as we observe that in practice, balancing this metric also establishes good row-balance.

### D. Optimizations for NUMA scalability

Performing MTTKRP for sparse tensors is an extremely memory bound operation as the tensor is very sparse in general, and the data accesses due to tensor nonzeros lack locality. Therefore, optimizing the memory footprint of the implementation plays a crucial role in obtaining high performance. Particularly on a NUMA architecture, one has to carefully allocate memory pages in NUMA nodes to be able to utilize the available memory bandwidth at maximum, and distribute the memory pages equitably across NUMA nodes. In most systems, this can be ensured by properly using memory first-touch policies after allocation, which in turn yields adequate memory page-to-socket bindings. In our implementation, after the allocation each thread performs a first-touch on the matrix rows as well as the rows of $rl^{(1)}$ and $rli^{(1)}$ that it owns. For the matrix $\mathbf{Z}$, each thread initializes a block of $\text{nnz}(\mathcal{X})/P$ vectors. This way, we not only maximize the NUMA bandwidth utilization, but also aim to reduce the inter-NUMA node memory requests as much as possible. This allocation scheme together with a balanced partitioning is

TABLE I. PER-ITERATION CP-ALS RUNTIME RESULTS (IN SECONDS) FOR SEQUENTIAL, SINGLE-SOCKET (14 THREADS) AND DUAL-SOCKET PARALLEL EXECUTIONS OF ALL METHODS.

| Method \| Data | ten-4D | ten-8D | ten-16D | ten-32D |
|---|---|---|---|---|
| | | $P = 1$ | | |
| **splatt** | 175.1 | 791.2 | 3766.9 | 19994.8 |
| **hypertensor** | **98.3** | 306.3 | 929.3 | 2873.8 |
| **cp-eps** | 130.3 | **284.9** | **586.9** | **1199.4** |
| | | $P = 14$ | | |
| **splatt** | 15.1 | 68.4 | 280.3 | 1292.2 |
| **hypertensor** | **11.8** | 33.3 | 88.5 | 354.5 |
| **cp-eps** | 13.1 | **27.5** | **56.12** | **111.31** |
| | | $P = 28$ | | |
| **splatt** | 11.5 | 47.2 | 190.7 | 683.8 |
| **hypertensor** | 13.0 | 36.6 | 69.1 | 215.0 |
| **cp-eps** | **8.3** | **17.5** | **36.2** | **65.3** |

shown in Figure 4 for two threads.

## V. Experiments

We compared our algorithm with two state-of-the-art implementations, SPLATT and HYPERTENSOR, and ran them on a workstation having 768GBs of memory and two Intel(R) Xeon(R) E5-2695 CPUs, each having 14 cores running at 2.30GHz as well as L1, L2, and L3 caches of sizes 32K, 256K, and 35M, respectively. We performed two types of experiments to measure the parallel scalability and the accuracy of our method. The first experiment compares the runtime of three methods using synthetically generated high dimensional sparse tensors. The second experiment uses a real-world tensor to compare the quality of approximation of the standard CP-ALS computation with our method. In all experiments, we use $\epsilon = 10^{-6}$ as the threshold parameter.

### A. Scalability

We compare the runtime of three methods using 4, 8, 16, and 32-dimensional randomly (uniform) generated tensors of size 10M at each dimension, and having 100M nonzero elements. We employ synthetic data instead of real-world tensors for two reasons. First, with random data we are able to control the dimensionality of the tensor while fixing other tensor parameters, e.g., dimension sizes, the number of nonzeros, and the distribution of nonzero indices; thereby, observe the performance of the algorithms with the increasing tensor dimensionality in a controlled manner. Second, there is a lack of available big high dimensional sparse tensors in the literature in parallel to the lack of efficient computational tools to handle such tensors. We run all three implementations using 1, 14 (single socket), and 28 cores/threads (two sockets) for 20 CP-ALS iterations using $R = 16$, and report the average time spent per iteration in Table I with labels **splatt**, **hypertensor**, and **cp-eps** corresponding to SPLATT, HYPERTENSOR, and our algorithm provided in Figure 3, respectively.

In Table I, we observe that using ten-4D, **hypertensor** runs the fastest using 1 and 14 cores, yet **cp-eps** surpasses **hypertensor** using 28-cores owing to better NUMA optimizations described in Section IV-D. In all other instances, **cp-eps** stays the fastest among all three methods, and the performance gains increase steadily as the tensor's dimensionality grows. Using 4-dimensional to 32-dimensional tensors, we observe that the

TABLE II. INITIAL SETUP TIME (IN SECONDS) FOR PARALLEL SPARSE CP-ALS.

| Method \| Data | ten-4D | ten-8D | ten-16D | ten-32D |
|---|---|---|---|---|
| **splatt** | 60 | 84 | 232 | 617 |
| **hypertensor** | 70 | 167 | 418 | 983 |
| **cp-eps** | **16** | **18** | **23** | **41** |

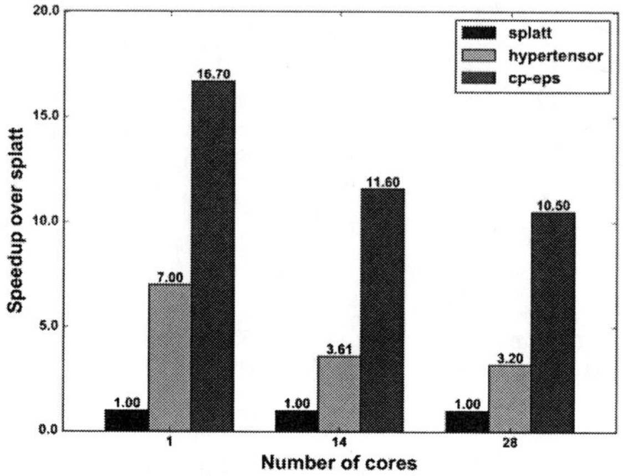


Figure 5. Speedup over **splatt** on ten32D.

speedup of **cp-eps** over **splatt** consistently increases from 1.39x to 10.47x using 28 threads, and from 1.34x to 16.67x using a single thread, which conforms with the algorithm complexities provided in Section IV-A. Similarly, the speedup of **cp-eps** over **hypertensor** varies from 1.56x to 3.29x using 28 threads, and from 0.75x to 2.40x using a single thread. Figure 5 demonstrates the speedup results of **cp-eps** and **hypertensor** over **splatt** for ten-32D.

In Table II, we compare the time spent on setting up data structures for MTTKRP using 28 threads on all datasets. We observe that **cp-eps** performs the preprocessing step up to 15x faster than **splatt**, and up to 24x faster than **hypertensor**. This significant improvement is possible owing to the smaller asymptotic complexity described in Section IV-B, as well as the parallelization using **cp-eps**.

### B. Accuracy

In computing Figure 3, we impose the constraint on factor matrices that they do not contain very small elements, which perturbs the decomposition slightly and can potentially affect the quality of approximation. To assess this, we compare the accuracy of this method with that of the original CP-ALS algorithm. We employ a 3-dimensional real-world tensor obtained from the Never Ending Language Learning (NELL) dataset of the "Read the Web" project [2], which consists of tuples of the form $(entity \times relation \times entity)$ such as ('Chopin', 'plays musical instrument', 'piano'). Nonzeros of this tensor correspond to such "facts" discovered by NELL from the web, while the values of nonzeros are set to the "belief" scores for these facts. The tensor is of size 1.6M×297×338K and has 2M nonzeros. We run **hypertensor** and **cp-eps** 100 times with the rank of approximation $R \in \{25, 50, 75, 100\}$, and compute the geometric mean of approximation quality in each case. In Figure 6 we detail all these results. We observe that both methods produce equally good approximations to the original

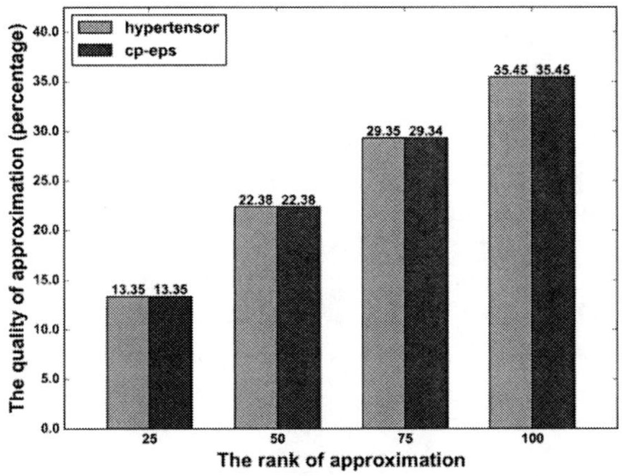


Figure 6. Accuracy comparison of **hypertensor** and **cp-eps** on NELL-2. We show the geometric mean of approximation values of 100 CP-ALS executions with random initial factor matrices using both methods.

tensor up to a small margin of error for $R = 75$ mostly due to randomization in factor matrix initialization. This shows that the nonzero constraint on factor matrices indeed has a negligible effect on the accuracy.

## VI. Conclusion

In this work, we propose an efficient parallel algorithm for computing a CP decomposition in which the factor matrices are assumed to not contain any zero elements. This constraint enables a computational scheme that provides $O(\log k)$ and $O(\log N \log k)$ faster preprocessing times for a tensor with $k$ nonzero entries, and performs $O(N)$ and $O(\log N)$ less MTTKRP work over two efficient state-of-the-art implementations **splatt** and **hypertensor** with a negligible effect on the accuracy. We achieve up to 16.7x speedup in sequential and 10.5x speedup in parallel executions over these methods, with up to 24x less data preprocessing time, using up to $O(\log N)$ less memory for storing intermediate computations. With these advancements, our approach renders the analysis of higher order big sparse datasets amenable both in terms of computational and memory requirements for real world applications.

## Acknowledgment

Part of this work was supported by GENCI-[TGCC/CINES/IDRIS] (Grant 2016-17 - i2016067501), and was performed using compute resources at ENS de Lyon.

## References

[1] T. G. Kolda and B. Bader, "The TOPHITS model for higher-order web link analysis," in Proceedings of Link Analysis, Counterterrorism and Security 2006, 2006, pp. 26–29.

[2] A. Carlson et al., "Toward an architecture for never-ending language learning," in AAAI, vol. 5, 2010, p. 3.

[3] S. Rendle and T. S. Lars, "Pairwise interaction tensor factorization for personalized tag recommendation," in Proceedings of the Third ACM International Conference on Web Search and Data Mining, ser. WSDM '10. New York, NY, USA: ACM, 2010, pp. 81–90.

[4] L. D. Lathauwer and B. D. Moor, "From matrix to tensor: Multilinear algebra and signal processing," in Institute of Mathematics and Its Applications Conference Series, vol. 67, 1998, pp. 1–16.

[5] M. A. O. Vasilescu and D. Terzopoulos, "Multilinear analysis of image ensembles: TensorFaces," in Computer Vision—ECCV 2002. Springer, 2002, pp. 447–460.

[6] I. Perros, R. Chen, R. Vuduc, and J. Sun, "Sparse hierarchical Tucker factorization and its application to healthcare," in Data Mining (ICDM), 2015 IEEE International Conference on, Nov 2015, pp. 943–948.

[7] T. G. Kolda and B. Bader, "Tensor decompositions and applications," SIAM Review, vol. 51, no. 3, 2009, pp. 455–500.

[8] B. W. Bader et al., "Matlab tensor toolbox version 2.6," Available online, Retrieved: March 2017.

[9] O. Kaya and B. Uçar, "Scalable sparse tensor decompositions in distributed memory systems," in Proceedings of the International Conference for High Performance Computing, Networking, Storage and Analysis, ser. SC '15. New York, NY, USA: ACM, 2015, pp. 77:1–77:11.

[10] ——, "High performance parallel algorithms for the Tucker decomposition of sparse tensors," in 45th International Conference on Parallel Processing (ICPP '16), Aug 2016, pp. 103–112.

[11] S. Smith, N. Ravindran, N. D. Sidiropoulos, and G. Karypis, "SPLATT: Efficient and parallel sparse tensor-matrix multiplication," in 29th IEEE International Parallel & Distributed Processing Symposium. Hyderabad, India: IEEE Computer Society, May 2015, pp. 61–70.

[12] S. Smith and G. Karypis, "Tensor-matrix products with a compressed sparse tensor," in Proceedings of the 5th Workshop on Irregular Applications: Architectures and Algorithms. ACM, 2015, p. 7.

[13] ——, "A medium-grained algorithm for sparse tensor factorization," in 2016 IEEE International Parallel and Distributed Processing Symposium, IPDPS 2016, Chicago, IL, USA, May 23-27, 2016, 2016, pp. 902–911.

[14] D. J. Carroll and J. Chang, "Analysis of individual differences in multidimensional scaling via an N-way generalization of "Eckart-Young" decomposition," Psychometrika, vol. 35, no. 3, 1970, pp. 283–319.

[15] R. A. Harshman, "Foundations of the PARAFAC procedure: Models and conditions for an "explanatory" multi-modal factor analysis," UCLA Working Papers in Phonetics, vol. 16, 1970, pp. 1–84.

[16] C. A. Andersson and R. Bro, "The N-way toolbox for MATLAB," Chemometrics and Intelligent Laboratory Systems, vol. 52, no. 1, 2000, pp. 1–4.

[17] U. Kang, E. Papalexakis, A. Harpale, and C. Faloutsos, "GigaTensor: Scaling tensor analysis up by 100 times - Algorithms and discoveries," in Proceedings of the 18th ACM SIGKDD International Conference on Knowledge Discovery and Data Mining, ser. KDD '12. New York, NY, USA: ACM, 2012, pp. 316–324.

[18] J. H. Choi and S. V. N. Vishwanathan, "DFacTo: Distributed factorization of tensors," in 27th Advances in Neural Information Processing Systems, Montreal, Quebec, Canada, 2014, pp. 1296–1304.

[19] O. Kaya and B. Uçar, "Parallel CP decomposition of sparse tensors using dimension trees," Inria - Research Centre Grenoble – Rhône-Alpes, Research Report RR-8976, Nov. 2016.

[20] B. W. Bader and T. G. Kolda, "Efficient MATLAB computations with sparse and factored tensors," SIAM Journal on Scientific Computing, vol. 30, no. 1, December 2007, pp. 205–231.

[21] E. C. Chi and T. G. Kolda, "On tensors, sparsity, and nonnegative factorizations," SIAM Journal on Matrix Analysis and Applications, vol. 33, no. 4, 2012, pp. 1272–1299.

[22] A. Pinar and C. Aykanat, "Fast optimal load balancing algorithms for 1D partitioning," Journal of Parallel and Distributed Computing, vol. 64, no. 8, 2004, pp. 974 – 996.

# Electrochemical Impedance Spectroscopy of Alkaline Methanol Oxidation

Tanja Clees, Igor Nikitin, Lialia Nikitina,
Daniela Steffes-lai and Sabine Pott
Fraunhofer Institute for Algorithms and Scientific Computing
Sankt Augustin, Germany
Email: {Tanja.Clees|Igor.Nikitin
|Lialia.Nikitina|Daniela.Steffes-lai
|Sabine.Pott}@scai.fraunhofer.de

Ulrike Krewer and Theresa Windorfer
Institute of Energy and Process Systems Engineering
Technische Universität Braunschweig, Germany
Email: {u.krewer|t.windorfer}
@tu-braunschweig.de

***Abstract*—Direct alkaline methanol fuel cell is a perspective technology for economic energy sources. The development of this technology requires advanced methods for the analysis of underlying chemical reactions. Electrochemical impedance spectroscopy is a popular method for analysis of dynamical processes in cells by a direct measurement of linear response function of the system to harmonic perturbations. In this paper, we propose a parameter identification procedure for electrochemical impedance spectroscopy of alkaline methanol oxidation. The procedure is based on decomposition of the linear response function in terms of poles and zeros and cross-fit of the obtained decomposition to the kinetic model using the methods of non-linear programming. The necessary conditions of the applicability of the proposed procedure have been derived and the stability of the method has been confirmed by the numerical experiments.**

***Keywords*–*Modeling of complex systems; Non-linear optimization; Parameter identification; Applications; Electrochemistry.***

## I. INTRODUCTION

Methanol-powered fuel cells combine very high energetic density of methanol with the highly efficient energy converter concept of the fuel cell. Therefore, they are very attractive for portable and mobile power supplies. A widespread type of methanol fuel cells is based on acid medium, where the layers with a noble metal catalyst are used for accelerating the electrochemical oxidation of methanol. Since only platinum or platinum-ruthenium catalyst is sufficiently stable and active in an acid medium, the resulting material costs are very high, which makes these fuel cell systems less competitive. The costs can be reduced by the use of alkaline media, where the stability and activity of base metals, such as nickel, may approach that of platinum.

Electrochemical Impedance Spectroscopy (EIS) is a method for experimental analysis of dynamical electrochemical processes, based on a measurement of response of the system to harmonic oscillations of small amplitude over a wide frequency range [1–4]. The measured linear response function carries the information about kinetics of the electrochemical processes and allows to reconstruct the related reaction constants. Similar methods use signals of high amplitude to trigger non-linear effects, one can also use signals of different profiles, e.g., triangular signals of high amplitude are used in Cyclic Voltammetry (CV, [5], [6]), harmonic signals of high amplitude – in analysis of Total Harmonic Distortion (THD, [7]), etc.

Interpretation of the response is aided usually by model-based analysis. This commonly involves fitting of experimental data by parametric models using a kind of Non-linear Least Squares Fit (NLSF, [8], [9]). The problem becomes more difficult when complex processes are investigated, comprising many reagents and multiple chains of reactions. The reason is that the underlying kinetic models produce highly non-linear systems of equations of increasing size, impairing stability of the fit.

On the other hand, there are well established methods in electrotechnics, based on system identification in terms of poles and zeros of its transfer function. These methods are commonly used, e.g., in analysis of stability of power networks and electronic devices [10–12].

In this paper, we use a synergy of both approaches. At first, we perform a general system identification in terms of poles and zeros, with a possible cancellation of unstable elements. After that, the observed spectra are well described by a small number of parameters, for which a cross-fit to a kinetic model is performed. As a result, we reduce the dimension of the problem and improve stability of the fit.

The purpose of our work is to verify the stability of this procedure on the example of methanol oxidation in alkaline medium. Our motivation is triggered by the necessity of new design of the fuel cells allowing to reduce the costs of energetic resources. The goal is to develop a stable procedure for the determination of electrochemical kinetics in such systems. Synthetic data are used for the analysis, allowing to compare directly the specified and the reconstructed values of model parameters. This way, the precision of the reconstruction can be controlled.

In Section II, we describe a general problem setting in EIS analysis and the proposed parameter identification procedure. Section III is devoted to the details of kinetic model of methanol oxidation in alkaline medium. In Section IV, numerical experiments are presented and the obtained results are discussed.

## II. ELECTROCHEMICAL IMPEDANCE SPECTROSCOPY

Electrochemical processes have kinetics described by a system of differential equations:

$$d\theta_i/dt = F_i(\theta,\eta),\ i = 1 \dots n-1, \qquad (1)$$
$$d\eta/dt = F_n(\theta,\eta) + I_{cell}/C_{dl},$$

where $\theta_i$ are surface coverages of the electrode by adsorbed reagents, $\eta$ is electrode potential, $I_{cell}$ is cell current, $C_{dl}$ is cell capacitance. Details of (electro)chemical reactions are encoded in functions $F_{1...n}$. These functions are generally polynomial w.r.t. $\theta_i$, while $\eta$-dependence has exponential form, defined by Tafel equation: $\exp(\pm\alpha F/(RT)\cdot\eta)$. Here, $\alpha$ is charge transfer coefficient, $F$ is Faraday constant, $R$ is universal gas constant, $T$ is absolute temperature. The measurable quantities in these equations are $\eta$ and $I_{cell}$, while the detailed dynamics of variables $\theta_i$ is not directly measurable. Particular reactions define the form of the polynomials, while the coefficients are defined by reaction constants, which are generally unknown. Parameter identification, EIS method in particular, has the purpose of reconstructing the reaction constants from the measured data.

Let us consider a stationary point of the system (1):

$$0 = F_i(\theta^*, \eta^*),\ i = 1 \dots n-1, \qquad (2)$$
$$0 = F_n(\theta^*, \eta^*) + I^*_{cell}/C_{dl},$$

and linearize the system in this point:

$$dv/dt = Jv + b,\ J_{ij} = \partial F_i/\partial x_j. \qquad (3)$$

Here, $J$ is $n\times n$ Jacobi matrix, evaluated in stationary point, $x = (\theta_1, ..., \theta_{n-1}, \eta)^T$ is $n$-dimensional vector of variables, $v = \delta x$, $b = (0, ..., 0, \delta I_{cell}/C_{dl})^T$ are variations of vectors. Equations (3) define the evolution of the system near the stationary point, when the current (or potential) is varied according to a given profile. In EIS method, the harmonic profiles are taken, in complex denotation: $\delta\eta = \eta_0\exp(i\omega t)$, $\delta I_{cell} = I_0\exp(i\omega t)$, while their ratio gives a transfer function, or complex resistance, impedance $Z = \eta_0/I_0$. Harmonic substitution $v = v_0\exp(i\omega t)$, $b = b_0\exp(i\omega t)$ transforms (3) to

$$(i\omega - J)v_0 = b_0 \qquad (4)$$

and we obtain as a result:

$$C_{dl}Z(\omega) = ((i\omega - J)^{-1})_{nn}. \qquad (5)$$

This expression can be written in a rational form

$$C_{dl}Z(\omega) = Q_{n-1}(i\omega)/Q_n(i\omega), \qquad (6)$$

i.e., as a ratio of two polynomials of $(n-1)$-th and $n$-th degree, respectively. Here, the denominator represents the determinant of the matrix $(i\omega - J)$ and nominator – its $(n,n)$-minor. For the rational functions, the following equivalent representations are often used:

$$C_{dl}Z(\omega) = \prod_{j=1}^{n-1}(i\omega - q_j)/\prod_{j=1}^{n}(i\omega - p_j), \qquad (7)$$

where $p_j$ are poles and $q_j$ are zeros of $Z$, or

$$C_{dl}Z(\omega) = \sum_{j=1}^{n} r_j/(i\omega - p_j), \qquad (8)$$

where $r_j$ are residues at the poles $p_j$. Equivalently, $p_j$ are eigenvalues of Jacobi matrix $J$ and $q_j$ are eigenvalues of its left-upper $(n-1)\times(n-1)$ submatrix.

The curve $Z(\omega)$ on a complex plane is known as Nyquist plot, see Figure 1 left. $Z$ is a complex resistance (impedance, in Ohm), $\omega$ is cyclic frequency (in rad/s). The green curve corresponds to experimentally relevant positive values of $\omega$. The red curve corresponds to negative $\omega$, artificially introduced to represent complete rational curves, closed by complex conjugation.

The plot on Figure 1 left represents a typical measurement result in the EIS method. To obtain decomposition of impedance in form (7) or (8), one can use rational fitting techniques. There is a variety of methods and software packages available for this purpose [13–15]. The forms (7),(8) can also be directly fitted to experimental data with general purpose optimizing routines [16–19]. These procedures are known to be extremely robust. They encode the whole set of measured curves in a small number of poles and zeros, giving a compact equivalent representation of the experimental data for further fits.

The advantage of poles-zeros representation is not only improvement of stability of fitting procedures, but also determination of important characteristics of electrochemical kinetics. In particular, the poles are eigenvalues of Jacobi matrix which determine such processes as relaxation of the system to the stationary state, delay and hysteresis effect in high-amplitude dynamic scans of the cell, etc.

Figure 1 right shows a typical pattern of poles and zeros displayed on a complex plane. In the considered case all eigenvalues are real, negative and strongly hierarchical, here shown in logarithmic scale. Indeed, in view of the stability of the system, the poles should be located at Re $< 0$, they can be real-valued (corresponding to exponential decay of $\exp(pt)$) or form complex conjugated pairs (corresponding to decaying oscillations). Closely located poles and zeros can be canceled from nominator and denominator of (7). Generally this will only influence small local features near the canceled poles and zeros, producing the effects under the limit of experimental precision, while the rest of the function will not be changed [10]. The cancellation can be useful, since it reduces the degrees of polynomials and a number of constraints used for cross-fit.

Cross-fit matches the reaction constants to the obtained pattern of poles and zeros. It can be formulated as a generic problem of Non-Linear Programming (NLP, [20]):

$$\text{find } \min_x f(x), \text{ such that } g(x) = 0 \text{ and } h(x) \geq 0, \qquad (9)$$

i.e., minimization of an objective function in a domain, specified by equality and inequality constraints. In our application, the optimization variables $x$ combine the reaction constants $k_r$ entering in (1) and position of stationary point $\theta^*$ in (2). The functions $g$ collect the equations for stationary point (2), the definition of Jacobi matrix in (3) and the definition of poles and zeros:

$$Q_{n-1}(q_j) = 0,\ Q_n(p_j) = 0. \qquad (10)$$

In these equations, $Q$ are recorded in terms of the minors, while $q, p$ are set to the values found from experimental data. The inequalities provide non-negativity of reaction constants and surface coverage:

$$k_r \geq 0,\ \theta^*_i \geq 0,\ \theta^*_0 = 1 - \sum \theta^*_i \geq 0. \qquad (11)$$

In the case if the number of equality constraints becomes greater than the number of optimization variables (overdetermined problem), a part of the constraints should be moved to

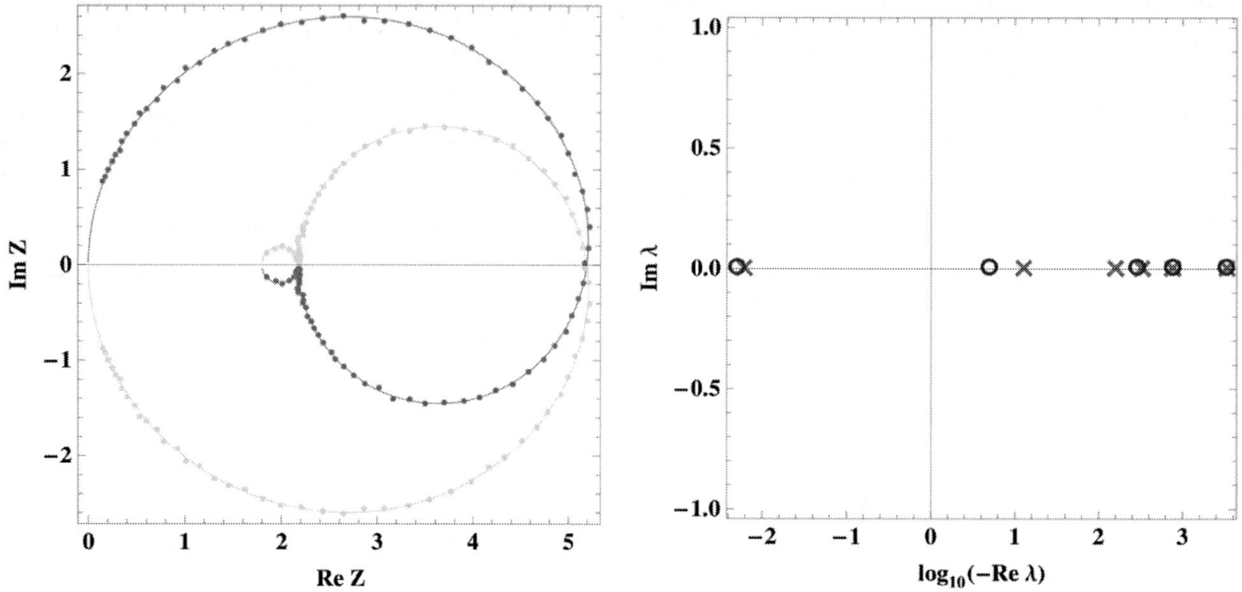


Figure 1. On the left: Nyquist plot $\mathrm{Re}(Z(\omega)), \mathrm{Im}(Z(\omega))$ for synthetic data. On the right: position of poles (red crosses) and zeros (blue circles) on the complex plane, formed by eigenvalues of linearized problem. See details in the text.

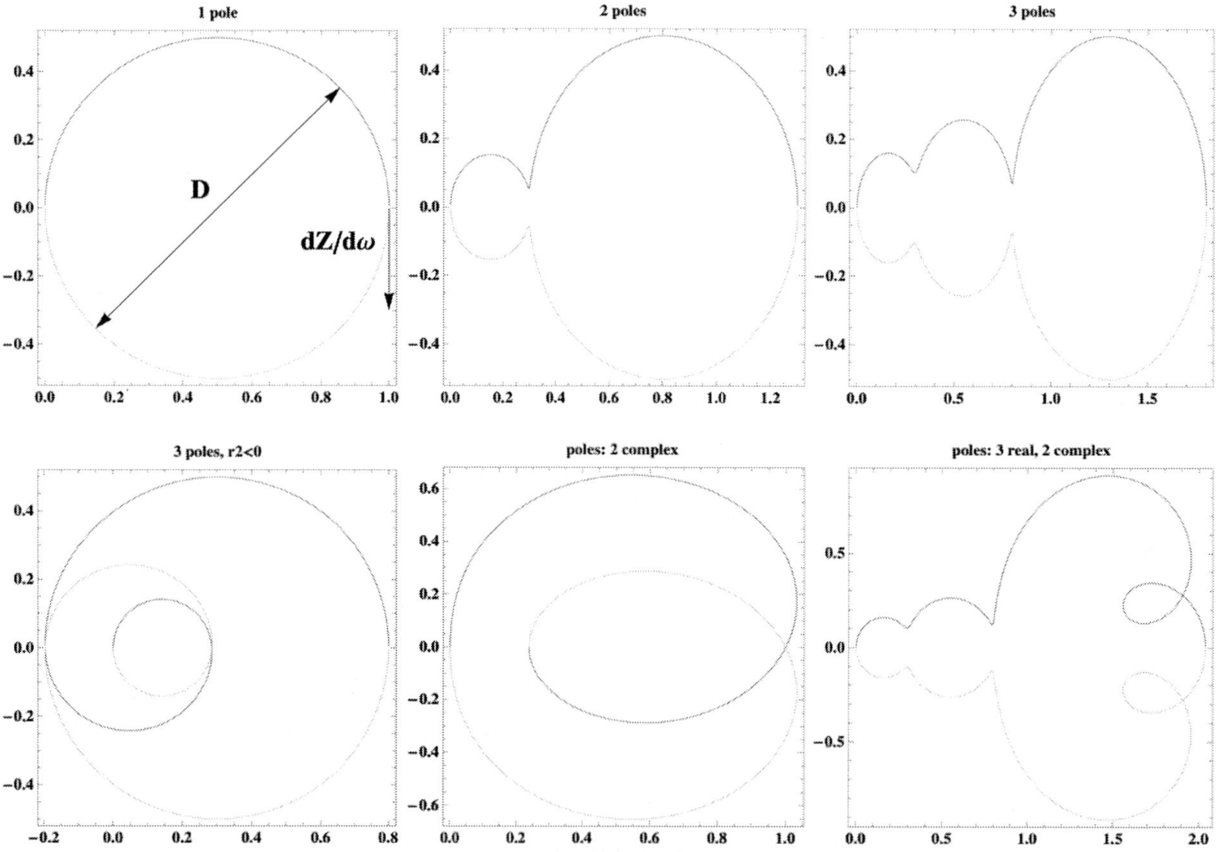


Figure 2. Nyquist plots for different types of the rational curves. The upper sequence shows the case of hierarchically separated real poles with positive residues. The bottom sequence shows the influence of the sign of the residue and the effects of complex poles.

the objective function, e.g.:

$$f(x): \ \chi^2 = \sum_j |Q_{n-1}(q_j)|^2 + \sum_j |Q_n(p_j)|^2. \quad (12)$$

There is a number of general purpose optimizing routines [16–19], suitable for the solution of so formulated problem.

We prefer to use algorithm *NMinimize* from Mathematica [16], since it comprises strategies for finding a global optimum and can be easily combined both with derivative-based and derivative-free optimization methods. Mathematica also possesses powerful capabilities for formulating the equations, computing partial derivatives in analytical form and provides a convenient interface for the modeling of complex dynamical systems. Typically, in the considered electrochemical problem *NMinimize* converges to the optimum in 5000 iterations, taking 35 minutes on 3GHz CPU.

The description in terms of poles and zeros (or residues) specifies a rich family of rational curves. Some typical representatives are shown in Figure 2. A single real pole defines a semi-circular arc. It closes the complete circle through the domain of negative frequencies, formally representing a complex conjugation of the transfer function. The diameter of the circle $D$ and the derivative $dZ/d\omega$ are defined by values of the pole and the residue: $D = |r/p|$, $|dZ/d\omega| = |r|/p^2$, $C_{dl} = 1$. Several poles give a combination of several arcs. If the poles are hierarchically separated: $|p_1| \ll |p_2| \ll |p_3|...$, there will be several clearly visible arcs, shown on upper sequence on Figure 2. The bottom sequence on Figure 2 shows the influence of the sign of the residue as well as the effects of complex poles, creating typical windings on the curves.

Analyzing the influence of noise in Nyquist data to the determination of poles and zeros, take a variation of (7):

$$\delta Z(\omega)/Z(\omega) = -\sum \delta q_j/(i\omega - q_j) + \sum \delta p_j/(i\omega - p_j). \quad (13)$$

In the case when the poles and/or zeros start to collide, i.e., there are nearly coincident complex numbers in the set of $\{q_j, p_j\}$, one can form unstable combinations, e.g.,

$$(\delta p_1 + \delta p_2)/(i\omega - p_{1,2}) \text{ at } p_1 \approx p_2. \quad (14)$$

In this way, one can select an arbitrary large but compensating variation of the poles without significant variation of the Nyquist plot. As a result, the reconstruction of such poles and zeros becomes unstable. This situation includes the case when a pole-zero pair wanders randomly on the complex plane without actual influence to the observable data. It also includes the cases when pole-pole or zero-zero collisions happen, e.g., collision of two real poles leading to their transformation to a complex conjugated pair. All such cases are highly singular and sensitive to the influence of noise in data.

In the case when poles and zeros are well separated from each other, the functions $(i\omega - q_j)^{-1}$, $(i\omega - p_j)^{-1}$ form linearly independent set. In this case vanishing variations of $Z(\omega)$ correspond to vanishing variations of poles and zeros, so that the reconstruction becomes more stable.

In the case if poles and zeros are hierarchically separated, i.e., well separated in logarithmic scale, the stability of reconstruction is drastically increased. The reason is that every pole and zero contributes to a wide range of frequencies, containing a lot of the measurement points ($N_{pt} \gg 1$). This leads to statistical improvement of precision by a factor of $\sqrt{N_{pt}}$, for the reconstructed poles and zeros in comparison to the noise in Nyquist data.

## III. Alkaline Methanol Oxidation

For the description of alkaline methanol oxidation, we will use the following model, based on the analysis of experimental data from [6].

Reactions:

$$\begin{aligned}
r_1 &: \ OH^- + Pt \rightleftharpoons OH_{ad} + e^- \\
r_2 &: \ CH_3OH + Pt \rightleftharpoons CH_3OH_{ad} \\
r_3 &: \ CH_3OH_{ad} + 3\,OH_{ad} \rightleftharpoons CHO_{ad} + 3\,H_2O \\
r_4 &: \ CHO_{ad} + OH_{ad} \longrightarrow CO_{ad} + H_2O \\
r_5 &: \ CO_{ad} + 2\,OH_{ad} \longrightarrow CO_2 + H_2O + 2\,Pt \\
r_7 &: \ CHO_{ad} + 2\,OH_{ad} \longrightarrow COOH_{ad} + H_2O + Pt \\
r_8 &: \ COOH_{ad} + e^- \rightleftharpoons HCOO^- + Pt \\
r_9 &: \ CO_{ad} + OH_{ad} \longrightarrow COOH_{ad} + Pt \\
r_{10} &: \ COOH_{ad} + OH_{ad} \longrightarrow CO_2 + H_2O + 2\,Pt
\end{aligned}$$

The corresponding formal reaction kinetics and the charge balance yield the following set of equations:

$$\begin{aligned}
F_1 &= (r_1 - 3r_3 - r_4 - 2r_5 - 2r_7 - r_9 - r_{10})/C_{act}, \\
F_2 &= (r_2 - r_3)/C_{act}, \\
F_3 &= (r_3 - r_4 - r_7)/C_{act}, \\
F_4 &= (r_4 - r_5 - r_9)/C_{act}, \\
F_5 &= (r_7 - r_8 + r_9 - r_{10})/C_{act}, \\
F_6 &= (-r_1 + r_8) \cdot FA/C_{dl},
\end{aligned} \quad (15)$$

where

$$\begin{aligned}
& r_1 = k_1 c_1 \theta_0 - k_{-1}\theta_1, \ r_2 = k_2 c_2 \theta_0 - k_{-2}\theta_2, \\
& r_3 = k_3 \theta_2 \theta_1^3 - k_{-3}\theta_3 c_3^3, \ r_4 = k_4 \theta_3 \theta_1, \\
& r_5 = k_5 \theta_4 \theta_1^2, \ r_7 = k_7 \theta_3 \theta_1^2, \ r_8 = k_8 \theta_5, \\
& r_9 = k_9 \theta_4 \theta_1, \ r_{10} = k_{10}\theta_5\theta_1, \ \theta_0 = 1 - \sum_1^5 \theta_i, \\
& k_1 = k_1^0 \exp(\alpha\beta\eta), \ k_{-1} = k_{-1}^0 \exp(-(1-\alpha)\beta\eta), \\
& k_8 = k_8^0 \exp(-(1-\alpha)\beta\eta), \ \beta = F/(RT).
\end{aligned} \quad (16)$$

The parameters in the equations are described in Tables I-III. Additional constants, introduced here are: $c_i$ – mole fractions of the reagents, $C_{act}$ – surface concentration of catalyst, $A$ – geometric electrode area.

TABLE I. Numeration of variables and constants.

| | | | |
|---|---|---|---|
| $\theta_1$ | $OH_{ad}$ | | |
| $\theta_2$ | $CH_3OH_{ad}$ | $c_1$ | $OH^-$ |
| $\theta_3$ | $CHO_{ad}$ | $c_2$ | $CH_3OH$ |
| $\theta_4$ | $CO_{ad}$ | $c_3$ | $H_2O$ |
| $\theta_5$ | $COOH_{ad}$ | | |

For generation of synthetic data for numerical experiments, we specify reaction constants as given in Table III. Then we find a stationary point by solving (2), Jacobi matrix by (3), impedance function by (5) and its poles and zeros by (7). The function is displayed on Figure 1 left and its poles and zeros

TABLE II. MODEL CONSTANTS.

| *Constant, units* | *Value* |
|---|---|
| $F$, C/mol | $9.649 \cdot 10^4$ |
| $R$, J/(K mol) | $8.314$ |
| $T$, K | $303.35$ |
| $\eta^*$, V | $-0.3$ |
| $A$, m$^2$ | $1.96 \cdot 10^{-5}$ |
| $C_{dl}$, F | $10^{-3}$ |
| $C_{act}$, mol/m$^2$ | $1.424 \cdot 10^{-4}$ |
| $\alpha$ | $0.5$ |

TABLE III. REACTION CONSTANTS.

| *Constant [mol/(m$^2$s)]* | *Specified* | *Reconstructed* |
|---|---|---|
| $k_1^0$ | $1.056 \cdot 10^2$ | $1.056 \cdot 10^2$ |
| $k_{-1}^0$ | $10^{-5}$ | $0.966 \cdot 10^{-5}$ |
| $k_2$ | $5.672 \cdot 10^{-1}$ | $5.665 \cdot 10^{-1}$ |
| $k_{-2}$ | $10^{-5}$ | $0.966 \cdot 10^{-5}$ |
| $k_3$ | $3.629 \cdot 10^3$ | $3.629 \cdot 10^3$ |
| $k_{-3}$ | $10^{-5}$ | $3.554 \cdot 10^{-5}$ |
| $k_4$ | $10^{-5}$ | $1.008 \cdot 10^{-5}$ |
| $k_5$ | $3.697 \cdot 10^{-4}$ | $3.921 \cdot 10^{-4}$ |
| $k_7$ | $6.192 \cdot 10^1$ | $6.192 \cdot 10^1$ |
| $k_8^0$ | $10^{-5}$ | $1.037 \cdot 10^{-5}$ |
| $k_9$ | $10^{-5}$ | $0.984 \cdot 10^{-5}$ |
| $k_{10}$ | $7.879 \cdot 10^{-1}$ | $7.879 \cdot 10^{-1}$ |

on Figure 1 right. Then we add a noise on the level of 3%, as shown by points on Figure 1 left, to simulate typical scatter in experimental data.

## IV. PARAMETER IDENTIFICATION

Solving the inverse problem, we take the noisy points on Figure 1 as input data and fit them by the rational function (8). The obtained poles and residues are used to find zeros in (7). Closely located poles and zeros are canceled. The remaining poles and zeros are used to reconstruct reaction constants by cross-fit procedure (9)-(12). Estimating the number of variables and equations in this procedure, we see that stable reconstruction is possible if the number of experiments $N_{exp}$, the number of obtained poles and zeros per experiment $N_{p,z}$ and the number of the reaction constants $N_k$ satisfy the condition $N_{exp}(N_p+N_z+1) \geq N_k$. In our case 2 experiments are sufficient for stable reconstruction. In the experiments we set different methanol concentrations 0.1mol/l and 0.075mol/l, while alkaline concentration was set to 1mol/l and 0.7mol/l respectively.

The result is shown in the right column of Table III. The reconstructed reaction constants are close to the specified values, 6 constants are reconstructed with the precision <1% and 5 constants with the precision in the range 1%-5%. One constant, $k_{-3}$, is increased by a factor of 3 after the reconstruction. The contribution of this constant in the reaction $r_3$, with account of all $\theta$-factors, is much smaller than the neighbour contribution of $k_3$. This is the reason why the constant $k_{-3}$ is reconstructed less precisely than the others.

In summary, our numerical experiment demonstrates that the reconstruction procedure generally does not amplify the noise in transition from input data to model parameters, except of the constants giving a negligible contribution to the reactions. Therefore, the proposed procedure is robust enough for the usage in practical applications of parameter identification in electrochemical impedance spectroscopy.

There are some possible modifications of the procedure. There are special cases, when the stationary point becomes inaccessible for experimental measurements, e.g., due to the effects of electrode poisoning with intermediates or byproducts of reactions, which can happen before the stationary point is reached. The described methodology is still applicable in this non-stationary situation, if the linearization point $\theta^*$ performs only a little change during the recording of EIS diagram. In such case the stationary equations (2) should be removed from the system, while the condition on poles and zeros (10) will remain in force. The condition of stable reconstruction becomes $N_{exp}(N_p+N_z-n+1) \geq N_k$. This condition can be satisfied at sufficient number of poles and zeros per experiment $N_p+N_z > n-1$ and sufficiently large number of experiments.

Such quasistationary approximation can be used for estimation of parameters and obtaining a starting point for more sophisticated methods. Currently, we are performing various measurements of alkaline-methanol oxidation in our laboratory in Braunschweig. They include not only EIS experiments, but also CV, THD, etc. Their analysis is similar, but due to the non-linear effects involved they require numerical integration and is, therefore, more complex. In particular, the search for the optimum requires extensive Monte Carlo runs with a typical complexity 120000 points per 6 hours on 3GHz CPU.

## V. CONCLUSION

We have proposed a parameter identification procedure for electrochemical impedance spectroscopy of alkaline methanol oxidation process. The procedure is based on decomposition of the measured linear response function in terms of poles and zeros, elimination of unstable elements and the cross-fit of the obtained decomposition to the kinetic model. The cross-fit is solved with the methods of non-linear programming. The number of experiments, necessary for stable reconstruction, is estimated. Numerical experiments are performed, demonstrating stability of the method.

With the developed method, two experiments with a typical Nyquist plot, shown on Figure 1, representing a problem with 12 parameters, 24 inequality constraints and containing 3% noise, have been analyzed. The kinetic is reconstructed in 5000 iterations, taking 35 min on 3GHz CPU. The precision of the reconstruction is <1% for 6 reaction constants, 1%-5% for 5 reaction constants. One constant has a negligible contribution in the reactions and escapes the identification.

## ACKNOWLEDGMENT

This work is supported by German Research Foundation, project DfG CL 494/2-1, Identification of reaction kinetic models using metamodeling on the example of the alkaline electrooxidation of methanol.

## REFERENCES

[1] U. Krewer, T. Vidakovic-Koch, L. Rihko-Struckmann, "Electrochemical oxidation of carbon-containing fuels and their dynamics in low-temperature fuel cells", ChemPhysChem, vol. 12, 2011, pp. 2518-2544.

[2] U. Krewer, M. Christov, T. Vidakovic, K. Sundmacher, "Impedance spectroscopic analysis of the electrochemical methanol oxidation kinetics", Journal of Electroanalytical Chemistry, vol. 589, 2006, pp. 148-159.

[3] F. Ciucci, "Revisiting parameter identification in electrochemical impedance spectroscopy: Weighted least squares and optimal experimental design", Electrochimica Acta, vol. 87, 2013, pp. 532-545.

[4] Gamry Instruments, Basics of Electrochemical Impedance Spectroscopy, online tutorial, http://www.gamry.com/application-notes/EIS/basics-of-electrochemical-impedance-spectroscopy [accessed: 2017-04-24]

[5] A. J. Bard and L. R. Faulkner, Electrochemical Methods: Fundamentals and Applications, Wiley 2000.

[6] B. Beden, F. Kardigan, C. Lamy, J. M. Leger, "Oxidation of methanol on a platinum electrode in alkaline medium: effect of metal ad-atoms on the electrocatalytic activity", J. Electroanalytical Chem., vol. 142, 1982, pp. 171-190.

[7] Q. Mao and U. Krewer, "Total harmonic distortion analysis of oxygen reduction reaction in proton exchange membrane fuel cells", Electrochimica Acta, vol. 103, 2013, pp. 188-198.

[8] W. H. Press, S. A. Teukolsky, W. T. Vetterling, B. P. Flannery, Numerical Recipes in C, Cambridge University Press 1992, Chap. 15.

[9] T. Strutz, Data Fitting and Uncertainty: A practical introduction to weighted least squares and beyond, Springer 2016.

[10] M. I. Bryzgunov, A. D. Goncharov, V. B. Reva, D. N. Skorobogatov, "Determination of transfer function of regulated object by characteristics of closed system with feedback", Reports of Novosibirsk State University, vol. 3, 2008, pp. 104-113, in Russian.

[11] B. Gustavsen and A. Semlyen, "Combined phase and modal domain calculation of transmission line transients based on vector fitting", IEEE Trans. Power Delivery, vol. 13, 1998, pp. 596-604.

[12] B. Gustavsen, "Wide band modeling of power transformers", IEEE Trans. Power Delivery, vol. 19, 2004, pp. 414-422.

[13] B. Gustavsen and A. Semlyen, "Rational approximation of frequency domain responses by vector fitting", IEEE Trans. Power Delivery, vol. 14, 1999, pp. 1052-1061.

[14] R. Zeng and J. Sinsky, "Modified Rational Function Modeling Technique for High Speed Circuits", IEEE MTT-S Int. Microwave Symp. Dig., San Francisco, CA, June 11–16, 2006.

[15] Rational Fitting Algorithm, MathWorks, https://de.mathworks.com/help/rf/ug/rationalfit.html [accessed: 2017-04-24]

[16] NMinimize Algorithm, Mathematica, http://reference.wolfram.com/language/ref/NMinimize.html [accessed: 2017-04-24]

[17] Interior Point OPTimizer, IPOPT, https://projects.coin-or.org/Ipopt [accessed: 2017-04-24]

[18] Sparse Nonlinear OPTimizer, SNOPT, http://www.sbsi-sol-optimize.com/asp/sol_product_snopt.htm [accessed: 2017-04-24]

[19] Modular In-core Nonlinear Optimization System, MINOS, http://www.sbsi-sol-optimize.com/asp/sol_product_minos.htm [accessed: 2017-04-24]

[20] A. Wächter and L. T. Biegler, "On the implementation of an interior-point filter line-search algorithm for large-scale nonlinear programming", Mathematical Programming, vol. 106, 2006, pp. 25-57.

# Advanced Modeling of Gas Compressors for Globally Convergent Stationary Network Solvers

Tanja Clees, Igor Nikitin, Lialia Nikitina
Fraunhofer Institute for Algorithms and Scientific Computing
Sankt Augustin, Germany
Email: {Tanja.Clees|Igor.Nikitin|Lialia.Nikitina}@scai.fraunhofer.de

*Abstract*—**The simulation of transport networks in civil engineering has become increasingly important for the planning and stable operation of modern infrastructure. Compressors are essential elements in gas transport networks; they create pressure necessary for driving gas towards the consumers. This paper presents mathematical modeling of gas compressors, taking into account their individually calibrated physical profiles. The approach is based on conversion of the measured profiles into an explicitly resolved form suitable for globally convergent solvers. In particular, a proper signature of derivatives for the element equation of a compressor is provided. The usability of the approach is demonstrated on a number of real-life network scenarios.**

***Keywords–modeling of complex systems; globally convergent solvers; applications; gas transport networks.***

## I. INTRODUCTION

In our previous paper [1], it has been shown that specific solvers for generic stationary network problems can be made globally convergent under special conditions on modeling of their elements. Stationary network problems combine linear Kirchhoff's equations and (generally non-linear) element equations. The first class of equations represents conservation laws, the second class describes transport. We have shown that under certain monotonicity conditions on element equations, i.e., a special signature of the derivatives, the whole system possesses a globally non-degenerate Jacobi matrix. As a result, the problem always has exactly one solution. Moreover, standard algorithms, like Armijo backtracking line search and Katzenelson piecewise linear tracing, provide convergence to this solution from an arbitrary starting point.

These ideas have been implemented in our multi-physics network simulator MYNTS as described in [2], [3]. Considering gas transport networks, these papers used a simplified modeling of gas compressors, known in the simulation community as *free compressors*. This type of compressors does not possess limits on their power, only input or output pressure or gas flow are restricted. The present work extends the modeling by realistic characteristics to so called *advanced compressors*. Such compressors are described by individually measured physical profiles, defining the limits on power, revolution number, working region, etc. We will show how to incorporate such realistic characteristics into our globally convergent solver.

Modeling of gas transport networks has been considered in full detail in paper [4]. The networks are composed of a variety of elements (pipes, valves, compressors, drives, regulators, resistors, etc.), each type possessing a particular element equation. For instance, the pressure drop in pipes is described either by an empiric quadratic law [5] or by more accurate formulae by Nikuradse [6] and Colebrook-White [7]. Compressors and regulators have a control logic, implemented in the form of control equations or inequalities [4], e.g., a compressor/regulator can have a control goal to keep fixed output pressure, input pressure or flow value. There are various models for compressors (turbo, piston) and their drives (gas turbine, steam turbine, gas motor, electro motor), with characteristic diagrams calibrated on real engines.

The nodal variables (pressure, density, temperature, etc.) are related by equations of state, including various gas laws (ideal, Papay, standards of the American Gas Assotiaciation – AGA and the International Organization for Standardization – ISO [8], [9]). Gas composition is defined in terms of molar components and effective gas properties (critical temperature and pressure, calorific value, molar mass, etc.), with appropriate equations describing their propagation and mixing. Thermal modeling [4] includes a number of physical effects (non-linear heat capacity, heat exchange with the soil, Joule-Thomson effect, i.e., a temperature drop due to free expansion of gas through a valve, regulator, etc.).

The obtained system of equations and inequalities is solved by non-linear programming methods [10], [11]. Due to the non-linearity of equations, the stability of the solver critically depends on the choice of the starting point. For this purpose, various empirical strategies are used [12], [13]. An alternative has been proposed in our papers [1], [2], employing globally convergent algorithms, able to find the solution from an arbitrary starting point.

In Section II, we recall conditions on the generic stationary network problem, necessary for global convergence, and concretize these conditions in application to gas transport networks. In Section III, we introduce advanced gas compressors. In Section IV, we present our implementation of advanced compressor modeling which fulfills the conditions for global convergence. In Section V, we apply the respective realization in MYNTS to a number of realistic gas transport network examples and discuss the results obtained.

MYNTS is a cross-platform application, available on request from [14].

## II. GLOBAL CONVERGENCE AND GAS TRANSPORT NETWORKS

A generic stationary network problem can be written as

$$\sum_e I_{ne} Q_e = Q_n^{(s)},\ n \notin N_P,\ P_n = P_n^{(s)},\ n \in N_P,$$
$$f_e(P_{in}, P_{out}, Q_e) = 0, \tag{1}$$

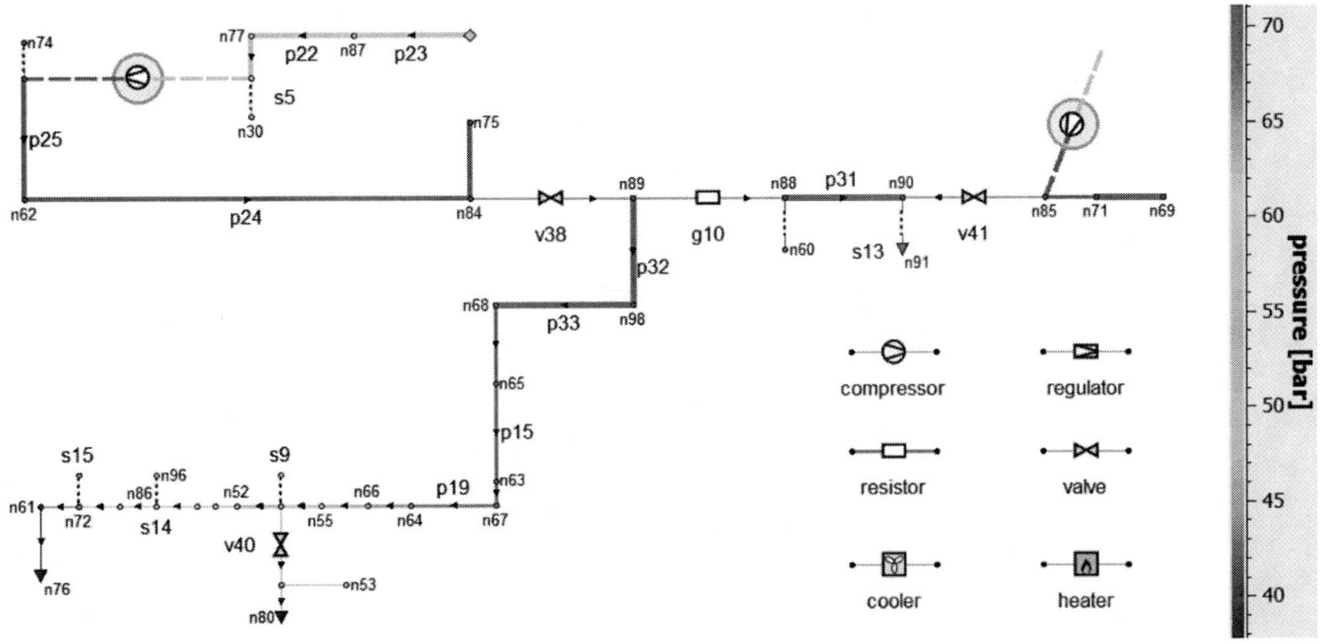


Figure 1. Test gas transport network N1 with 100 nodes, 111 edges.

where indices $n = 1...N$ denote the nodes and $e = 1...E$ the edges of the associated network graph, $I_{ne}$ is an incidence matrix of the graph, $Q_e$ are flows through the edges, $Q_n^{(s)}$ are source/sink contributions, localized in supply/exit nodes, $P_n$ are nodal variables (pressure for gas transport networks), $P_n^{(s)}$ are set values, localized in the subset $N_P$ of supply/exit nodes, at least one value per connected component of the graph. Let the element equations possess derivatives of the signature:

$$\partial f_e/\partial P_{in} > 0,\ \partial f_e/\partial P_{out} < 0,\ \partial f_e/\partial Q_e < 0. \quad (2)$$

It has been proven in [1] that the system (1) under condition (2) possesses a globally non-degenerate Jacobi matrix.

Gas transport networks, e.g., the networks shown in Figure 1, consist of several types of elements, all possessing the property (2). The gas networks are mostly composed of pipes with a non-linear (nearly quadratic) element equation. Some elements (valves and shortcuts) have linear equations, but most complex elements (compressors and regulators) possess piecewise linear equations. According to [13], all continuous piecewise linear functions can be represented in a max-min form:

$$f(x) = \max_i \min_j \sum_k a_{ijk} x_k + b_{ij}, \quad (3)$$

where $a, b$ are coefficient lists. In particular, free compressors are described by the following element equation:

$$\begin{aligned} &\max(\min(\ P_{in} - \epsilon P_{out} - \epsilon Q - P_L, \quad (4)\\ &\epsilon P_{in} - P_{out} - \epsilon Q + P_H, \epsilon(P_{in} - P_{out}) - Q\\ &+Q_H), P_{in} - P_{out} - \epsilon Q, \epsilon(P_{in} - P_{out}) - Q) = 0. \end{aligned}$$

The compressor tries to satisfy one of the following control goals: a specified pressure on output (SPO), a specified pressure on input (SPI) or a specified mass flow (SM). Being combined with the given upper and lower bounds: $PH = \min(SPO, POMAX)$, $PL = \max(SPI, PIMIN)$, $QH = \min(SM, MMAX)$, the element equation defines a polyhedral surface shown in Figure 2, top. Here, $PH$ stands for high pressure limit, $PL$ – low pressure limit, $QH$ – high flow limit; $POMAX$ is an upper safety bound on output pressure, $PIMIN$ is a lower safety bound on input pressure, $MMAX$ is an upper safety bound on the flow. Every face of the diagram corresponds to the best possible satisfaction of the control goal, e.g., $P_{out} = PH$ (typical for SPO-mode), $Q = QH$ (typical for SM-mode), $P_{in} = P_{out}$ (bypass BP, equivalent to an open valve), $Q = 0$ (OFF, equivalent to a closed valve), etc. A small $\epsilon$ value is used for regularization purposes. Every compressor is part of a compressor station, the simplest one is shown on Figure 2, bottom. This figure presents a compressor station with one machine unit, including (in flow direction) input resistor, compressor, cooler, output resistor, exit valve, (in an oblique direction) bypass valve, bypass regulator, both currently closed. In more complex stations, the compressors with accompanying elements are cascaded to parallel or sequential configurations.

## III. Advanced Modeling of Gas Compressors

In addition to pressure $P$, the nodes in gas transport networks possess other common variables, including: $\rho$ – mass density, $T$ – temperature, $z$ – compressibility factor, $\mu$ – molar mass. In addition to conserving mass flow $Q$, measured in kg/s, sometimes volume flow $Q_x$ is also considered. It is measured in m$^3$/s with explicit reference to the measurement conditions, e.g., $Q_{norm}$ represents the volume flow under normal conditions (1 bar, 273.15 K), $Q_{in,out}$ refers to the volume flow under conditions in the input and output nodes. Different flow definitions are related by the formula:

$$Q = Q_{norm}\rho_{norm} = Q_{in}\rho_{in} = Q_{out}\rho_{out}. \quad (5)$$

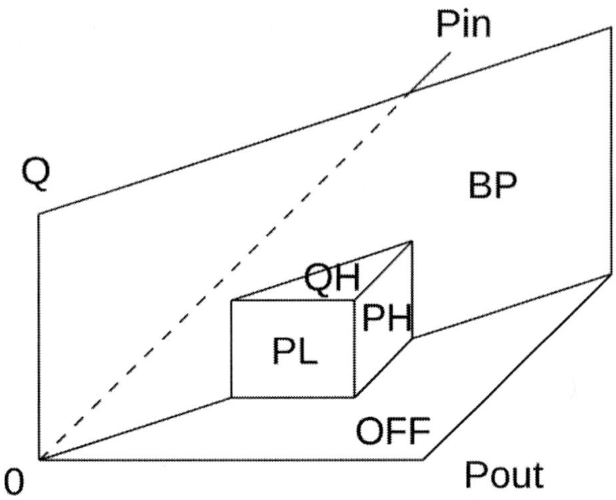


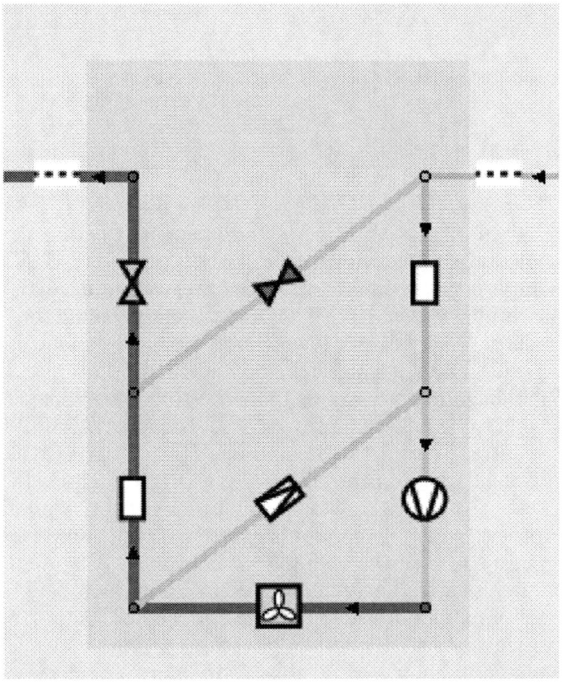

Figure 2. On the top: control diagram of free compressor. On the bottom: a compressor station with one typical machine unit.

Advanced compressors bring four new variables: $H_{ad}$ – adiabatic enthalpy increase, $\eta_{ad}$ – adiabatic efficiency, $r$ – revolution number of compressor drive, $W$ – power of compressor drive. Also, four equations are added [4]:

$$\begin{aligned} &H_{ad} = RT_{in}z_{in}/(\mu\alpha) \cdot ((P_{out}/P_{in})^{\alpha} - 1), \\ &W = QH_{ad}/\eta_{ad}, \\ &H_{ad} = (1, r, r^2) \cdot A \cdot (1, Q_{in}, Q_{in}^2)^T, \\ &\eta_{ad} = (1, r, r^2) \cdot B \cdot (1, Q_{in}, Q_{in}^2)^T, \end{aligned} \quad (6)$$

where $R$ is the universal gas constant, $\kappa$ the adiabatic exponent, $\alpha = (\kappa - 1)/\kappa$. $A$ and $B$ are (3x3)-matrices filled with calibration constants. In addition, working limits for compressors are defined by the following inequalities:

$$\begin{aligned} &r_{min} \le r \le r_{max}, \ \eta_{ad} \ge \eta_{min}, \\ &Q_{in} \ge Q_{min}, \ W \le W_{max}, \\ &Q_{min} = (1, H_{ad}, H_{ad}^2) \cdot C^T, \\ &W_{max} = (1, r, r^2) \cdot D^T, \end{aligned} \quad (7)$$

where the constants $r_{min}$, $r_{max}$ define limits of the revolution number, $\eta_{min}$ – the lower limit on efficiency (so called choke line; $Q_{min}$ is a lower limit on the input volume flow (a surge line), $W_{max}$ is an upper limit on power. $C$, $D$ are (3)-vectors filled with calibration constants.

The constants in $(A, B, C, D)$ are found by fitting the measured data for the compressor considered as part of a calibration procedure and further represent the individual profiles for this compressor. Here, we described the modeling for a common class of turbo compressors and gas turbine drive engines. The other types are simpler in implementation and can be modeled analogously.

Figure 3 (top) shows profiles for a typical turbo compressor. In this plot, the horizontal axis represents input volume flow $Q_{in}$, the vertical axis – adiabatic enthalpy increase $H_{ad}$. Solid blue curves are the lines of constant revolution number $r$, their uppermost curve corresponds to $r_{max}$, the lowest curve – to $r_{min}$. The red curve is the surge line $Q_{in} = Q_{min}$, while the rightmost green curve – the choke line $\eta_{ad} = \eta_{min}$. The points in this diagram depict the data measured, a blue cross denotes the current working point of the compressor.

The equations (6) serve as definitions of newly introduced variables, while the inequalities (7) define the restrictions, in addition to (4) of those for a free compressor. The upper bounds $r = r_{max}$ and $W = W_{max}$ define new upper bounds for the flow and should be combined with the one defined by the diagram for a free compressor, shown in Figure 2 top. The lower bounds $r = r_{min}$ and $Q_{in} = Q_{min}$ show the points where the station automatically opens its bypass regulator, shown in Figure 2 bottom. After that the gas starts to circulate inside the station, so that the compressor never violates its bounds. The choke line $\eta_{ad} = \eta_{min}$ cuts off a region of unstable calibration related with the small $\eta_{ad}$ in the denominator of (6). Usually, the working point of a compressor is not located in this region, except of the starting procedure. On necessity the diagram can be continued in this region by a convenient monotone formula.

If $P_{in}$ and $P_{out}$ are fixed and the compressor is on its $r = r_{max}$ limit, it is straightforward to resolve the equations analytically, finding $H_{ad}$, $Q_{in}$, $\rho_{in}$, $Q$, $\eta_{ad}$ and $W$, in this order. If $r$ and $Q_{in}$ are fixed and the compressor is on its $W = W_{max}$ limit, the equations can be resolved in the order $H_{ad}$, $\eta_{ad}$, $W_{max}$, $Q$, $\rho_{in}$, $P_{in}$, $P_{out}$. The first analytic formula gives an explicit representation $Q(P_{in}, P_{out})$ for the surface, defining a patch of the element equation. The second one represents the other patch in a parametric form $(r, Q_{in}) \to (P_{in}, P_{out}, Q)$. By numerical differentiation, it is possible to find the normals to both surfaces, which directly define the signatures of the corresponding patches. We recall that the correct signature reads $(+--)$, see (2). In Figure 3 (bottom) green points show the area of wrong signature. The

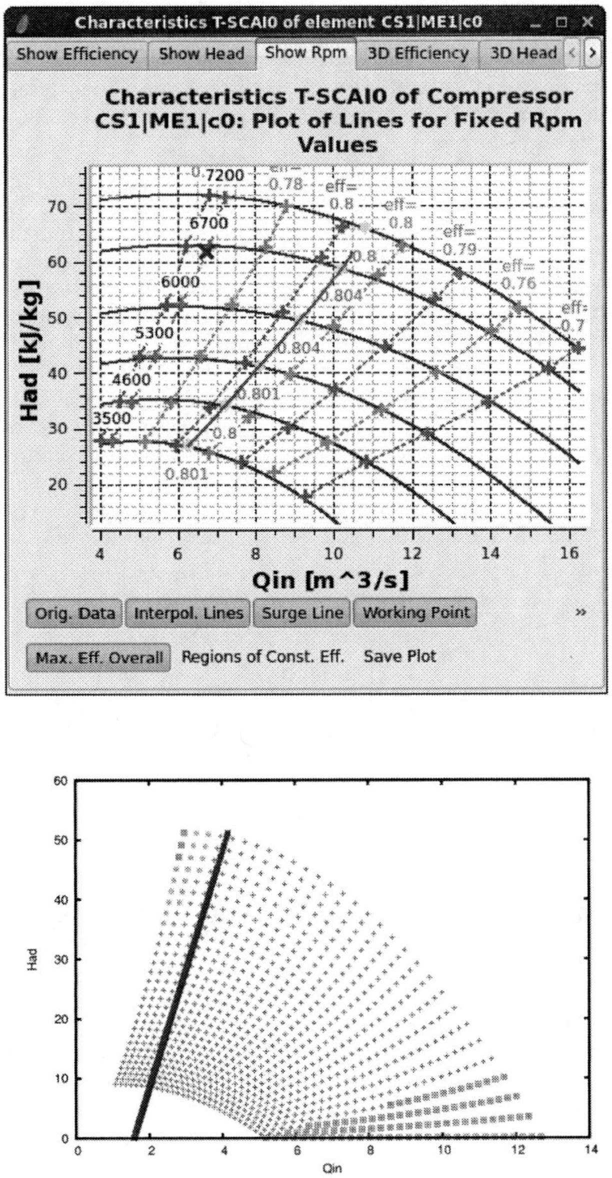


Figure 3. Advanced modeling of compressors. On the top: typical characteristic diagram. Solid blue curves are lines of constant revolution number. On the bottom: stability analysis.

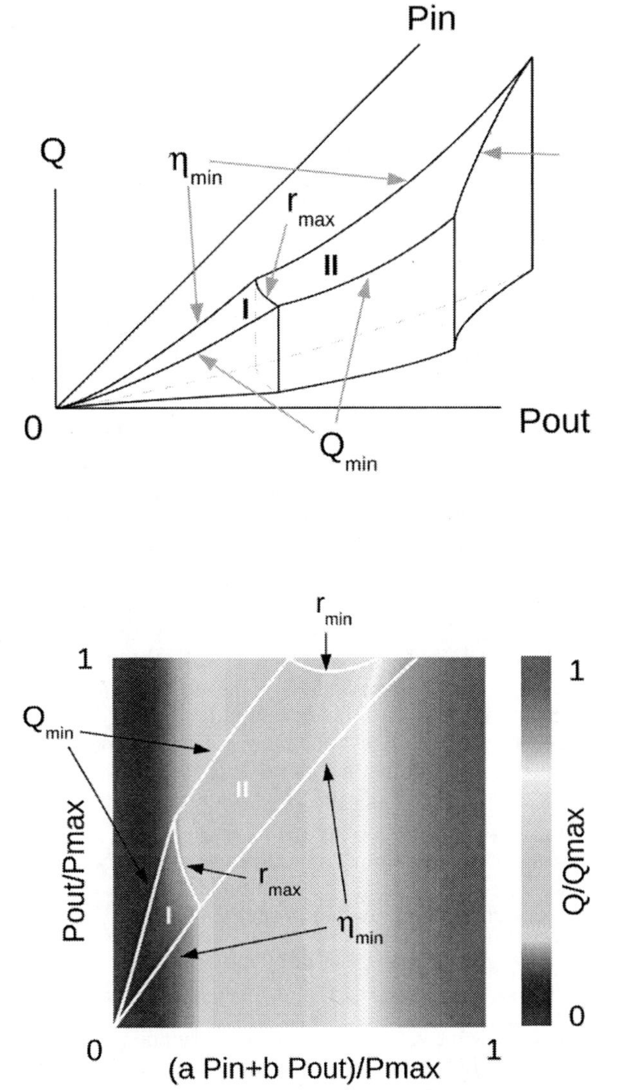


Figure 4. Advanced modeling of compressors (cont'd). On the top: control diagram of an advanced compressor. On the bottom: the same diagram in affine coordinates and color map representation.

blue curve is the surge line, magenta points show the area $\eta_{ad} < \eta_{min}$. Normally, the unstable green area is cut off by the surge and choke lines, so that the whole working region of the compressor is stable. In rare cases, when it is not so, the surge and choke lines should be modified accordingly.

## IV. GLOBALLY CONVERGENT IMPLEMENTATION

Figure 4 (top) shows the surface $Q_{adv}(P_{in}, P_{out})$ defined by the characteristics of the advanced compressor. The calibrated part of the surface is located between the curves $Q_{min}$ and $\eta_{min}$ and consists of two patches I and II, connected on the $r_{max}$ line. Patch I is located between the $r_{max}$ line and the origin. Here, the input and output pressures are small and the compressor's performance is limited by its maximal revolution number: $r = r_{max}$. Patch II is located between the $r_{max}$ and $r_{min}$ lines. Here, the pressures are large and the compressor is limited by the maximal power of the drive: $W = W_{max}$. On $Q_{min}$ and $r_{min}$ curves the surface vertically falls down. This behavior corresponds to the open bypass regulator. $Q$ in that case denotes a total mass flow through the compressor and bypass regulator. The flow through the compressor remains equal to $Q_{min}$ or the equivalent flow on the $r_{min}$ line, while the negative difference $\Delta Q$ circulates through the bypass regulator. A slope of the vertically falling faces should be $\epsilon$-regularized to provide the necessary signature $(+ - -)$. The surface should be continued beyond $\eta_{min}$ curve by any function supporting the same signature.

Figure 4 (bottom) shows the same diagram as a color map. Patch II requires a conversion from parametric to explicit representation. For this purpose, we adopt resampling algorithms well known in computer graphics (CG). At first, we perform an affine transformation:

$$\begin{pmatrix} x \\ y \end{pmatrix} = \begin{pmatrix} a & b \\ 0 & 1 \end{pmatrix} \begin{pmatrix} P_{in} \\ P_{out} \end{pmatrix} \cdot \frac{1}{P_{max}}, \quad (8)$$

with $a + b = 1$. The square on the $(x, y)$-plane is represented as a $N_{px} \times N_{px}$ pixel buffer, storing floating point values of $Q$ in double precision. Patches I and II are regularly sampled and represented as triangle strip sets. Then, the patches are rendered onto the $(x, y)$-plane using the Z-buffer algorithm. Finally, the remaining gaps are filled by copying a constant $Q$-value along the columns and to the right – by a linearly increasing function in the row. As a result, the $Q_{adv}$-function in these regions becomes dependent only on $x$. Monotonous increase of $Q$ on the border lines and a choice of affine coefficients $a > 0$, $b < 0$ support correct signature of the function $Q_{adv}(P_{in}, P_{out})$. If the bypass regulator is activated, the part above the upper border lines must be reset towards $Q = 0$, providing a regularized vertical fall of the surface on this bound.

The described algorithms provide a transformation from the calibration coefficients $(A, B, C, D)$ and characteristic diagram in Figure 3 (top) to the tabulated function $Q_{adv}(P_{in}, P_{out})$, represented by the color map in Figure 4 (bottom). This transformation should be done once per advanced compressor. For a moment, we use an implementation of the CG algorithms on Central Processing Unit (CPU) and plan their acceleration with Graphics Processing Unit (GPU).

In the solver, the lookup function $Q_{adv}(P_{in}, P_{out})$ is made available via rapid bilinear interpolation of tabulated values inside the $(x, y)$-square. It is continued to the whole $(x, y)$-plane by an explicit analytic formula:

$$f(x, y) = f(\hat{x}, \hat{y}) + k(\min(x, 0) + \max(x - 1, 0)), \quad (9)$$
$$\hat{x} = \min(\max(x, 0), 1), \ \hat{y} = \min(\max(y, 0), 1),$$

with a constant $k > 0$. This global function is constructed similarly to the continuation formulas in [1]. In our special case it provides monotonous increase in $x$ and constancy in $y$ outside of the tabulated region.

Finally, the element equation for an advanced compressor is obtained by extending (4) as follows:

$$\begin{aligned} &\max(\min(\ P_{in} - \epsilon P_{out} - \epsilon Q - P_L, \quad (10)\\ &\epsilon P_{in} - P_{out} - \epsilon Q + P_H, \underline{Q_{adv}(P_{in}, P_{out}) - Q},\\ &\epsilon(P_{in} - P_{out}) - Q + Q_H), P_{in} - P_{out} - \epsilon Q,\\ &\epsilon(P_{in} - P_{out}) - Q) = 0. \end{aligned}$$

For clarity, the inserted term is underlined.

We have implemented the algorithms described above in our network simulator MYNTS in a preliminary version (solver strategy “stable”).

## V. RESULTS

For benchmarking the algorithms, we have received a number of realistic test scenarios from our partners. The simplest gas transport network N1 from our test set is shown in Figure 1. It contains two compressor stations, each equipped with two machine units, cf. Figure 2 (bottom), working in parallel mode. It has two supplies and three major consumers. The color shows the pressure distribution over the network, arrows – the direction of gas flow, thickness of lines – the diameter of the pipes. Supplies are shown by rhombi, consumers (n76, n80, n91) are shown by triangles. The main elements are shown in the legend.

A closeup to one of the compressors is shown in Figure 2 (bottom), and its characteristics are displayed in Figure 3 (top). Parameters of more complex networks are presented in Table I. In particular, medium-sized network N2 contains about a thousand nodes and edges and is equipped with 7 compressors. The largest considerd network N3 has about five thousand nodes and edges and is driven by 25 compressors. Topological connection of elements in the network together with geographic coordinates, the lengths and diameters of pipes form so called *geometry* of the network. Physical setting, such as supply pressures and consumer flows, control settings of compressors and regulators, define *scenario* for the particular simulation case. All networks in our test set were simulated with the same gas composition at 20°C environmental temperature.

TABLE I. PARAMETERS OF TEST NETWORKS

| network | nodes | edges | compressors |
|---|---|---|---|
| N1 | 100 | 111 | 4 |
| N2 | 931 | 1047 | 7 |
| N3 | 4466 | 5362 | 25 |

In Table II, we compare the performance of the newly implemented algorithms (strategy “stable”) with the performance of the solver with standard settings. For each network in the test set two scenarios are considered, with different numerical values of set points for input pressures and output flows and compressor/regulator $SM$, $SPO$ settings. Divergent cases are marked as 'div'. The number of iterations (iter.) and timing (t) are given. The simulation is performed on a 3 GHz Intel i7 CPU 8 GB RAM workstation.

TABLE II. COMPARISON OF THE ALGORITHMS

| scenario | solver_strategy | | | | | | | |
|---|---|---|---|---|---|---|---|---|
| | standard | | | | stable | | | |
| | free | | advanced | | free | | advanced | |
| | iter. | t, sec | iter. | t, sec | iter. | t, sec | iter. | t, sec |
| N1S1 | 3 | 0.01 | 32 | 0.12 | 2 | 0.01 | 2 | 0.01 |
| N1S2 | 57 | 0.17 | 70 | 0.21 | 11 | 0.03 | 4 | 0.02 |
| N2S1 | 11 | 0.27 | 19 | 0.64 | 12 | 0.31 | 12 | 0.37 |
| N2S2 | div | – | div | – | 13 | 0.36 | 15 | 0.48 |
| N3S1 | div | – | div | – | 26 | 3.3 | 23 | 3.5 |
| N3S2 | 47 | 6.5 | div | – | 26 | 3.3 | 24 | 3.6 |

All scenarios are tested both with free and advanced compressor models. We see that the standard solver provides worse convergence and even diverges in certain scenarios. Some scenarios show divergence already for free compressors, some diverge on advanced ones only. The new algorithm converges in all cases, in agreement with its theoretical properties. We also see that the table lookup implemented for advanced modeling has a negligible computational overhead in strategy "stable".

## VI. Conclusion

In this paper, we presented mathematical modeling of gas compressors with their individually calibrated physical profiles. The measured profiles are converted to an explicitly resolved form using algorithms inspired by computer graphics. The control element equation for a free compressor has been extended by a lookup function representing the working region of the advanced compressor. The resulting equation possesses the desired signature of derivatives necessary for global non-degeneracy of the Jacobi matrix. As a result, the globally convergent algorithm developed for the solution of network problems with free compressors remains applicable, with a negligible computational overhead. The usability of the approach has been demonstrated for a number of real-life network scenarios. The algorithm significantly overperforms a standard Newtonian solver in terms of stability, number of iterations and computational time.

## Acknowledgment

This work is supported by German Federal Ministry for Economic Affairs and Energy, project BMWI-0324019A, MathEnergy: Mathematical Key Technologies for Evolving Energy Grids.

## References

[1] T. Clees, I. Nikitin, L. Nikitina, "Making Network Solvers Globally Convergent", in Advances in Intelligent Systems and Computing, Springer, 2017 (in print).

[2] T. Clees, N. Hornung, I. Nikitin, L. Nikitina, "A Globally Convergent Method for Generalized Resistive Systems and its Application to Stationary Problems in Gas Transport Networks", In Proc. SIMULTECH 2016, SCITEPRESS, 2016, pp. 64-70.

[3] T. Clees et al., "MYNTS: Multi-phYsics NeTwork Simulator", In Proc. SIMULTECH 2016, SCITEPRESS, 2016, pp. 179-186.

[4] M. Schmidt, M. C. Steinbach, B. M. Willert, "High detail stationary optimization models for gas networks", Optimization and Engineering, vol. 16, num.1, 2015, pp. 131-164.

[5] J. Mischner, H.G. Fasold, K. Kadner, System-planning basics of gas supply, Oldenbourg Industrieverlag GmbH, 2011 (in German).

[6] J. Nikuradse, "Laws of flow in rough pipes", NACA Technical Memorandum 1292, Washington, 1950.

[7] C. F. Colebrook and C. M. White, "Experiments with Fluid Friction in Roughened Pipes", in Proc. of the Royal Society of London, Series A, Mathematical and Physical Sciences, vol. 161, num. 906, 1937, pp. 367-381.

[8] J. Saleh, ed., Fluid Flow Handbook, McGraw-Hill Handbooks, McGraw-Hill, 2002.

[9] DIN EN ISO 12213-2: Natural Gas – Calculation of compression factor, European Committee for Standartization, 2010.

[10] A. Wächter and L. T. Biegler, "On the implementation of an interior-point filter line-search algorithm for large-scale nonlinear programming", Mathematical Programming, vol. 106, num. 1, 2006, pp. 25-57.

[11] R. Fletcher, Practical Methods of Optimization, Wiley, 2013.

[12] M. Schmidt, M. C. Steinbach, B. M. Willert, "High detail stationary optimization models for gas networks: validation and results", Optimization and Engineering online, 2015, DOI: 10.1007/s11081-015-9300-3

[13] A. Griewank, J.-U. Bernt, M. Radons, T. Streubel, 'Solving piecewise linear systems in abs-normal form", Linear Algebra and its Applications, vol. 471, 2015, pp. 500-530.

[14] Multiphysical Network Simulator MYNTS, www.scai.fraunhofer.de/en/products.html

# Sensitivity of Linear Construction Project Performance to Correlation in Task Durations

Ricardo Eiris Pereira and Ian Flood
Rinker School, College of Design, Construction and Planning,
University of Florida
Gainesville, United States
email: reiris@ufl.edu, flood@ufl.edu

*Abstract–* **The performance of construction work and thus the optimality of a plan are impacted directly by uncertainty in the performance of productive resources. For repetitive projects, smooth work flow is necessary to minimize or eliminate interruptions and idle time with the objective of reducing costs and meeting schedule deadlines. Earlier research suggests that correlation in the duration of repeated activities (where durations are stochastic) may be important in determining the most favorable plan. This study assesses the significance of correlation in this respect, using a Linear Scheduling framework for modeling repetitive construction work. A range of levels of correlation is considered using linear correlation between immediate successor repetitions of an activity. The results provide insight into the effects of different degrees of correlation on the expected project duration, cost, crew and equipment idle times and interruptions. The potential impact of correlation on the optimality of a project plan was found to be sufficiently high to justify further investigation of the nature and impact of correlation in construction.**

***Keywords - Linear Correlation; Project Planning; Repetitive Construction Work; Risk Management; Stochastic Linear Scheduling.***

## I. INTRODUCTION

Activity repetition is most prevalent at a low level in a work breakdown of construction tasks, such as the cycling of equipment in an earthmoving operation or the laying of bricks, but it is also common at intermediate and high levels, such as the laying of utility lines or the construction of many similar floors in a high-rise building. Modeling repetitive activities requires careful attention to ensure accuracy since a small error in the estimate of a single repetition translates to a large error over many repetitions. Effects, such as learning and forgetting [1] in repetitive activities can be dramatic and if not properly addressed can lead to significant errors in the estimation of project performance. Uncertainty in activity performance must also be taken into account since it can significantly impact the accuracy of project performance estimates. Interactions between construction processes are usually sufficiently complicated that stochastic effects can only be modeled accurately using statistical sampling techniques, the most popular of which is the Monte Carlo method.

Rachmat et al. [2] investigated stochastic simulation on repetitive projects to incorporate activity performance uncertainty in look-ahead scheduling. In this analysis, it was concluded that including uncertainty on linear schedules improves the forecasting capability of project performance and thus helps a scheduler anticipate problem areas and formulate new plans that improve project performance.

Processes that are stochastic can also demonstrate correlation between the duration of repeated activities. Positive correlation means that if one activity (or repetition of an activity) takes longer than expected then the correlated activities (or repetitions of that activity) are also more likely to take longer. Work on correlation between construction activities (repeated or otherwise) is limited, but it is easy to demonstrate that positive correlation affects the statistical performance of a project by increasing kurtosis, meaning that more of the variance in the performance of a project results from occasional larger deviations as opposed to more frequent smaller deviations. An outstanding question, however, is whether the effects of correlation significantly impact the optimality of a plan. This paper reports on ongoing research into this question, presenting a series of experiments designed to assess the potential impact of correlation on project plan optimality. If correlation is found to impact plan optimality, then this will justify further work into the nature and impact of correlation.

The paper continues in Section II with a general definition of the concept of correlation and a formal definition of correlation as it is measured in this paper. Section III introduces the modeling framework adopted for assessing the impact of correlation on the performance of a plan, and the objective functions used for measuring optimality. The results from this study and their analysis are presented in Section IV, and the conclusions along with recommendations for continuing the study are presented in Section V.

## II. ACTIVITY DURARTION CORRELATION

In this study, correlation is concerned with the relationship between the duration of activities that are subject to uncertainty. That is, once the uncertainty about the duration for one of the correlated activities has been resolved (such as when the activity has been executed on site) then we can make a statistically more accurate estimate of the duration of the correlated activities. Correlation occurs when the durations of different activities are determined by common factors, such as excavation activities that operate in similar ground conditions, utilize the same crew, and/or are overseen by the same superintendent. This study is concerned with determining the significance of correlation in terms of its impact on the optimality of a project schedule. For this reason, a range of levels of correlation from 0.0 (no correlation) to 1.0 (perfect correlation) will be considered. Activities that are repeated are strong candidates for demonstrating correlation since the durations of the repetitions will likely be determined by many common factors. Moreover, the impact such correlation may have on the optimality of a plan could compound over many repetitions and thus quickly become significant. For this reason, this study will consider correlation that occurs between repetitions of an activity but not between different activities.

Correlation between the durations of repeated activities will be implemented by calculating a normalized weighting of the previous repetition duration and a stochastically generated duration. That is:

$$D_n = \begin{cases} D'_n & ; n = 1 \\ k \cdot D_{n-1} + (1-k) \cdot D'_n & ; n \geq 2 \end{cases} \quad (1)$$

where: $D_n$ = the duration for the n[th] repetition of the activity;

$D'_n$ = a stochastically generated component for the duration of the nth repetition of the activity;

$D_{n-1}$ = the duration of the (n-1)[th] repetition of the activity; and

$k$ = the correlation between the durations of subsequent repetitions (ranging from 0.0 for no correlation to 1.0 for perfect correlation).

While there is no published work to support any particular model for representing correlation of durations for repetitive construction activities, the authors chose this approach since it is simple to implement. Further work in this aspect of correlation modeling is required to determine the most appropriate model. While the studies by Trofin [3] and Flood et al. [4] were concerned with how stochastic effects in repetitive activities impact project performance, they gave no consideration to correlation. Implicitly their model had correlation set to k = 1.0 in that all repetitions of a given activity had the same duration. Rachmat et al. [2] also gave no consideration to correlation, although in their case correlation was set implicitly to k = 0.0 in that a new duration was generated stochastically for each repetition of a given activity.

## III. Approach

### A. Modeling Methods

The Monte Carlo method has been implemented within a number of construction planning tools for modeling uncertainty, including the linear scheduling method (LSM) (see, for example, Wyrozębski, and Wyrozębska, [5]). This study will use the SciPy package from IPython [6] for Monte Carlo sampling since it provides a convenient framework for model development and analysis. For this study, the expected durations and variances of different activities will be allowed to differ, while the expected durations and variances for repetitions of a given activity will be fixed.

The LSM methodology represents repetitive activities as a production line in time and space on a two-dimensional graph, such as illustrated in part (b) of Fig. 1. Time, in this illustration, is represented on the horizontal axis and space (location of crew or repetition number) on the vertical axis. The slope of a production line represents its production rate. The slope of the line may be straight if the productivity rate is constant or variable if the productivity changes from unit to unit.

### B. Objective Function and Objective Variables

The aim of the study is to determine the impact of correlation between the durations of repeated activities on the optimality of the project plan. Two objective variables were adopted: Crew Idle Time; and Missed Opportunities. Crew Idle Time refers to the total period of time that the crews spend idle or inoperative between their start and finish times. It is caused by interference between dependent crews, and requires one or other of the crews to cease operations intermittently or lower their production rate to avoid any conflict. Fig. 1.a shows two examples where Crew Idle Time would have to be introduced (to activities B and D) to avoid the conflict. In either case, the clash may have been caused by the preceding activity progressing more slowly than expected and/or the succeeding activity progressing more quickly than expected. The Crew Idle Time would be the sum of these two periods of time. Missed Opportunities refer

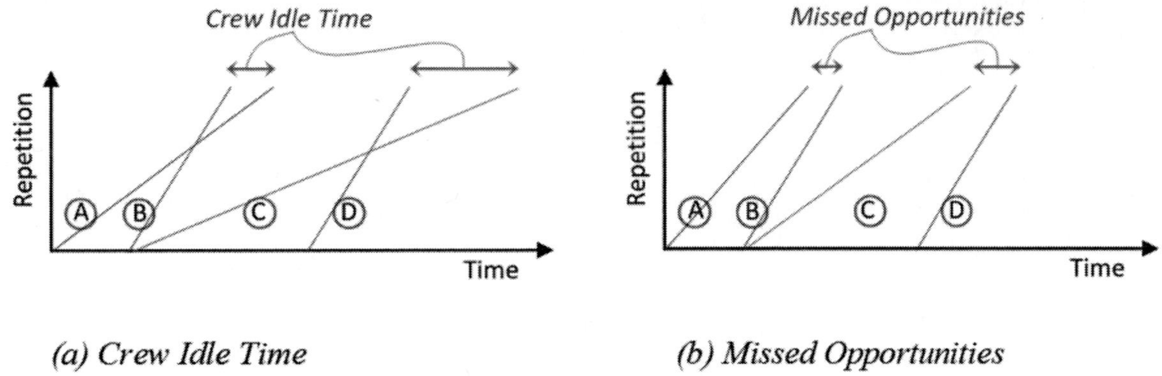


Figure 1. Examples of Inefficiencies in Performance Optimality.

to periods of time that could have been saved in the execution of a project by starting crews earlier. Fig. 1.b includes two examples of Missed Opportunities for completing work sooner, between activities A and B and between activities C and D. The Missed Opportunities would be the sum of these two periods of time.

Missed Opportunities and Crew Idle Time are caused by stochastic and correlation effects that result in crew performance rates that are different from the deterministically derived optimum base plan. This base plan assumes that each activity progresses at its expected rate and the start times for each activity are set to ensure that crews neither spend time idle nor miss any opportunities for starting and finishing work sooner. Crew Idle Time represents an additional direct cost to the project in that the crews are employed for longer periods of time to complete the specified amount of work. Missed Opportunities represent an indirect cost to the project in that they lead to a longer than necessary project duration and therefore result in unnecessary project overhead costs.

### C. *Synthetically Generated Test Projects*

Investigation of the research question was completed for a sample of synthetically generated projects, similar to the approach reported by Trofin [3] for assessing the impact of uncertainty on LSM plan optimality. The number of activities in each synthetically generated project was set to 10, a large enough number to permit complicated interactions between crews. Each activity was represented by its own Beta distribution which was used to generate the stochastic component of the duration of each repetition of that activity,

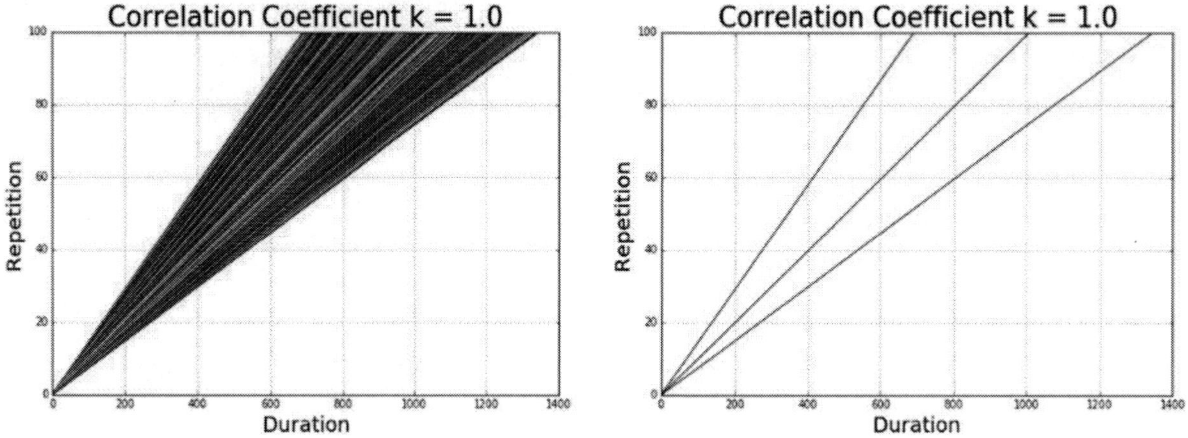


Figure 2. Activity Boundary Generation

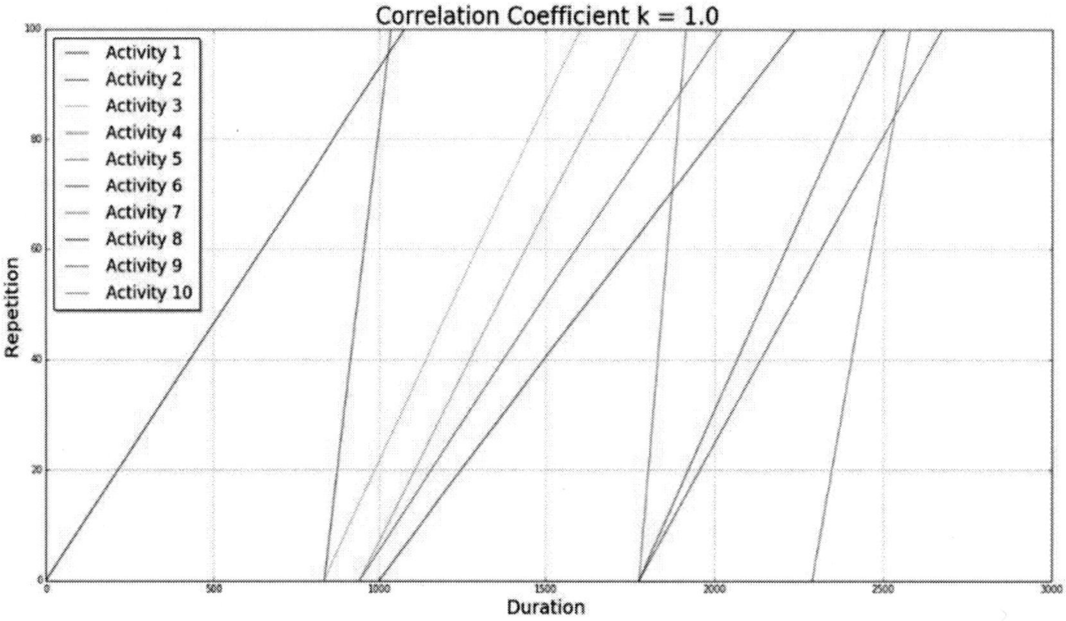


Figure 3. LSM Construction.

the parameter $D'_n$ in (1). The Beta distribution parameters for each activity were selected using Monte Carlo sampling based on the characteristic range of values for these parameters published in AbouRizk and Halpin [7] for earthmoving operations, as detailed in Eiris [8]. For construction simulation, the Beta distribution has been found to provide a good representation of the stochastic variance apparent in construction activities [9].

The synthetically generated 10 activity projects were tested for sensitivity to changes in the level of correlation relative to the deterministically derived optimum base plan. This was undertaken for a range of correlation levels from k = 0.0 to k = 1.0. For each level of k, 1,000 alternative outcomes for the project were generated using Monte Carlo sampling, and each activity was run for 100 repetitions. Fig. 2 shows an example of 1,000 samples for one activity (for k=1.0) and its corresponding boundaries and mean. Fig. 3 shows one of the 1,000 stochastically sampled outcomes for this project, for all 10 activities, where k=1.0. The deviation from the optimal plan in Fig. 3 is apparent by both the clashes between activities (resulting in Crew Idle Time) and the gaps between succeeding activities (amounting to Missed Opportunities), which are numerous. The following section provides a detailed statistical analysis of how such inefficiencies in project performance result from the level of correlation between activity repetitions.

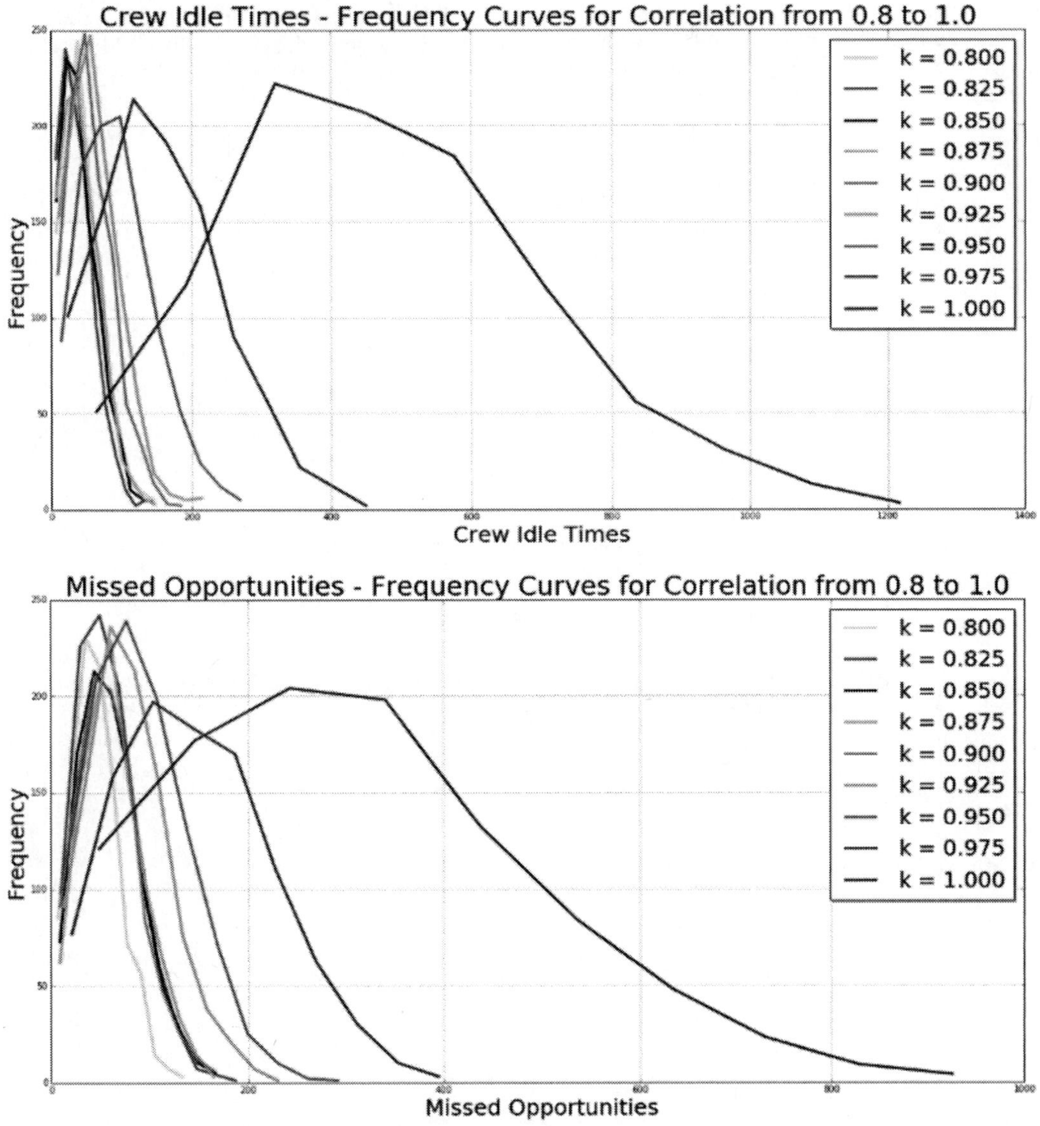


Figure 4. Distribution of Impact of Correlation, k, on *Crew Idle Time* and *Missed Opportunities*.

## IV. RESULTS AND ANALYSIS

The results of the experiments described above indicated that lower levels of correlation, between 0.00 and 0.80, did not show a significant impact on either Crew Idle Time or Missed Opportunities. However, for higher levels of correlation both variables were found to increase geometrically. Therefore, an additional 1,000 LSM scenarios were generated for each level of correlation ranging from k = 0.80 to 1.00 in increments of 0.025, to provide a higher resolution in the results for the region where performance was found to change most dramatically.

The results of these experiments are presented in Fig. 4, with the first graph plotting the frequency of occurrence of different Crew Idle Time for different levels of correlation, k, and the second graph plotting the same for Missed Opportunities. Fig. 5 summarizes these results showing, how the mean Crew Idle Time and Missed Opportunities change with respect to the level of correlation. The performance of the project was most severely impacted when correlation was perfect (k=1.0), in which case the Crew Ide Time was found to be on average approximately 7% of the total time the crews were active and the Missed Opportunities were approximately 12% of the optimum base plan's project duration. Both of these values are considered to be significant, warranting further investigation of the nature and impact of correlation on project planning.

The *Crew Idle Time* and the *Missed Opportunities* data were assessed in a single sample t-test to determine the statistical margin of standard error of the sample mean. Each level of correlation was tested independently using a confidence level of 95%. Table 1 and 2 show the results of this test for different correlation levels. For *Crew Idle Time* the average margin of error from the sample mean for all the correlation levels was 3.7%. Similarly, for *Missed Opportunities* the average margin of error from the sample mean for all the correlation levels was 3.61%. Given that these margins of error are all below 5% at the 95% confidence level, the sample size of 1,000 LSM test scenarios was considered sufficiently large.

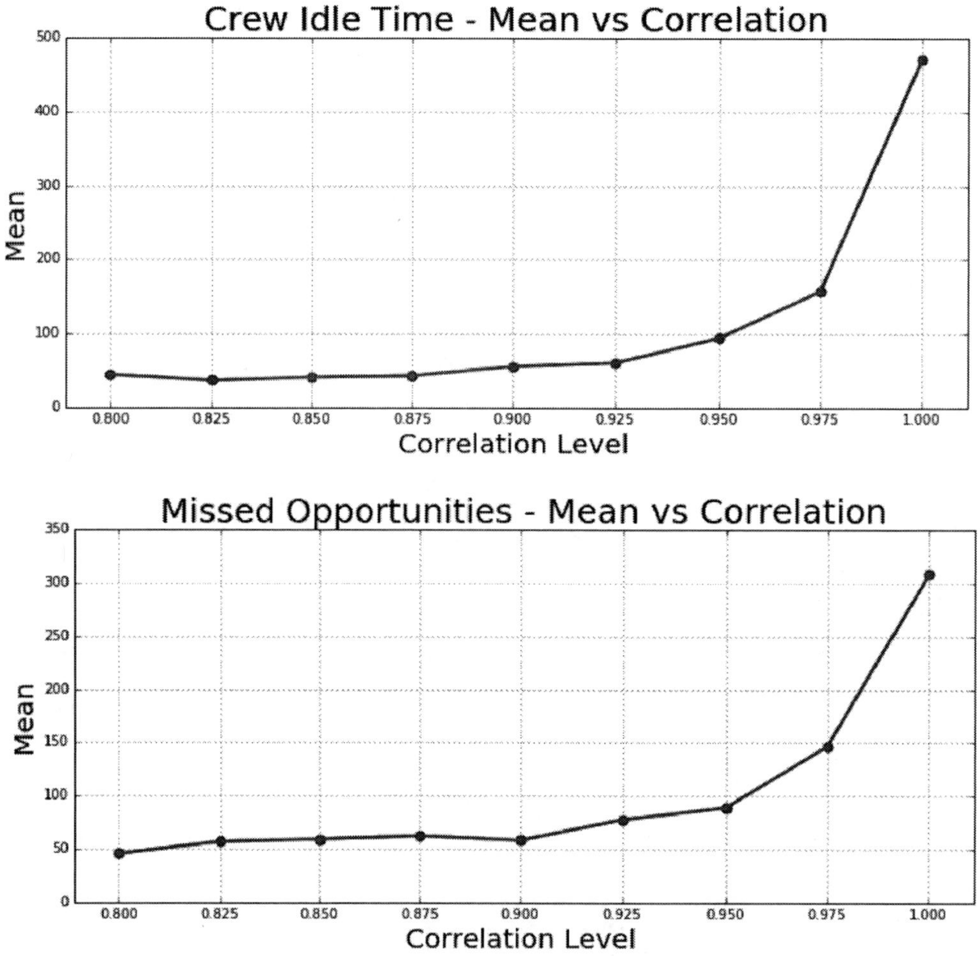


Figure 5. Summary of Impact of Correlation, k, on *Crew Idle Time* and *Missed Opportunities*.

Table 1. EXPERIMENTAL MARGIN OF ERROR AT 95% CONFIDENCE LEVEL, FOR CORRELATION LEVELS 0.0 TO 0.5.

| Correlation Level (k) | 0.0 | 0.1 | 0.2 | 0.3 | 0.4 | 0.5 |
|---|---|---|---|---|---|---|
| % Error – Crew Idle Time | 3.74 | 3.69 | 3.81 | 3.82 | 3.73 | 3.80 |
| % Error – Missed Opportunities | 3.76 | 3.62 | 3.73 | 3.65 | 3.58 | 3.74 |

Table 2. EXPERIMENTAL MARGIN OF ERROR AT 95% CONFIDENCE LEVEL, FOR CORRELATION LEVELS 0.60 TO 1.0.

| Correlation Level (k) | 0.6 | 0.7 | 0.8 | 0.9 | 1.0 |
|---|---|---|---|---|---|
| % Error – Crew Idle Time | 3.75 | 3.76 | 3.92 | 3.64 | 3.06 |
| % Error – Missed Opportunities | 3.67 | 3.47 | 3.32 | 3.45 | 3.73 |

## V. CONCLUSIONS AND RECOMMENDATIONS

The impact of correlation between activities on the performance of construction projects is not well understood. Moreover, existing models of correlation are limited in sophistication and largely untested in terms of their accuracy. Before investing resources in the development of more appropriate models of correlation for construction it was decided to first test whether correlation may affect project performance significantly. Specifically, this study had the goal of determining whether the optimality of a project plan is prone to disruption by unaccounted correlation. The study was limited to correlation between repetitions of an activity in a LSM framework, using a simple model of linear compounding correlation. Project performance was assessed in terms of two objective variables: Crew Idle Time and project Missed Opportunities. The results showed that both performance indicators are significantly impacted if the level of correlation is high (between k=0.8 and k=1.0), in the worst case having an expected crew idle time of 7% of crew active time and an expected extension to the project duration of 12%.

These results provide justification for undertaking further work developing our understanding of how correlation can best be modeled in construction and its impact on project performance.

## REFERENCES


[1] M. Gates and A. Scarpa. Learning and experience curves. Journal of the Construction Division, ASCE, 98(CO1), March, proceedings papers 8778, pp. 79–101, 1972.

[2] F. Rachmat , L. Song, and S. Lee. "Applying a Stochastic Linear Scheduling Method to Pipeline Construction", 3rd International Conference on Construction Engineering and Management, ICCEM & ICCPM, May 2009, pp 154-162, 2009.

[3] I. Trofin. "Impact of Uncertainty on Construction Project Performance Using Linear Scheduling", Master Thesis, Rinker School of Construction, University of Florida, Gainesville, FL, 2004.

[4] I. Flood, R. R. A. Issa, and I. Troffin. "Optimization of Stochastic Linear Schedules", in proceedings of 11th International Workshop, EG-ICE, Weimar, May 2004, pp 182-189, 2004.

[5] P. Wyrozębski and A. Wyrozębska. "Challenges of Project Planning in the Probabilistic Approach Using PERT, GERT and Monte Carlo", Journal of Management and Marketing, JMM, Vol. 1, Issue 1, November 2013, pp 1-8, 2013.

[6] F. Pérez and E. G. Granger. "IPython: A System for Interactive Scientific Computing", Computing in Science and Engineering, Vol. 9, No. 3, pp. 21-29, doi:10.1109/MCSE.2007.53, 2007.

[7] S. AbouRizk and D. Halpin. "Statistical Properties of Construction Duration Data", Journal of Construction Engineering and Management, 10.1061/(ASCE)0733-9364(1992)118:3(525), 525-544, 1992.

[8] R. Eiris Pereira. "Impact of Linear Correlation on Construction Project Performance Using Stochastic Linear Scheduling", Master Thesis, Rinker School of Construction, University of Florida, Gainesville, FL, 2016.

[9] S. AbouRizk, D. Halpin, J. and Wilson. "Fitting Beta Distributions Based on Sample Data", Journal of Construction Engineering and Management, 10.1061/(ASCE)0733-9364(1994)120:2(288), 288-305, 1994.

# Extending the Portfolio and Strategic Planning Horizon by Stochastic Forecasting of Unknown Future Projects

Alireza Shojaei, Ian Flood
M.E. Rinker, Sr. School of Construction Management, University of Florida
Gainesville, Florida, USA.
Email: a.shojaei@ufl.edu, flood@ufl.edu

*Abstract*— **Providing a practical and comprehensive methodology to facilitate management and coordination of multiple projects in a company's portfolio is a challenging task. Historically, the focus of research has been limited to the selection and prioritization of the set of known projects, current and near future. It is argued that existing portfolio planning models can be improved by adding a stochastic generator of project streams that extends the portfolio and strategic planning horizon to include future unknown projects. The study both identifies the historical factors in the market that are strong predictors of the profile of future project streams and evaluates alternative modeling approaches to the problem. The outputs from the generator are those parameters most critical to a company, namely the occurrence and letting date of a project, its expected duration, and its expected cost. A preliminary case study is presented developing, validating and testing the project stream generator for design-bid-build highway construction projects let by the Florida Department of Transportation (FDOT).**

*Keywords - Project Portfolio Management; Stochastic Forecasting; Time Series Modeling; Strategic Planning; Uncertainty.*

## I. INTRODUCTION

Construction companies are usually involved in multiple projects at any given time. While different projects progress concurrently, they have different goals and objectives. For instance, some projects may have financial objectives while other projects' may be more focused on marketing or strategic networking. Consequently, a key managerial duty is to allocate resources (such as financial, material, and human resources) between these concurrently ongoing projects and manage their workflow together to maximize the company's performance [1]. The process of coordinating multiple projects as such is a challenging task because each incoming project affects all other ongoing projects in terms of their schedule and progress [2], and without foreseeing these effects, the consequences can be devastating. The goal of this study is to develop a stochastic project stream generator to forecast unknown future projects in order to extend the horizon of strategic planning for construction companies.

The success of a construction company is strongly impacted by its ability to strategically plan for and manage a stream of projects, many of which will overlap in time, and all of which are subject to uncertainty about their occurrence, scope and resource needs. This task can be broadly classified as Project Portfolio Management (PPM). Reference [3] describes PPM as "...dealing with the coordination and control of multiple projects pursuing the same strategic goals and competing for the same resources, whereby managers prioritize among projects to achieve strategic benefit." Modern portfolio theory was introduced by Markowitz [4] within the finance context. McFarlan [5] introduced the concept of PPM in an information technology project management context. He suggested using projects as the elements of a portfolio (instead of investments) to better achieve an organization's objectives as well as reduce the overall risk that the organization encounters during execution of those projects.

Providing a practical and comprehensive methodology to facilitate management and coordination of multiple projects in a company's portfolio is a challenging task. There are no appropriate analytical solutions available for dynamic scheduling and resource allocation of project portfolios in real-time [2]. Existing proposed mathematical models (such as those of [6]–[9]) cannot handle the complexity of real world challenges due to a limited consideration of significant uncertainties within their models and a lack of provision for dynamic and real-time analysis. The primary focus of PPM research was initially to improve organizational performance by introducing good practices to choose and prioritize projects and ensure that the right mix of projects was adopted. A recurring theme is the alignment of the projects with the organization's strategy. There is also extensive literature on project selection with a mathematical approach. In this research, it is not proposed that developed models are incorrect. Instead, it is argued they can be advanced by adding a stochastic project generator to extend the portfolio and strategic planning horizon by stochastically forecasting the unknown future projects.

The rest of this paper is organized as follows. Section 2 provides a review of the shortcomings of existing PPM models and discusses the impact of uncertainties in PPM. Section 3 describes the project stream generator and the data used for its development. Section 4 discusses the modeling approach and results. Section 5 presents the conclusions and identifies future directions for the research.

## II. PROJECT PORTFOLIO MANAGEMENT AND UNCERTAINTY

Selecting projects from available options and planning and scheduling for them have recently received a considerable amount of attention [10]. For construction related organizations, such as investors, developers, and contractors, it is critical to gather and analyze project information to select the best options according to their strategic goals and schedule them within the required time frame and the financial constraints. This is a complex and multifaceted process, which has many contributing factors, such as the market condition, the organization's structure, resource availability and so on [11]. Research on this topic has come from several different points of view, such as selection model criteria and scheduling mechanisms [12], yet the primary focus has been choosing the most appropriate projects rather than providing a real-time dynamic model to address the project selection and scheduling issues [2]. Another shortcoming has been to disregard the importance of multiple project scheduling and resource allocation under influential factors and uncertainties, such as the economic situation of the construction industry and companies' organizational changes. Despite the available modeling proposals, companies still struggle to optimize and manage changes among their projects [12]. One of the reasons for this is that the proposed mathematical models cannot address the complexity of the real world situation [2]. Excluding uncertainties, such as the impact of possible upcoming projects or changes in the economic and financial situation of the construction industry, are some other noteworthy contributing factors to the poor performance of existing models.

The concept of uncertainty is very significant within the field of project portfolio management. This has led to an extensive literature on uncertainty and the ways to manage it. Duncan [13] and Daft [14] demonstrated that changes in the business environment combined with projects with high complexity always result in an increase in uncertainty in parameters, such as the number of projects, their performance, and their adherence to the project plan.

The impact of uncertainty on organizations is well established across many disciplines from psychology to economics [15]. Environmental uncertainties and their relation to organizations are analogous to the state of a person with a shortage of critical information about the environment. Scott [11] provides an example of the definition of environmental uncertainty as variability or the extent of predictability of the environment where work is executed. They also introduce some measures for uncertainty, such as variability of inputs, the number of deviations in work process, and the number of changes in the main products. In the project management context, uncertainty in a project is defined as the accuracy of predicting the variation of resource consumption, output, and work process. Uncertainty in a project can be seen as a variation from expected performance of the system under investigation.

The Project Management Institute (PMI) standard for portfolio management despite introducing the risk management concept at a portfolio level does not provide much information on how managers should handle uncertainty and risk within their portfolio. They only provide guidelines on categorizing different possible stages and processes plus naming some of the possible techniques available to handle uncertainties. The PMI only suggests monitoring risks and the performance of the project portfolio under the monitoring and control process group. The proposed framework by the PMI also includes monitoring changes in business strategy. This is an important task because when it occurs, it might result in a complete realignment of the portfolio. The mechanisms involved in this realignment are not specified other than restarting the whole PPM process from the beginning. Also, ad-hoc disturbances to the ongoing and approved project portfolios are almost entirely neglected. This oversight is not because the topic lacks interest or that authors assume a stable and predictable environment. Rather, it can probably be explained by the fact that the subject of PPM is relatively young and that the researchers and academics preferred to focus on more pressing issues in this area. For many companies, the environment is unstable, and the high level of uncertainty and unknowns resulting from the dynamic environment lead to some challenges. Upcoming projects significantly affect the performance of a project portfolio [2]. The typical approach when a new project is added to the portfolio is to update the project portfolio's plans and to try to re-optimize everything.

## III. PROJECT STREAM GENERATOR

This paper presents an approach to statistically represent unknown future projects to extend the portfolio and strategic planning horizon. Forecasting a company's unknown future projects can be based on the company's past and current portfolio data, or it can use historical data from market to forecast all the upcoming projects as project streams and filter those by bidding success models. In an environment, where the supply of the projects is scarce and very competitive, using just the company's past projects to forecast the future unknown projects is potentially less accurate. Arguably it is more valid to forecast streams of unknown projects (all the available projects in the future) considering the uncertainties in the context and filter those projects by bidding success models to get the final future projects in a company's portfolio. The forecast can statistically generate a single set of outputs or stochastically produce streams of values as output. Considering the uncertainties in the market, the PPM context, and the availability of future projects, stochastic forecasting appears to be the right choice.

A preliminary study is underway developing, validating and testing a project stream generator for design-bid-build highway construction projects let by the Florida Department of Transportation (FDOT). The primary data for this study were obtained from FDOT's historical project lettings database covering 14 years (from 2003 to 2017). The last two years (2015 and 2016) data are withheld to be used as a test set for the final model. The model training and selection are based on the data from 2003 to 2015, which contains 2,816 design-bid-build project-letting reports. The outputs from the generator are those parameters most critical to a company, namely the occurrence and letting date of a project, its expected duration, and its expected cost. Other factors, such as economic condition can have an impact on the project stream. Table I shows a pool of candidate variables containing 24 potentially relevant predictors including the macroeconomics metrics and construction indices that were compiled from the related sources and literature [16]. The authors suggest applying a recursive feature elimination with a greedy optimization algorithm to prune down this list. This method iteratively builds models and separates best and worst variables at each iteration. This process continues until all reductions have been made. The result is the ranking of the variables based on their order of elimination.

The data should be split into three sections as a training set, a validating and model selection set, and a testing set for the final model. In the preliminary stage, the test set is the data from 2015 and 2016, and the data from 2003 to 2015 is divided to seventy percent for training and thirty percent for validating the model. However, the aim of the study is to use cross-validation to show the robustness of the model.

TABLE I. POTENTIALLY RELEVANT PREDICTORS.

| CANDIDATE VARIABLES | SOURCE |
|---|---|
| GROSS DOMESTIC PRODUCTS (GDP) | U.S. Bureau of Economic Analysis |
| GDP IMPLICIT PRICE DEFLATOR | U.S. Bureau of Economic Analysis |
| INFLATION RATE | World Bank |
| CONSUMER PRICE INDEX | U.S. Bureau of Labor Statistics |
| NATIONAL HIGHWAY COST INDEX (NHCCI) | U.S. Department of Transportation |
| FDOT'S ANNUAL BUDGET | Florida Department of Transportation |
| FDOT'S PRODUCT BUDGET | Florida Department of Transportation |
| FEDERAL FUNDS RATE | Federal Reserve Systems |
| UNEMPLOYMENT RATE | U.S. Bureau of Labor Statistics |
| FLORIDA UNEMPLOYMENT RATE | U.S. Bureau of Labor Statistics |
| NUMBER OF EMPLOYEES IN CONSTRUCTION | U.S. Bureau of Labor Statistics |
| NUMBER OF EMPLOYEES IN CONSTRUCTION IN FL | U.S. Bureau of Labor Statistics |
| AVERAGE WEEKLY HOURS | U.S. Bureau of Labor Statistics |
| PRIME LOAN RATE | Federal Reserve System |
| BUILDING PERMITS | U.S. Bureau of Census |
| MONEY SUPPLY | Federal Reserve System |
| AVERAGE HOURLY EARNINGS | U.S. Bureau of Labor Statistics |
| EMPLOYMENT COST INDEX (ECI) CIVILIAN | U.S. Bureau of Labor Statistics |
| DOW JONES INDUSTRIAL AVERAGE | Yahoo Finance |
| CRUDE OIL PRICE | U.S. Energy Information Administration |
| BRENT OIL PRICE | U.S. Energy Information Administration |
| PRODUCER PRICE INDEX | U.S. Bureau of Labor Statistics |
| HOUSINGS STARTS | U.S. Bureau of Census |
| CONSTRUCTION SPENDING | U.S. Census Bureau |

The data under study can be categorized as time series type so the integrity of the data is important and should not be tampered with by randomly dividing into different sections for validation. In this case, as shown in Figure 1, using an evaluation on a rolling forecasting origin method is advisable. This method, in general, has two variations, fixed window (Figure 1-A) where the training (orange bar) and test (blue bar) sets duration is fixed and rolls through time, or the training set (as shown in Figure 1-B) window can be extended in each trial. Using both methods can help better understand the model's performance and give more insights into the characteristics of different time spans of the data.

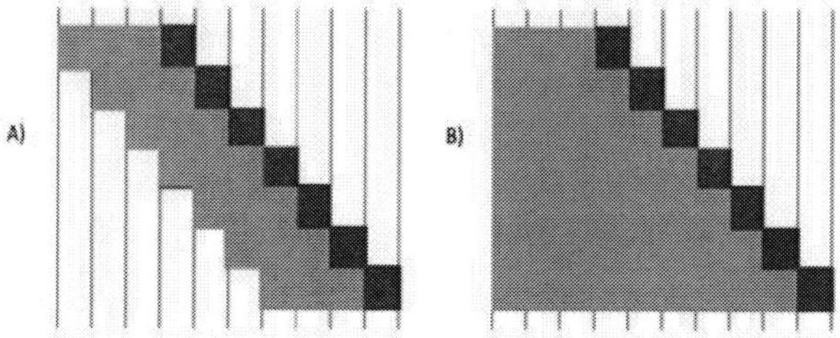


Figure 1. Evaluation of a rolling forecasting.

The sequence of generating information in the proposed model is shown in Figure 2. The first step is to forecast the number of projects (project frequency), for the desired time span, using the optimal model based on the training and validation from historical data. Next, sampling from project cost distribution takes place. At each point in time, the number of samples from the distribution is based on the number of projects forecasted in the previous step. Finally, the same process applies to the duration distribution while the possible correlation between cost and duration should be considered in the sampling process.

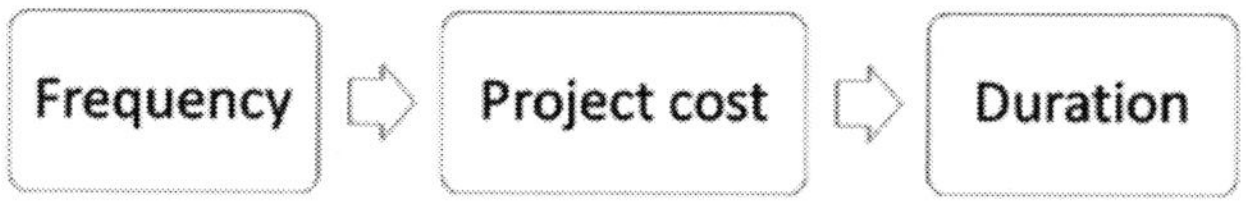


Figure 2. The Sequence of Generating Information.

The complete set of results from the proposed framework can be used as an input to any PPM model to consider unknown future projects in strategic planning.

## IV. MODELING APPROACH

The scheme used to develop the model is shown in Figure 3. The purpose of this scheme is to look for characteristics of data, to capture them in the model's projections, and then to check to see if the model reproduces them by using the cross-validation models discussed. The univariate model was adopted as a benchmark, which the more complex multivariate models should be compared to it for improvements in forecast accuracy.

The first step is modeling the main variables through univariate modeling methods, such as Autoregressive (AR), Moving Averages (MA), Autoregressive Moving Average (ARMA), and exponential smoothing. More sophisticated approaches such as artificial neural networks can also be implemented considering the availability of the necessary data size. After establishing a benchmark, potentially relevant predictors were identified to populate a pool of candidate independent variables based on a literature review and cognitive theories. This brings in the environmental uncertainties into the forecast with the aim of improving the accuracy of the simulation. These variables are not going to have necessarily a causal relationship with the main variables; the only concern here is to be helpful in forecasting the dependent variable.

The next step is exploratory data analysis. It starts with a graphical comparison of the independent and dependent variables, such as scatterplots of pairs of variables. Pearson correlation, unit root (stationary or non-stationary test), Granger causality (helpful for short term forecasting), and cointegration (helpful for long term forecasting) tests are among diagnosis tests that are relevant.

The last step is to choose a set of multivariate modeling approaches based on the result of the exploratory data analysis and test whether including explanatory variables and models that are more complex can improve the accuracy of the forecast. The range of the models should test for linear and non-linear relationships based on the result of the previous step along with variable selection (pruning), parameter optimization and finding the appropriate lag between variables.

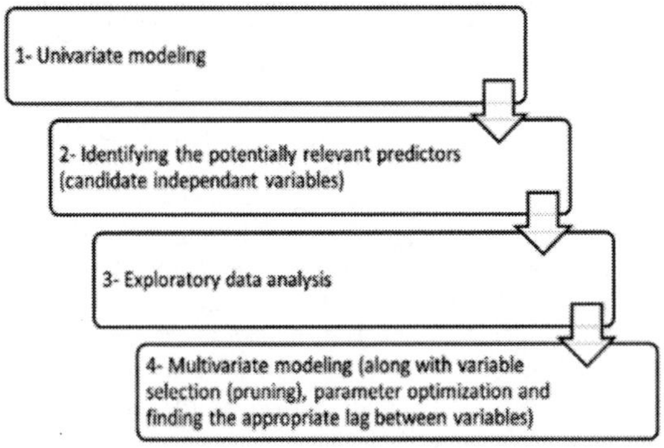


Figure 3. Model Development Scheme.

Models concerning time series data frequently involve using the value from one or more previous time steps to forecast values at the succeeding point in time; in other words, they regress based on past values. In conventional modeling, the assumption is that the independent values are known, and the dependent values are forecast. However, in multivariate time series forecasting, even the independent variables' values in the future are unknown and need to be forecast. As a result, the model contains a system of equations that forecast both independent and dependent variables in the future. This system is recursive when all the causal relationships are unidirectional and non-recursive (simultaneous) when there is reciprocal causation between variables.

Figure 4 shows four of the possible internal structures of the model. Figure 4-A shows the dependencies between the inputs and output in a univariate AR model with a lag of two. In this example, the forecast value at each point in time is based on the two preceding past values. Figure 4-B shows a recursive multivariate model where the dependent variable forecast is based on past values of itself and the independent variables. However, each independent variable is only based on its past values. Figure 4-C shows another recursive model, which differs from model 4-B in that the independent variables also act as input to each other. Figure 4-D shows a sample of a non-recursive (simultaneous) model where all the variables work as inputs for each other. There is no discrimination between dependent and independent variables in this approach.

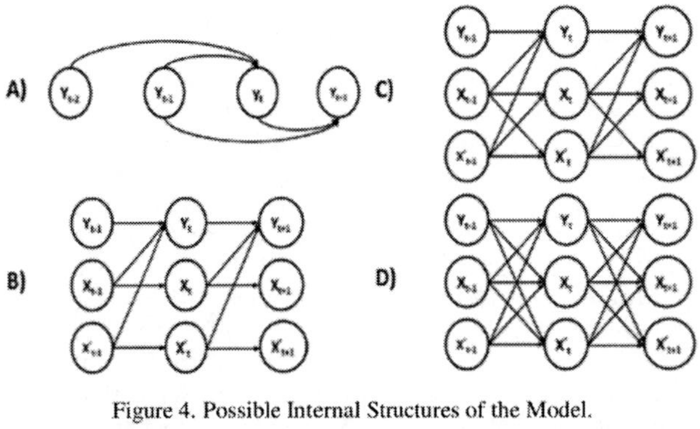


Figure 4. Possible Internal Structures of the Model.

After training and validating the model, some diagnostic tests should be conducted to check the stability of the model. For instance, checking to see if there is an autocorrelation between the residuals of the forecast is an appropriate tool for time series forecasts. Also, checking the way error compounds and undertaking a sensitivity analysis to see how the values of model parameters affect the model's output can give more insight into the performance of the model.

## A. *Modeling Project Frequency*

Before modeling the project frequency, it is necessary to conduct some preliminary data analysis to quantify the data's characteristics. Correlogram of autocorrelation and partial autocorrelation reveals that lag 8 and 12 exceeds the significance bounds.

Testing the stationarity of the project frequency is also important. Figure 5 shows the rolling mean and standard deviation of project frequency plotted along with the actual data. It is visually plausible that the data fluctuate around a fixed mean and variance. It can be further justified by using an Augmented Dickey–Fuller test (ADF) to see if the data is stationary. There are three variations of the ADF test, all with the null hypothesis that a unit root is present in a time series sample (series is not stationary). If under any of the three variations the null hypothesis is rejected it can be inferred that the time series is stationary. The ADF test's result (the appropriate lag is chosen based on the Akaike Information Criterion (AIC)) shows that the null hypothesis can be rejected at 95 percent confidence level. Therefore, the frequency series is stationary.

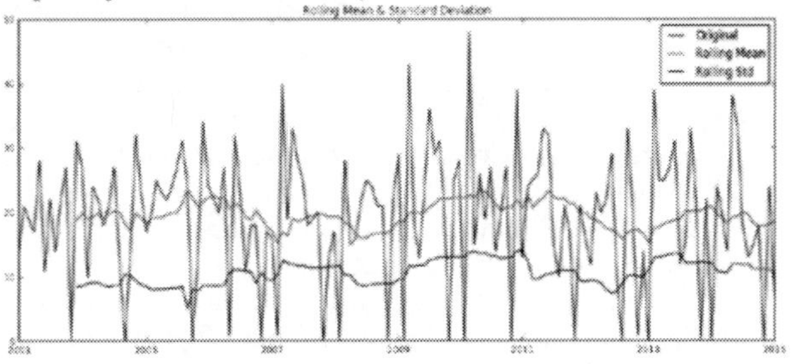

Figure 5. Rolling Mean and Standard Deviation of Project Frequency.

Two approaches can be implemented to forecast project frequency: univariate and multivariate modeling. Table 2 shows the summary of the best univariate models and their performance to forecast the project frequency. ARMA and exponential smoothing are among the most widely used methods to model a univariate time series. ARMA is used to model stationary time series data and is typically represented as ARMA (p,q), where, p is the autoregressive order and q is the moving average order. The order of autoregressive and moving average is selected via autocorrelation and partial autocorrelation correlograms. Based on the preliminary data analysis of project frequency an ARMA (p=8, q=8) is the best choice to model the project frequency series. Also, a set of seasonal ARMA models fitted to the data and the best model is selected via AIC. Moreover, a triple exponential smoothing (Holt-Winters) method is implemented, which takes into account both seasonal changes and trends. This analysis is conducted on two sets, the first containing seventy percent of the data as training data and the second comprising the remaining thirty percent of the data as a test set.

Table 2 presents the performance of the models on training and test sets using Root Mean Squared Error (RMSE) and Mean Absolute Error (MAE). The performance on the test set is the critical measure to compare the performance of the models. The results show that the ARMA model outperformed the other models both on the training and, more importantly, test sets.

TABLE II. SUMMARY OF THE UNIVARIATE MODELS' PERFORMANCE.

| Model | Set | RMSE | MAE |
|---|---|---|---|
| Holt winter (additive seasonal) | Training | 8.10 | 6.58 |
| | Test | 11.73 | 8.99 |
| ARMA(8,8) | Training | 7.93 | 6.28 |
| | Test | 8.82 | 6.84 |
| ARIMA(0,0,1)(0,0,2)[12] | Training | 9.28 | 7.46 |
| | Test | 10.22 | 8.15 |

Figure 6 provides a more in-depth understanding of the results by a visual illustration of the performance of the ARMA model, showing the difference between the actual data and the best performing model. The predicted values are shown in blue, and the actual data are plotted in red. Visual inspection of Figure 6 shows that the model performs better forecasting later values (after 2008) and, likewise, better captures the variance of the actual data in these later years. However, it is evident that the model's variance (blue) is less than the actual data (red) through the whole data set. The gray area represents the prediction intervals for the test data set. The dark grey shows the 80% interval and light grey shows 95% interval.

Based on the literature [16]–[18] including explanatory variables and using multivariate models can yield more accurate results. The next step in this research is to continue following the scheme illustrated in Figure 3 using multivariate methods to improve project frequency forecast.

*B. Modeling Cost and Duration*

Cost and duration are the two variables that are going to be sampled from a fitted distribution from past projects. Checking for the correlation between the two variables is essential. A Pearson correlation test shows 0.662 correlation coefficient with 0.000 significance between the duration and cost at the project level. This shows a moderately linear relationship between the two variables, and it should be incorporated in the model.

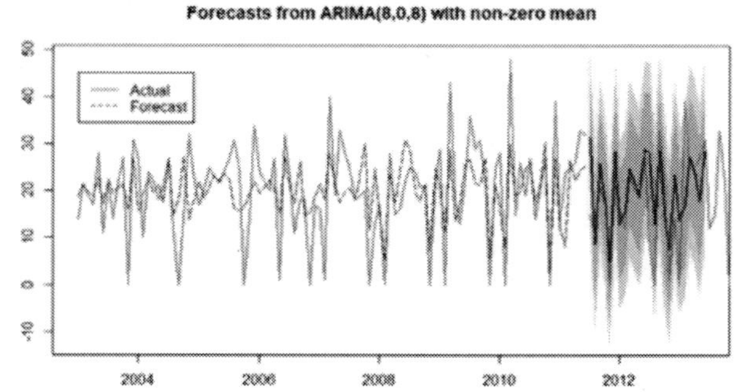


Figure 6. ARIMA (8,0,8) Forecast.

Figure 7 shows the histogram, and the corresponding fitted distribution for the duration and cost of the projects. An Inverse Gaussian distribution with $\mu$= 244.67 and $\lambda$= 273.93 was found to provide the best fit using AIC for the duration. A lognormal distribution with (mean log) $\mu$= 14.413319 and (standard deviation log) $\sigma$ = 1.524961 was found to provide the best fit using AIC for the cost.

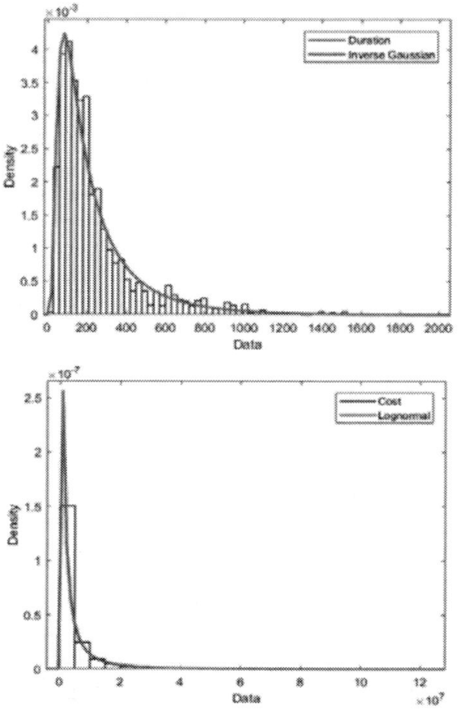


Figure 7. Duration (Up) and Cost (down) Distribution.

The performances of the various model components presented in this section indicate the viability of an integrated project stream forecaster that predicts, within a simulation environment, the frequencies of projects and empirical distributions of project duration and cost. Specifically, the generator will produce stochastic streams of unknown future FDOT projects.

## V. CONCLUSION AND FUTURE WORK.

This paper has proposed an extension to the body of existing project portfolio planning models and discussed a methodology for its development. The proposed model will extend the horizon of the portfolio and strategic planning by enabling users to look more into the future and consider unknown (but statistically quantifiable) projects alongside the known and current projects in their planning process.

The proposed model is an additional component to the current portfolio management models. A general modeling approach with different possible training and validating methods is discussed and results of the preliminary research on developing, validating and testing a stream generator to forecast FDOT projects, in terms of time of occurrence, expected duration and expected cost, is presented. It is shown how univariate models can be used to forecast project frequency and the representing distributions for project cost and duration along with the relationship between these two variables is discussed.

A set of potentially relevant predictors including the macroeconomics metrics and construction indices are identified to further improve the model by using multivariate methods in future steps of the research. The next stages of this research include further implementation of the suggested modeling approach and testing using a real case study.

It is also proposed to expand the scope of the research by adding other characteristics to the project stream generator (such as different project types) and implementing it within various environmental contexts.

The complete framework will allow the user to examine different bidding and project selection strategies to see the impact on a company's portfolio and the future resource demands. Furthermore, it will lead to the selection of a closer to optimal strategy and optimal resource distribution for the future. Finally, taking into account uncertainties in future project streams might decrease the required extent of continuous adjustments to a company's portfolio plan resulting from new projects being added to the portfolio.

## ACKNOWLEDGMENT

This work was funded by the University of Florida graduate student fellowships program.

## REFERENCES

[1] B. S. Blichfeldt and P. Eskerod, "Project portfolio management - There's more to it than what management enacts," Int. J. Proj. Manag., vol. 26, no. 4, pp. 357–365, May 2008.

[2] J. A. Araúzo, J. Pajares, and A. Lopez-Paredes, "Simulating the dynamic scheduling of project portfolios," Simul. Model. Pract. Theory, vol. 18, no. 10, pp. 1428–1441, Nov. 2010.

[3] R. G. Cooper, S. J. Edgett, and E. J. Kleinschmidt, "Portfolio management in new product development: Lessons from the leaders I," Res. Manag., vol. 40, no. 5, pp. 16–28, 1997.

[4] H. Markowitz, "Portfolio Selection," J. Finance, vol. 7, no. 1, pp. 77–91, Mar. 1952.

[5] W. F. McFarlan, "Portfolio approach to information systems," Harv. Bus. Rev., vol. 59, no. 5, pp. 142–150, 1981.

[6] N. Archer and F. Ghasemzadeh, "An integrated framework for project portfolio selection," Int. J. Proj. Manag., vol. 17, no. 4, pp. 207–216, Aug. 1999.

[7] T. R. Browning and A. A. Yassine, "Resource-constrained multi-project scheduling: Priority rule performance revisited," Int. J. Prod. Econ., vol. 126, no. 2, pp. 212–228, Aug. 2010.

[8] A. F. Carazo, et al., "Solving a comprehensive model for multiobjective project portfolio selection," Comput. Oper. Res., vol. 37, no. 4, pp. 630–639, Apr. 2010.

[9] M. Engwall, "No project is an island: Linking projects to history and context," Res. Policy, vol. 32, no. 5, pp. 789–808, May 2003.

[10] S. S. Liu and C. J. Wang, "Optimizing project selection and scheduling problems with time-dependent resource constraints," Autom. Constr., vol. 20, no. 8, pp. 1110–1119, Dec. 2011.

[11] W. R. Scott, "Organizations: Rational, Natural, and Open Systems," Englewood Cliffs, NJ Pren-tice-Hall.ScottOrganizations Ration. Nat. Open Syst., 2003.

[12] M. Martinsuo, "Project portfolio management in practice and in context," Int. J. Proj. Manag., vol. 31, no. 6, pp. 794–803, Aug. 2013.

[13] R. B. Duncan, "Characteristics of Organizational Environments and Perceived Environmental Uncertainty," Adm. Sci. Q., pp. 313–327, 1972.

[14] R. L. Daft, "Organziation Theory and Design," in South-Western Cengage Learning, 2009, pp. 138–157.

[15] Y. Petit and B. Hobbs, "Project portfolios in dynamic environments: Sources of uncertainty and sensing mechanisms," Proj. Manag. J., vol. 41, no. 4, pp. 46–58, Sep. 2010.

[16] S. M. Shahandashti and B. Ashuri, "Highway Construction Cost Forecasting Using Vector Error Correction Models," J. Manag. Eng., vol. 32, no. 2, p. 4015040, Mar. 2016.

[17] S. Thomas Ng, S. O. Cheung, R. Martin Skitmore, K. C. Lam, and L. Y. Wong, "Prediction of tender price index directional changes," Constr. Manag. Econ., vol. 18, no. 7, pp. 843–852, Oct. 2000.

[18] J. M. W. Wong and S. T. Ng, "Forecasting construction tender price index in Hong Kong using vector error correction model," Constr. Manag. Econ., vol. 28, no. 12, pp. 1255–1268, 2010.

# Social Representation Networks

Júlia Góth, Bálint File
Faculty of Information Technology and Bionics
Pázmány Péter Catholic University
Budapest, Hungary
email: goth.julia@itk.ppke.hu, file.balint@ttk.mta.hu

Zsolt Keczer
Doctoral School of Psychology
Eötvös Loránd University
Budapest, Hungary
email: keczer.zsolt@ppk.elte.hu

***Abstract*—The present study aimed to find patterns in free word associations. Associations were gathered from two nationally comprehensive samples in Hungary (N1 = 505; N2 = 505) to the cue "migrant". We demonstrated that network analysis based on co-occurrences reveals distinct clusters based on attitudes and emotions.**

***Keywords-social representation; natural language processing; free word association***

## I. INTRODUCTION

Our social environment provides access to a large amount of information on social phenomena. This information is accumulated and shared via communication. In social psychology, the collection of opinions shared by a social group regarding a social object is called a social representation [1]. Social representation studies frequently apply free associations [2]. However, the data-driven grouping of associations reflecting psychologically meaningful dimensions is a challenge to social psychology. Furthermore, opinions have a dynamic nature [3] and they can also polarize into multiple views [4].

In Section 2, we describe the procedure and the methods. In Section 3, we summarize our results. In Section 4, we discuss results and limitations. In Section 5, we point out prospects for future work.

## II. METHODS AND PROCEDURE

We gathered multiple response free associations from two nationally comprehensive samples in Hungary (N1 = 505; N2 = 505) and the cue was the word 'migrant' (currently a highly sensitive societal issue in Europe). Each respondent had to associate five words. We also applied a psychological measure to assess respondents' attitudes toward migrants (validated Hungarian version [5] of the Social Distance (SD) scale [6]). We constructed networks from these associations for both samples separately. Nodes were the different associations. Edge weights were defined based on co-occurrences in individual responses. To find psychologically-relevant dimensions behind individual opinions, we used module detection (Louvain algorithm [7] and consensus partitioning [8]). We validated the modular structure with the help of the SD scale. Independent sample t-tests were applied with Bonferroni correction.

## III. RESULTS

The two most frequent associations are displayed in Table I. and Table II. for Sample 1 and Sample 2, respectively.

TABLE I.

| | *Associations* | *Z-score* |
|---|---|---|
| ***Module 1*** | war | 3.99 |
| | refugee | 3.94 |
| ***Module 2*** | immigrant | 3.58 |
| | stranger | 2.70 |
| ***Module 3*** | terrorism | 4.52 |
| | Islam | 1.16 |
| ***Module 4*** | violence | 4.91 |
| | fear | 3.70 |

TABLE II.

| | *Associations* | *Z-score* |
|---|---|---|
| ***Module 1*** | refugee | 5.36 |
| | war | 3.46 |
| ***Module 2*** | immigrant | 4.14 |
| | Islam | 1.74 |
| ***Module 3*** | terrorism | 5.53 |
| | violence | 4.49 |

In case of Sample 1, respondents assigned to the Module 1 showed the lowest SD score. ($M = 3.9$, $SD = 2.2$). Respondents assigned to Module 2 reported higher level of SD score ($M = 4.6$, $SD = 2.2$). Respondents assigned to the Module 3 reported even higher level of SD score ($M = 5.2$, $SD = 2.1$). Respondents assigned to Module 4 showed the highest SD score ($M = 6$, $SD = 1.6$). Module 1 showed significantly lower score than Module 2 ($t(481) = -3.4$, $p = .02$), Module 3 ($t(484) = -6.4$, $p < .001$) and Module 4 ($t(600) = -13.3$, $p < .001$.) Module 2 had significantly lower d SD score than Module 3 ($t(403)=-2.6$, $p<.001$) and Module 4 ($t(519) = -7.8$, $p < .001$.) Module 3 had significantly lower SD score than Module 4 ($t(522) = -4.9$, $p < .001$).

In case of Sample 2 respondents assigned to Module 1 showed the lowest SD score (M = 4.4, SD = 2.2). Respondents assigned to Module 2 (M = 5.1, SD = 2). Respondents assigned to Module 3 showed the highest SD score (M = 6.2, SD = 1.5). Module 1 had significantly lower SD score than Module 2 ($t(597) = -4$, $p < 0.001$) and Module 3 ($t(717) = -12.4$, $p < .001$). Module 3 had significantly lower SD score than Module 4 ($t(602) = -6.9$, $p < 0.001$).

## IV. Discussion

Our results indicate that module detection in association networks yields a psychologically meaningful mapping of the rich symbolic context behind attitudes in a structured way. The modules reflected distinct attitudes toward asylum seekers based on pairwise statistical comparisons of attitude scores between respondents who were affiliated with different modules.

Our networks can be seen as a subtype of large-scale semantic networks [9]–[11] map constant lexical relations among words of a language. As opposed to these models, our study focuses on a single social object which generates polarized opinions. Furthermore, opinions in social issues fluctuate over time [3]. They can be significantly reshaped by events (e.g., war, terrorism or economic changes). Such changes can be observed in our social representation networks. For example, the association "terrorism" is one of the most frequent associations in both samples, which is in line with previous results on the stability of frequent components [1]. However, it appeared in completely different contexts in the two samples. In the first sample, it had a stereotypical connection to Arab/Islam-related concepts (this associative relation had already been found before the current migration-related events by other researchers as well [12]). In the second sample, its frequency increased and it had stronger relations to other associations indicating threat, violence and crime. A possible explanation can be that in the time-interval between the two data gatherings, a significant terror attack happened in Nice in July, 2016 and this event could be perceived as result of the increased number of migrants after the Syrian war. A future study could investigate how social representations are updated according to changes in the environment.

A limitation is that multiple response free associations are sparse datasets. As a consequence of sparsity, we have to be careful with interpretations based on a single connection in our networks and rely more on the modules which are derived from multiple connections. Another limitation is that the method was demonstrated regarding only one social object.

## V. Conclusion

Our research can provide an empirical basis for constructing knowledge graphs to analyze texts in political, social and ideological domains. Modules constructed from individual word usage patterns indicated significantly different attitudes toward migrants. Human respondents provide more relevant associations than corpus-based association extraction [13]. The downside is that collecting associations from human respondents is tedious, the datasets can be sparse and they expire. However, combining human associations with extracted associations yields a promising performance [13]. This implies that associations can be used as representative signals to build more comprehensive databases for text comprehending in a given domain. For example, our empirically-validated word clustering can be extended with web-mining and natural language processing techniques.

## References


[1] J. C. Abric, "Central system, peripheral system: their functions and roles in the dynamics of social representations," *Pap. Soc. Represent.*, vol. 2, no. 2, pp. 75–78, 1993.

[2] L. Dany, I. Urdapilleta, and G. Lo Monaco, "Free associations and social representations: some reflections on rank-frequency and importance-frequency methods," *Qual. Quant.*, vol. 49, no. 2, pp. 489–507, 2015.

[3] D. Acemoglu, G. Como, F. Fagnani, and A. Ozdaglar, "Opinion fluctuations and disagreement in social networks," *Math. Oper. Res.*, vol. 38, no. 1, pp. 1–27, 2013.

[4] P. Dandekar, A. Goel, and D. T. Lee, "Biased assimilation, homophily, and the dynamics of polarization," *Proc. Natl. Acad. Sci.*, vol. 110, no. 15, pp. 5791–5796, 2013.

[5] G. Orosz, E. Bánki, B. B\Hothe, I. Tóth-Király, and L. R. Tropp, "Don't judge a living book by its cover: effectiveness of the living library intervention in reducing prejudice toward Roma and LGBT people," *J. Appl. Soc. Psychol.*, vol. 46, no. 9, pp. 510–517, 2016.

[6] E. S. Bogardus, "A social distance scale.," *Sociol. Soc. Res.*, 1933.

[7] V. D. Blondel, J.-L. Guillaume, R. Lambiotte, and E. Lefebvre, "Fast unfolding of communities in large networks," *J. Stat. Mech. Theory Exp.*, vol. 2008, no. 10, p. P10008, 2008.

[8] A. Lancichinetti and S. Fortunato, "Consensus clustering in complex networks," *Sci. Rep.*, vol. 2, 2012.

[9] S. De Deyne and G. Storms, "Word associations: Network and semantic properties," *Behav. Res. Methods*, vol. 40, no. 1, pp. 213–231, 2008.

[10] D. L. Nelson, C. L. McEvoy, and T. A. Schreiber, "The University of South Florida free association, rhyme, and word fragment norms," *Behav. Res. Methods, Instruments, Comput.*, vol. 36, no. 3, pp. 402–407, 2004.

[11] G. A. Miller, "WordNet: a lexical database for English," *Commun. ACM*, vol. 38, no. 11, pp. 39–41, 1995.

[12] A. Ernst-Vintila, S. Delouvée, and C. Roland-Lévy, "Under threat. Lay thinking about terrorism and the three-dimensional model of personal involvement: a social psychological analysis," *J. Risk Res.*, vol. 14, no. 3, pp. 297–324, 2011.

[13] D. Heath, D. Norton, E. Ringger, and D. Ventura, "Semantic models as a combination of free association norms and corpus-based correlations," in *Semantic Computing (ICSC), 2013 IEEE Seventh International Conference on*, 2013, pp. 48–55.

# Machine Learning for Chemogenomics on HPC in the ExCAPE Project

Tom Vander Aa and Tom Ashby
IMEC,
Leuven, Belgium
email:*firstname.lastname*@imec.be

Yves Vandriessche
Intel corp.
Belgium
email:yves.vandriessche@intel.com

Vojtech Cima, Stanislav Böhm and Jan Martinovič
IT4Innovations, VŠB – Technical University of Ostrava,
Ostrava, Czech Republic
email:*firstname.lastname*@vsb.cz

***Abstract*—The ExCAPE project is a Horizon 2020 project to advance the state of the art of machine learning (ML) implementations on supercomputing hardware. We have adopted bioactivity predictions for chemogenomics as a challenging use-case to drive development. In this paper, we will give an overview of the challenges in ExCAPE to use supercomputing efficiently. We will touch on three key examples dealing with efficient ML workflow execution, support for multi-task learning using matrix factorization methods and the challenges originating from the large and very sparse datasets in ExCAPE.**

***Index Terms*—Machine Learning, High-Performance Computing, Collaborative Filtering, Distributed Task Scheduling**

## I. Introduction and Context

Traditional users of High Performance Computing (HPC) have mostly been concerned with simulation of physics of one type or another and at various different scales. In the last decade, a new breed of user of very large machines has appeared, those concerned with Big Data. Carrying out simulations is mostly about doing large amounts of computation to observe the behavior of a sophisticated model with few parameters. Big Data problems, by contrast, usually deal with less sophisticated models but with many more parameters, and try to choose the model parameters by analyzing large amounts of data with relatively little associated computation. Folk wisdom in this field states that the ability to capture and analyze more data is more valuable than making more sophisticated models, and this works well when data is cheap and easy to get. However, there are problems in this area for which the data are very expensive to generate. In this case, it becomes important to be able to use more sophisticated models to be able to squeeze as much knowledge as possible out of the data. Such problems are at the juncture of HPC and Big Data in that they have large data sets to analyze, yet should exploit more sophisticated models through computation to make the most of the available data.

The ExCAPE project [1] is about how to tackle such problems. The core of the project is about mathematics and software and how they work on HPC machines. However, to be able to advance the state of the art it helps to have a concrete problem to tackle. For this, we take the chemogenomics problem, that of predicting the activity of compounds in the drug discovery phase of the pharmaceutical industry, leading to the project name *Exascale Compound Activity Prediction Engines* (ExCAPE). Making such predictive models belongs to the field of Machine Learning.

More general than chemogenomics, we want to find methods and systems that can tackle large and complex machine learning problems. This will require algorithms and software that make efficient use of the latest HPC machines. Creating these, along with preparing the data to give the system something to work on, is the main work of the project.

Many interesting open challenges need to be overcome to be able to run machine learning efficiently at scale on HPC hardware in all cases. In the following sections of this paper we explain three very relevant and interesting example challenges, namely:

- how to execute machine learning workflows with many dependent tasks (Section II);
- how to take advantage of the fast interconnect (like inifiniband) typically only found on true HPC hardware for multi-node machine learning tasks (Section III);
- how to support very large but sparse datasets (Section IV)

More details can be found in the referenced documents.

## II. Efficient Workflows using HyperLoom

Solutions for scheduling problems on HPC systems exist when dispatching tasks (computational units) of known duration and resource requirements. However, real-world applications such as those in machine learning, encompass tasks with no requirement annotations in addition to the overhead of handling massive amounts of data only manageable by large-scale distributed environments. To address these challenges, we developed HyperLoom [2]. HyperLoom is a platform for defining and executing pipelines in large-scale distributed environments. Unlike other scheduling systems, HyperLoom is specifically tailored to work efficiently on high-performing computing (or HPC) systems and offers a user-friendly representation of tasks as acyclic computational graphs. An example of such a scientific pipeline is shown in Figure 1.

Our resulting pipelines for both synthetic and real-world use cases are successfully distributed leveraging HPC resources covering up to a hundred thousand tasks, across ten or more physical compute nodes. We analyzed HyperLoom performance for both synthetic and real test cases scaling up to hundreds of thousands tasks and tens of physical computational nodes. HyperLoom significantly outperforms Dask/Distributed

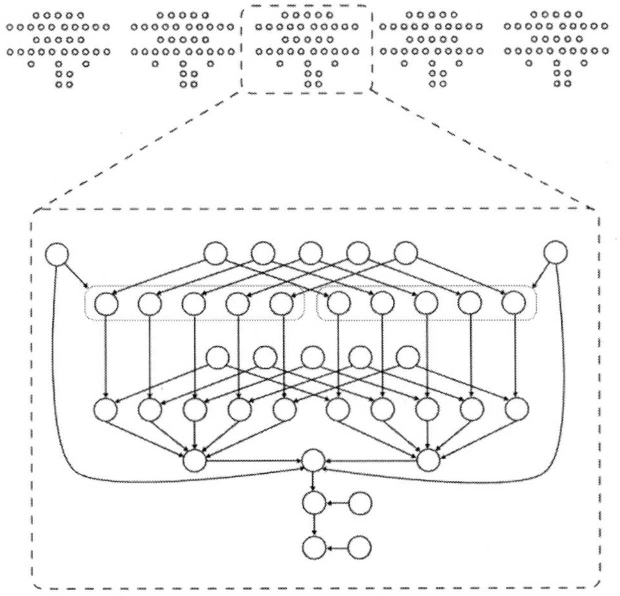

Figure 1. Example of a scientific pipeline visualized as a directed acyclic graph.

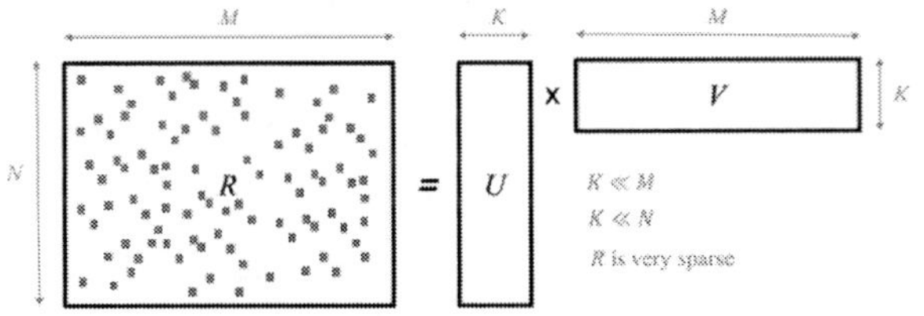


Figure 2. Low-rank Matrix Factorization

ranging from 6.3× to 2.2× better performance for two test cases [2].

## III. Scalable Matrix Factorization using Asynchronous Communication

While single-task learning methods for compound-activity prediction result in many small tasks, which can easily be solved using HyperLoom, multi-task learning methods combine and solve multiple tasks at the same time [3], by exploiting commonalities and differences across tasks. This generally results in improved prediction accuracy but also in much fewer and much larger tasks. Such tasks need to be parallelized themselves to be able to run them efficiently.

Matrix Factorization (MF) is a class of multi-task methods that have been successfully used. As sketched in Figure 2, the idea of these methods is to approximate the compound-activity matrix $R$ as a product of two low-rank matrices $U$ and $V$ such that $R \approx U \times V$. In this way, $U$ and $V$ are constructed from the known ratings in $R$, which is usually very sparsely filled. The recommendations can be made from the approximation $U \times V$, which is dense.

We have built a high-performance distributed implementation [4] of the popular and effective matrix factorization algorithm called Bayesian Probabilistic Matrix Factorization (BPMF [5]). We have shown that load balancing and low-overhead asynchronous communication are essential to achieve good parallel efficiency, clearly outperforming more common synchronous approaches like GraphLab [6]. The achieved speed-up allowed us to speed up machine learning for drug discovery on an industrial dataset from 15 days for the initial Julia-based version to 5 minutes using the distributed version with Intel Threading Building Blocks (TBB) and the Global Address Space Programming Interface (GASPI) [7].

## IV. Support for Large Binary Sparse Matrices

There is one class of routines that is ubiquitous for all involved Machine Learning algorithms on ExCAPE-like data: sparse linear algebra. In many cases, these operations dominate the runtime of the computation, which means that even small optimizations translate into large efficiency and performance gains.

Unlike dense linear algebra routines, where ready-made heavily optimized libraries are available, the performance of sparse routines is determined by the nature of the data, which makes it impossible to make a routine that is optimal in general.

Sparse matrix-vector (SPMV) was identified as a key bottleneck low-level operation is the ExCAPE ML-algorithms. The two main workloads we are analyzing are matrix-factorization and neural network training on ExCAPE's activity and the compounds' fingerprint data.

After optimization [8] of those SPMV routines on ExCAPE data [9] we can say that:

- Linear algebra optimizations on the Compressed Storage of Rows (CSR) format performs best from those formats tested, but
- although the Coordinate Format (COO) is less efficient, it gets close to CSR by sorting non-zero elements by Hilbert-order [10], making it a good choice in case the matrix contents are changing dynamically.
- Optimizing for binary matrix data and parallel task imbalances yields a 2.7× speedup over the more general mkl_scsrgemv() Intel Math Kernel Library (MKL) SparseBlas routine.
- Operating on multiple right-hand sides obtains another 2.4× proportional speedup due to both vectorization and improved cache locality.

## V. Conclusions

This short paper provided insight into what is needed to run large scale machine learning efficiently on HPC hardware for three key examples. We have indicated the importance of efficient *i)* workflow execution, *ii)* support for multi-task learning, and *iii)* low lever sparse algebra routines. Solutions for all three will need to be combined for the project to succeed.

## ACKNOWLEDGMENTS

This work is partly funded by the European project ExCAPE with reference 671555 and by the IT4Innovations infrastructure, which is supported from the Large Infrastructures for Research, Experimental Development and Innovations project "IT4Innovations National Supercomputing Center – LM2015070".

## REFERENCES

[1] The ExCAPE Consortium, "ExCAPE: Exascale Compound Activity Prediction Engine," http://excape-h2020.eu/, retrieved: June 2017.

[2] V. Cima *et al.*, "HyperLoom possibilities for executing scientific workflows on the cloud," in *Proceedings of the CISIS 2017 : The 11th International Conference on Complex, Intelligent, and Software Intensive Systems*, 2017.

[3] R. Caruana, "Multitask learning," in *Learning to learn.* Springer, 1998, pp. 95–133.

[4] T. Vander Aa, I. Chakroun, and T. Haber, "Distributed bayesian probabilistic matrix factorization," in *ICCS 2017: International Conference on Computational Science*, June 2017.

[5] R. Salakhutdinov and A. Mnih, "Bayesian probabilistic matrix factorization using Markov chain Monte Carlo," in *Proceedings of the International Conference on Machine Learning*, vol. 25, 2008, pp. 880–887.

[6] Y. Guo, A. L. Varbanescu, A. Iosup, C. Martella, and T. L. Willke, "Benchmarking graph-processing platforms: A vision," in *Proceedings of the 5th ACM/SPEC International Conference on Performance Engineering*, ser. ICPE '14. New York, NY, USA: ACM, 2014, pp. 289–292. [Online]. Available: http://doi.acm.org/10.1145/2568088.2576761

[7] D. Grünewald and C. Simmendinger, "The GASPI API specification and its implementation GPI 2.0," in *7th International Conference on PGAS Programming Models*, vol. 243, 2013, pp. 243–248.

[8] Y. Vandriessche and T. Vander Aa, "ExCAPE deliverable D2.6: Simulation report 1," Tech. Rep., 2017.

[9] J. Sun *et al.*, "ExCAPE-DB: an integrated large scale dataset facilitating Big Data analysis in chemogenomics," *Journal of Cheminformatics*, vol. 9, no. 1, p. 17, dec 2017. [Online]. Available: http://jcheminf.springeropen.com/articles/10.1186/s13321-017-0203-5

[10] A. N. Yzelman, D. Roose, and K. Meerbergen, "Sparse matrix-vector multiplication: parallelization and vectorization," in *High Performance Parallelism Pearls: Multicore and Many-core Programming Approaches*, J. Reinders and J. Jeffers, Eds. Elsevier, 2014, ch. 27, p. 20.

# Using GPI-2 for Distributed Memory Paralleliziation of the Caffe Toolbox to Speed up Deep Neural Network Training

Martin Kuehn, Janis Keuper and Franz-Josef Pfreundt

Competence Center High Performance Computing
Fraunhofer Institute for Industrial Mathematics
Fraunhofer-Platz 1
D-67663 Kaiserslautern, Germany
Email: {Martin.Kuehn, Janis.Keuper, Franz-Josef.Pfreundt}@itwm.fraunhofer.de

***Abstract*—Deep Neural Network (DNN) are currently of great interest in research and application. The training of these networks is a compute intensive and time consuming task. To reduce training times to a bearable amount at reasonable cost we extend the popular Caffe toolbox for DNN with an efficient distributed memory communication pattern. To achieve good scalability we emphasize the overlap of computation and communication and prefer fine granular synchronization patterns over global barriers. To implement these communication patterns we rely on the the "Global address space Programming Interface" version 2 (GPI-2) communication library. This interface provides a light-weight set of asynchronous one-sided communication primitives supplemented by non-blocking fine granular data synchronization mechanisms. Therefore, CaffeGPI is the name of our parallel version of Caffe. First benchmarks demonstrate better scaling behavior compared with other extensions, e.g., the Intel™Caffe. Even within a single symmetric multiprocessing machine with four graphics processing units, the CaffeGPI scales better than the standard Caffe toolbox. These first results demonstrate that the use of standard High Performance Computing (HPC) hardware is a valid cost saving approach to train large DDNs. I/O is an other bottleneck to work with DDNs in a standard parallel HPC setting, which we will consider in more detail in a forthcoming paper.**

*Keywords–GPI-2; Caffe; DNN; SGD; GASPI.*

## I. Introduction

Deep Neural Network (DNN) architectures have improved considerably the accuracy in data classification opening the door for a plethora of use cases in image classification, speech recognition or semantic text understanding. However, the training of DNNs is a very compute intensive task. So, the raising interest in these architectures created a tremendous demand for compute resources which is further intensified by a race to greater sizes of DNNs.

Another important factor is the time necessary for training DNNs. To train a popular architecture like, e.g., GoogLeNet can easily take several days on a Graphics Processing Unit (GPU). To make things worse the training usually is an iterative process of trials and modifications in the DNN architecture. So, keeping training times tolerably is a key requirement to actually apply DNNs in research and industry.

In response to this challenge, hardware vendors brought to market special hardware, e.g., the DGX-1 sold by NVIDIA or the S822LC ("Minsky") sold by IBM. They try to integrate as much compute power in terms of floating point operations per second (FLOP/s) as possible in a single compute node. While this special hardware comes also with a special price it is also not as flexible to apply to other problems in computer science. On the other hand, there already exists a plethora of compute systems in the world used for High Performance Computing (HPC) [1]. Usually these consist of hundreds of nodes usually connected with high bandwidth, low latency networks like InfiniBand networks. A considerable number of them are even equipped with GPU accelerators.

TABLE I. APPROXIMATE COMPUTATION TIMES FOR ALEXNET WITH BATCH SIZE $B = 256$ AND 450k ITERATIONS, GOOGLENET AND INCEPTION V3 WITH $B = 32$ AND 1400k,2000k ITERATIONS. SETUP CAFFE WITH CUDA 8 AND CUDNN 6 FOR GPUS AND INTEL™CAFFE WITH MKL17 FOR CPUS.

| | CPU | K80 | P100 | KNL |
|---|---|---|---|---|
| AlexNet [2]: | | | | |
| time per iteration | 2s | 0.9s | 0.1s | 0.6s |
| time till convergence | 250h | 112h | 13h | 75h |
| GoogLeNet [3]: | | | | |
| time per iteration | 1.3s | 0.36s | 0.08s | 0.32s |
| time till convergence | 361h | 100h | 31h | 89h |
| Inception V3: | | | | |
| time per iteration | - | - | 0.33s | - |
| time till convergence | - | - | 180h | - |

Our aim is to make these HPC resources available to the field of data analytics. The advantage of this approach is twofold. First, it provides the data analytics community access to the needed hardware quickly because it is already up and running. Secondly, in the long run it avoids the separation of resources that are used in the field of data analytics and in the traditional HPC field. This not only simplifies the buildup and the operation of these compute resources but it also increases the flexibility to mix data analytics and other compute jobs on the same cluster. The latter increases the load factor and reduces costs.

The toolbox Caffe [4] is very popular to build and train DNNs. It is easy to use and a wealth of predefined DNNs are available to get to results quickly. The popular Convolutional Neural Networks usually have a performance advantage on Caffe versus the TensorFlow framework. However, the parallelization of Caffe, as it is provided in its original version, is limited to a single Symmetric Multi Processing (SMP) compute node. Intel™developed a MPI based prallel version of Caffe, which we will use as benchmark. Our goal is to provide a parallel version of Caffe based on a Partitioned Global Address Space (PGAS) Application Programming Interface (API), that can exploit one sided commmunication more efficiently than MPI. This speeds up the DNN training by distributing the computational load on several servers equipped with a GPU or a set of powerful Central Processing Units (CPUs).

To ensure high scalability it is crucial to organize the inter node communication efficiently. To exploit the precious network bandwidth to the maximum it is important to overlay as much of the inter node communication with computation as possible. The Global address space Programming Interface version 2 (GPI-2) library [5] developed by our group provides an efficient interface for one sided, asynchronous data transfers. This interface is the basis of an efficient and well scaling distributed memory parallelization of the Caffe toolbox. So, we call our parallel version of Caffe CaffeGPI.

The rest of the text is organized as follows. In Section II details on our parallelization approach and communication pattern are given. In Section III the implementation of the communication pattern is described. In Section IV our first benchmarks are presented and in Section V the results are discussed.

## II. Parallelization Approach

Although the numerical operations involved in the training of DNNs are typically basic linear algebra operations on dense matrices, which have a rather good FLOP to byte ratio, the bandwidth of the communication networks must be used efficiently to keep the latency low between the training iterations.

### A. Stochastic Gradient Descend

The Stochastic Gradient Descend (SGD) [6] algorithm is a standard for training DNN and is implemented in the Caffe toolbox. It is the standard choice for such famous DNNs like, e.g., GoogLeNet or AlexNet. The training data $x_i$ is partitioned into batches which are iteratively applied to the DNN to modify the weights $w$ which are also called the model. Each iteration consists of a forward propagation and a backward propagation. In the forward propagation, the data batch is inferred while during the backward propagation a gradient on the weights is computed and later on applied on the model.

**Require:** $\epsilon > 0$
**for all** $t = 0 \dots T$ **do**
  **randomly draw** batch $M \leftarrow B$ samples from $X$
  **Init** $\Delta w_t = 0$
  **for all** $x \in M$ **do**
    **aggregate update** $\Delta w \leftarrow \partial_w x_j(w_t)$
  **end for**
  **update** $w_{t+1} \leftarrow w_t - \epsilon \Delta w_t$
**end for**
Return $w_T$

Figure 1. Mini-Batch SGD with samples $X = \{x_0, \dots, x_m\}$, iterations $T$, step-size $\epsilon$, batch size $B$

The two basic parallelization strategies commonly used for SGD are data parallelism or model parallelism [7]. In the model parallelism, the net and its weights are distributed among different ranks of the parallel computer, while the batch stays the same for all ranks. In data parallelism the DNN is duplicated on every rank while the data batch is split into equal fractions for each rank. The computed gradients on each rank are aggregated and then applied to the model which is distributed back to all the ranks. We concentrate on the data parallelism approach here which is favorable for DNN containing many convolutional layers like the popular AlexNet or GoogLeNet. An advantage of this approach is a constant aggregated IO turnover over the ranks fetching the training data.

As the DNN is organized in layers we write the model of layer $l$ in the iteration $k$ as $w^{(l,k)}$, the partial gradient on rank $r$ as $\Delta w_r^{(l,k)}$. Using this notation the iterative data parallel SGD algorithm can be shortly noted as

$$w^{l,k+1} := w^{l,k} - \epsilon \sum_{r=1}^{s} \Delta w_r^{l,k}. \quad (1)$$

Higher order terms are neglected here without loss of generality. These terms usually depend on the history of the models $w^{l,k}$, which are inherently broadcasted to all the ranks to perform the next forward propagation phase.

### B. Design Principles

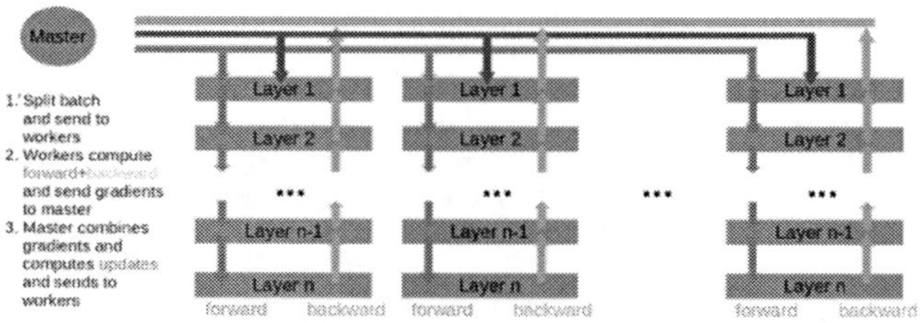


Figure 2. Data Parallel SGD as frequently implemented.

To exploit the full potential of this parallelization approach the data transfers of the model and gradients have to be designed very carefully, since the total amount of data that has to be transferred during each iteration grows with the number of compute ranks.

As a consequence a typical HPC interconnect, like EDR InfiniBand, should be used to provide enough bandwidth to exploit the scalability of the problem. These networks are commonly used to connect the nodes in current HPC clusters. Another important aspect is to use these interconnects efficiently. Foremost this means to overlap computation and communication to avoid that their run times add up fully. Instead both should ideally take place at the same time so that no additional time for communication is necessary. Unfortunately this is not the case for the standard Caffe which enters separate phases for computation and communication (see Figure 2). The second principle is to avoid global synchronization points between the ranks. Instead data dependencies are enforced locally and very fine granular. The communicated data chunks are pipelined to keep the ranks busy most of the time with either computing, communication or both. Barriers to synchronize the ranks are avoided and used only where absolutely necessary. However, it is important to note that our approach strictly regards all the data dependencies immanent of the SGD algorithm unlike the so called "asynchronous SGD" algorithms described in literature [8].

### C. Overlapping Computation and Communication

During the backward propagation the partial gradients $\Delta w_r^{(l,k)}$ are computed separately for each layer and in an inverse order. The next read access to the model of a certain layer is in the forward propagation of the following time step. So, especially for the layers at the bottom of the DNN quite some time is available to reduce the partial gradients and to update the model of that layer (see Figure 4 for illustration).

The communication pattern is turn based, one layer of the DNN per turn. In each turn, a partial gradient $\Delta w_r^{(l,k)}$ is computed for the respective layer $l_i$ and forwarded to the receiving ranks. Incoming partial gradients of previous layers from other ranks are checked, aggregated if available and forwarded to receiving ranks as well. In the same manner, updates on the model of previous layers are forwarded to the receiving nodes. In all these cases the data transfers are only triggered but not awaited for conclusion.

**for all** $l = L, \ldots, 1$ **do**
  **compute** local gradient $\Delta w_r^{(k,l)}$
  **check** for arrived gradients from previous layers
  **reduce** arrived gradient data locally
  **trigger** sends of available gradient data
  **trigger** sends of arrived model data
**end for**
**finalize** local communication phase

Figure 3. Turn based communication pattern on rank r.

In the finalization phase, all loose ends of the communication to the local rank $r$ are finalized. After that the local instance of the DNN is ready for the next iteration. Please note that even between iterations there is no global barrier applied. So, every rank that received a complete update of the model can immediately start with the next training phase without having to wait for other ranks to get their full update.

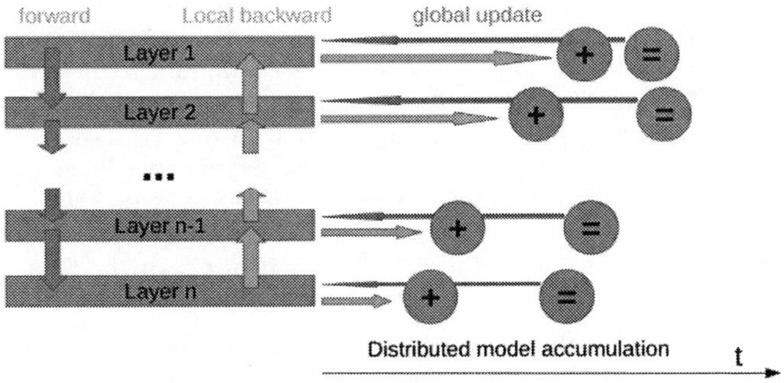


Figure 4. Sketch of the data parallel SGD communication pattern implemented in this work.

Particularly, this scheme allows to overlap the computation of the gradient $\Delta w_r^{(l,k)}$ with the communication of gradients and models of previous layers. And it avoids global barriers between the ranks.

## III. IMPLEMENTATION

Our parallel version of the Caffe framework is done as minimally invasive as possible. Basically, the setup routine of the DDN and the backward propagation routines are modified. Additionally, a layer-wise model update is introduced in the Solver class.

During the backward propagation over the layers, the calculations of the gradients are followed by calls to the newly added communication routines to reduce the local gradients and to broadcast the updated model.

### A. Basics of GPI-2

To implement the overlapping, one sided communication pattern the GPI-2 library has been used, which is a PGAS communication API for C/C++ and Fortran applications. Fulfilling the Global Address Space Programming Interface (GASPI) specification (see webpage [9]), it provides truly asynchronous one-sided communication primitives supplemented by a non-blocking light-weight and fine granular data synchronization mechanism. GPI-2 exploits interconnects supporting Remote Direct Memory Access (RDMA) as, e.g., InfininBand networks. On these networks the data transfers can be almost completely offloaded to the network infrastructure reducing the load on the computational resources to a minimum. No intermediate copies are necessary which saves memory bandwidth. Apart from that, GPI-2 is a very lean library and gives the user more direct control over the particular data transfers as, e.g. the usual Message Passing Interface (MPI) library.

All these features make GPI-2 a perfect match to implement the overlap of computation and inter node communication in Caffe. Being an open source library GPI-2 can be downloaded at [5].

### B. Implementation of Data Transfers

In the Caffe data structures that define the DNN the arrays that carry the model and the gradient data are placed inside GPI-2 data segments. Providing the gaspi_segment_use function, GPI-2 cooperates perfectly with special memory regions in Caffe which are allocated by cudaMallocHost to enhance data transfers to the GPU. The GPI-2 library allows to write remotely (inter node) and directly to these segments. All the data transfers are triggered with a gaspi_write_notify call to the library. The receiver of the data chunk checks on the respective notification and acts on the received data if necessary.

The gradient data is reduced in a reduction tree pattern aggregating the final gradient on the master rank. The master rank performs the update on the current model to compute an update for the next iteration. Then the updated model is broadcasted to all the other ranks in another tree pattern. The gradient data is always sent from higher rank numbers to lower rank numbers while the updated model is broadcasted from lower rank numbers to higher rank numbers. As the size of the gradients equals the size of the models we take advantage of the full duplex feature of switched networks.

The reduction and the broadcast trees are build from scratch to keep control over the tree topolgy and to interwine closely the communication pattern with the computation.

*1) Reduction of the Gradient:* To reduce the local gradients in a binomial, tree each rank checks for incoming gradient data in its receive buffer. If available the gradient data is reduced (added to) with its own gradient data of that layer. If the rank has a receiver in the tree pattern the reduced gradient is forwarded to this receiver using a call to gaspi_write_notify. The communication tasks are performed once in the loop over the layers as depicted in section II-C. The gradient data is processed as available. No waiting takes place for a specific data chunk.

*2) Broadcast of the model:* The broadcast of the model is performed similarly as the gradient reduction. As no reduction steps are necessary the incoming model data from the sender is just forwarded to its receiver ranks using a call to gaspi_write_notify.

## IV. First Benchmarks

To evaluate our parallelization approach we start to compare CaffeGPI with the original Caffe on a SMP machine containing 4 GPUs. This setup is quite similar to specialized workstations produced to train DNNs. The original Caffe uses the standard thread parallel communication pattern in this benchmark. In the CaffeGPI benchmark, 4 independent processes are started on the same node, one for each GPU, communicating through the network card. The SMP machine is a single node of the Taurus cluster at the ZIH in Dresden containing 2 Intel™Xeon E5-2680v3 CPUs, 64GB Random-access memory (RAM) and 4 NVIDIA K80 GPU. The network is InfiniBand FDR. As DNN we choose the familiar AlexNet. Figure 5 depicts the scaling behavior at 1, 2, and 4 GPU.

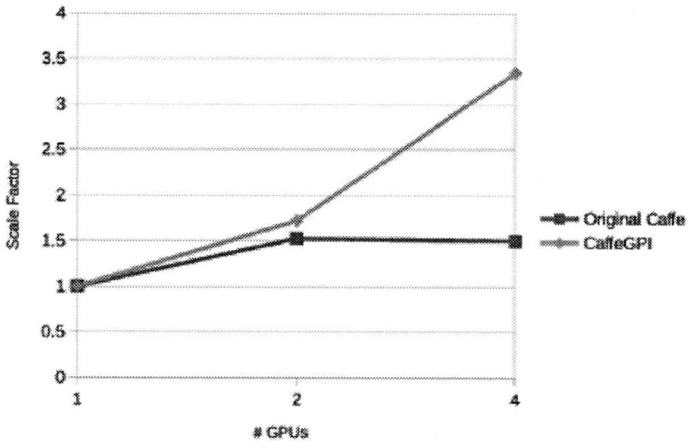


Figure 5. Scaling results for AlexNet an overall batch size of 256 on a single node with multiple GPUs interconnected via PCIe. Based on Caffe 1.15, Cuda 8, CuDNN 5.1.

On a first glance our CaffeGPI should have a small disadvantage in this benchmark compared with the standard Caffe toolbox because it needs to communicate via memory copies inside the node. At a closer look the reduction of the partial gradients puts a lot of load on the memory system, the PCIe bus and the QuickPath Interconnect between the CPUs. In both cases, memory copies between GPU-RAM and CPU-RAM have to be performed. However in the benchmark of the standard Caffe all the GPUs execute their communication phase at the same time leaving precious bandwidth idle during the computation phase. In the CaffeGPI benchmark, the memory copies between GPU-RAM and CPU-RAM are not overlapped but interleaved with computation of the partial gradients. As not all the GPUs perform their copies at the same time, the memory transfers are distributed over a longer period of time. The memory copies across the two sockets are performed by the network card and overlapped with the computation. Finally our implementation can demonstrate superior scaling behavior as depicted in Figure 5. The second benchmark compares CaffeGPI to Intel™Caffe (see webpage [10]), a distributed memory extension of Caffe based on the MPI. In this benchmark, 1, 2 or 4 nodes of the same cluster were used, but only one GPU per node. Here distributed memory data transfers are performed in both scenarios. The benchmark in Figure 6 demonstrates a superior scaling behavior of our implementation in comparison to the Intel™Caffe framework. A speedup of 2.4 on 4 nodes compared to one node delivers a reasonable performance figure to train AlexNet in a reasonable time frame on standard HPC hardware.

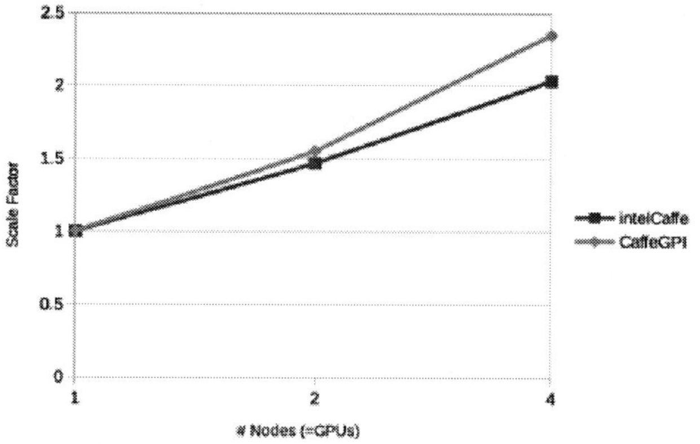


Figure 6. Scaling results for AlexNet with an overall batch size of 256 on distributed nodes with single GPUs interconnected via Infiniband. Based on Intel™Caffe 1.14, Cuda 8, CuDNN 5.1

## V. Conclusion and Future Work

The preliminary benchmarks presented in this work demonstrate that our distributed memory communication pattern implemented in the CaffeGPI framework scales well on four distributed memory nodes equipped with one GPU per node. The total performance is similar or even better than using the standard SMP-parallel approach of Caffe on a SMP node equipped with 4 GPU. Even on this single SMP node with 4 GPUs, our CaffeGPI scales much better than the standard Caffe framework.

These results demonstrate that data scientists can rely on available HPC compute resources to train their DNNs in a reasonable time frame. Our toolbox CaffeGPI can help to satisfy the need for more compute power in the area of data science without having to buy vast amounts of specialized hardware, which is difficult to apply economically for other tasks in computer science.

We will continue to benchmark various hardware configurations, e.g. a NVIDIA DGX-1 or an IBM S822LC ("Minsky"). Further benchmarks will be done to analyze the communication pattern introduced in CaffeGPI. Alternative patterns will be evaluated that might improve the reduction and the broadcast operations. We will also extend our benchmarks on more DNNs and to wider batch sizes to evaluate their scaling behavior and to find performance optimized training parameters.

## ACKNOWLEDGMENT

The authors thank the Center for Information Services and High Performance Computing (ZIH) at TU Dresden for generous allocations of computer time.

## REFERENCES

[1] "TOP 500," http://www.top500.org, accessed: 2017-05-15.

[2] A. Krizhevsky, I. Sutskever, and G. E. Hinton, "Imagenet classification with deep convolutional neural networks," in Advances in neural information processing systems, 2012, pp. 1097–1105.

[3] C. Szegedy et al., "Going deeper with convolutions," in Proceedings of the IEEE Conference on Computer Vision and Pattern Recognition, 2015, pp. 1–9.

[4] Y. Jia et al., "Caffe: Convolutional architecture for fast feature embedding," arXiv preprint arXiv:1408.5093, 2014.

[5] "GPI 2.0," http://www.gpi-site.com/gpi2, accessed: 2017-05-15.

[6] L. Bottou, "Large-scale machine learning with stochastic gradient descent," in Proceedings of COMPSTAT'2010. Springer, 2010, pp. 177–186.

[7] J. Keuper and F.-J. Preundt, "Distributed training of deep neural networks: Theoretical and practical limits of parallel scalability," in Proceedings of the Workshop on Machine Learning in High Performance Computing Environments, ser. MLHPC '16. Piscataway, NJ, USA: IEEE Press, 2016, pp. 19–26. [Online]. Available: https://doi.org/10.1109/MLHPC.2016.6

[8] J. Keuper and F.-J. Pfreundt, "Asynchronous parallel stochastic gradient descent: A numeric core for scalable distributed machine learning algorithms," in Proceedings of the Workshop on Machine Learning in High-Performance Computing Environments, ser. MLHPC '15. New York, NY, USA: ACM, 2015, pp. 1:1–1:11. [Online]. Available: http://doi.acm.org/10.1145/2834892.2834893

[9] "GASPI," http://www.gaspi.de, accessed: 2017-05-15.

[10] "Intel$^{TM}$caffe," https://github.com/intelcaffe/caffe, accessed: 2017-05-15.

# AUTHOR INDEX